Get the eBook FREE!

(PDF, ePub, Kindle, and liveBook all included)

We believe that once you buy a book from us, you should be able to read it in any format we have available. To get electronic versions of this book at no additional cost to you, purchase and then register this book at the Manning website.

Go to https://www.manning.com/freebook and follow the instructions to complete your pBook registration.

That's it!
Thanks from Manning!

Interpretable AI

Interpretable AI

BUILDING EXPLAINABLE MACHINE LEARNING SYSTEMS

AJAY THAMPI

MANNING

SHELTER ISLAND

For online information and ordering of this and other Manning books, please visit
www.manning.com. The publisher offers discounts on this book when ordered in quantity.
For more information, please contact

Special Sales Department
Manning Publications Co.
20 Baldwin Road
PO Box 761
Shelter Island, NY 11964
Email: orders@manning.com

Manning Publications Co.
20 Baldwin Road
PO Box 761
Shelter Island, NY 11964

Development editor:	Lesley Trites
Technical development editor:	Kostas Passadis
Review editor:	Mihaela Batinić
Production editor:	Deirdre Hiam
Copy editor:	Pamela Hunt
Proofreader:	Melody Dolab
Technical proofreader:	Vishwesh Ravi Shrimali
Typesetter:	Gordan Salinovic
Cover designer:	Marija Tudor

ISBN 9781617297649
Printed in the United States of America

To Achan, Amma, Ammu, and my dear Miru

brief content

contents

preface

I've been fortunate to have worked with data and machine learning for about a decade now. My background is in machine learning, and my PhD was focused on applying machine learning in wireless networks. I have published papers (http://mng.bz/zQR6) at leading conferences and journals on the topic of reinforcement learning, convex optimization, and classical machine learning techniques applied to 5G cellular networks.

After completing my PhD, I began working in the industry as a data scientist and machine learning engineer and gained experience deploying complex AI solutions for customers across multiple industries, such as manufacturing, retail, and finance. It was during this time that I realized the importance of interpretable AI and started researching it heavily. I also started to implement and deploy interpretability techniques in real-world scenarios for data scientists, business stakeholders, and experts to get a deeper understanding of machine-learned models.

I wrote a blog post (http://mng.bz/0wnE) on interpretable AI and coming up with a principled approach to building robust, explainable AI systems. The post got a surprisingly large response from data scientists, researchers, and practitioners from a wide range of industries. I also presented on this subject at various AI and machine learning conferences. By putting my content in the public domain and speaking at leading conferences, I learned the following:

- I wasn't the only one interested in this subject.
- I was able to get a better understanding of what specific topics are of interest to the community.

These learnings led to the book that you are reading now. You can find a few resources available to help you stay abreast of interpretable AI, like survey papers, blog posts, and one book, but no single resource or book covers all the important interpretability techniques that would be valuable for AI practitioners. There is also no practical guide on how to implement these cutting-edge techniques. This book aims to fill that gap by first providing a structure to this active area of research and covering a broad range of interpretability techniques. Throughout this book, we will look at concrete real-world examples and see how to build sophisticated models and interpret them using state-of-the-art techniques.

I strongly believe that as complex machine learning models are being deployed in the real world, understanding them is extremely important. The lack of a deep understanding can result in models propagating bias, and we've seen examples of this in criminal justice, politics, retail, facial recognition, and language understanding. All of this has a detrimental effect on trust, and, from my experience, this is one of the main reasons why companies are resisting the deployment of AI. I'm excited that you also realize the importance of this deep understanding, and I hope you learn a lot from this book.

acknowledgments

Writing a book is harder than I thought, and it requires a lot of work—really! None of this would have been possible without the support and understanding of my parents, Krishnan and Lakshmi Thampi; my wife, Shruti Menon; and my brother, Arun Thampi. My parents put me on the path of lifelong learning and have always given me the strength to chase my dreams. I'm also eternally grateful to my wife for supporting me throughout the difficult journey of writing this book, patiently listening to my ideas, reviewing my rough drafts, and believing that I could finish this. My brother deserves my wholehearted thanks as well for always having my back!

Next, I'd like to acknowledge the team at Manning: Brian Sawyer, who read my blog post and suggested that there might a book there; my editors, Matthew Spaur, Lesley Trites, and Kostas Passadis, for working with me, providing high-quality feedback, and for being patient when things got rough; and Marjan Bace, for green-lighting this whole project. Thanks as well to all the other folks at Manning who worked with me on the production and promotion of the book: Deirdre Hiam, my production editor; Pamela Hunt, my copyeditor; and Melody Dolab, my page proofer.

I'd also like to thank the reviewers who took the time to read my manuscript at various stages during its development and who provided invaluable feedback: Al Rahimi, Alain Couniot, Alejandro Bellogin Kouki, Ariel Gamiño, Craig E. Pfeifer, Djordje Vukelic, Domingo Salazar, Dr. Kanishka Tyagi, Izhar Haq, James J. Byleckie, Jonathan Wood, Kai Gellien, Kim Falk Jorgensen, Marc Paradis, Oliver Korten, Pablo Roccatagliata, Patrick Goetz, Patrick Regan, Raymond Cheung, Richard Vaughan, Sergio Govoni, Shashank Polasa Venkata, Sriram Macharla, Stefano Ongarello, Teresa Fontanella De

Santis, Tiklu Ganguly, Vidhya Vinay, Vijayant Singh, Vishwesh Ravi Shrimali, and Vittal Damaraju.Special thanks to James Byleckie and Vishwesh Ravi Shrimali, technical proof-readers, for carefully reviewing the code one last time shortly before the book went into production.

about this book

Interpretable AI is written to help you implement state-of-the-art interpretability techniques for complex machine learning models and to build fair and explainable AI systems. Interpretability is a hot topic in research, and only a few resources and practical guides cover all the important techniques that would be valuable for practitioners in the real world. This book aims to address that gap.

Who should read this book

Interpretable AI is for data scientists and engineers who are interested in gaining a deeper understanding of how their models work and how to build fair and unbiased models. The book should also be useful for architects and business stakeholders who want to understand models powering AI systems to ensure fairness and protect the business's users and brand.

How this book is organized: a roadmap

The book has four parts that cover nine chapters.

Part 1 introduces you to the world of interpretable AI:

- Chapter 1 covers different types of AI systems, defines interpretability and its importance, discusses white-box and black-box models, and explains how to build interpretable AI systems.
- Chapter 2 covers white-box models and how to interpret them, specifically focusing on linear regression, decision trees, and generalized additive models (GAMs).

Part 2 focuses on black-box models and understanding how the model processes the inputs and arrives at the final prediction:

- Chapter 3 covers a class of black-box models called tree ensembles and how to interpret them using post hoc model-agnostic methods that are global in scope, such as partial dependence plots (PDPs) and feature interaction plots.
- Chapter 4 covers deep neural networks and how to interpret them using post hoc model-agnostic methods that are local in scope, such as local interpretable model-agnostic explanations (LIME), SHapley Additive exPlanations (SHAP), and anchors.
- Chapter 5 covers convolutional neural networks and how to visualize what the model is focusing on using saliency maps, specifically focusing on techniques such as gradients, guided backpropagation, gradient-weighted class activation mapping (Grad-CAM), guided Grad-CAM, and smooth gradients (SmoothGrad).

Part 3 continues to focus on black-box models but moves to understanding what features or representations have been learned by them:

- Chapter 6 covers convolutional neural networks and how to dissect them to understand representations of the data that are learned by the intermediate or hidden layers in the neural network.
- Chapter 7 covers language models and how to visualize high-dimensional representations learned by them using techniques like principal component analysis (PCA) and t-distributed stochastic neighbor embedding (t-SNE).

Part 4 focuses on fairness and bias and paves the way for explainable AI:

- Chapter 8 covers various definitions of fairness and ways to check whether models are biased. It also discusses techniques for mitigating bias and a standardizing approach of documenting datasets using datasheets that will help improve transparency and accountability with the stakeholders and users of the AI system.
- Chapter 9 paves the way for explainable AI by understanding how to build such systems and also covers contrastive explanations using counterfactual examples.

About the code

This book contains many examples of source code. In most cases, source code is formatted in a `fixed-width font like this` to separate it from ordinary text.

In many cases, the original source code has been reformatted; we've added line breaks and reworked indentation to accommodate the available page space in the book. In rare cases, even this was not enough, and listings include line-continuation markers (➥). Additionally, comments in the source code have often been removed from the listings when the code is described in the text. Code annotations accompany many of the listings, highlighting important concepts.

You can get executable snippets of code from the liveBook (online) version of this book at https://livebook.manning.com/book/interpretable-ai. The complete code for the examples in the book is available for download from the Manning website at https://www.manning.com/books/interpretable-ai and from GitHub at http://mng.bz/KBdZ.

liveBook discussion forum

Purchase of *Interpretable AI* includes free access to liveBook, Manning's online reading platform. Using liveBook's exclusive discussion features, you can attach comments to the book globally or to specific sections or paragraphs. It's a snap to make notes for yourself, ask and answer technical questions, and receive help from the author and other users. To access the forum, go to https://livebook.manning.com/book/interpretable-ai/discussion. You can also learn more about Manning's forums and the rules of conduct at https://livebook.manning.com/discussion.

Manning's commitment to our readers is to provide a venue where a meaningful dialogue between individual readers and between readers and the author can take place. It is not a commitment to any specific amount of participation on the part of the author, whose contribution to the forum remains voluntary (and unpaid). We suggest you try asking the author some challenging questions lest his interest stray! The forum and the archives of previous discussions will be accessible from the publisher's website as long as the book is in print.

about the author

**AJAY THAMPI** has a strong background in machine learning. His PhD focused on signal processing and machine learning. He has published papers at leading conferences and journals on the topics of reinforcement learning, convex optimization, and classical machine learning techniques applied to 5G cellular networks. Ajay is currently a machine learning engineer at a large tech company, primarily focused on responsible AI and fairness. In the past, Ajay was a lead data scientist at Microsoft, where he was responsible for deploying complex AI solutions for customers across multiple industries such as manufacturing, retail, and finance.

about the cover illustration

The figure on the cover of Interpretable AI is "Marchante d'Orange de Mourcy," or "An orange merchant," taken from a collection by Jacques Grasset de Saint-Sauveur, published in 1797. Each illustration is finely drawn and colored by hand.

In those days, it was easy to identify where people lived and what their trade or station in life was just by their dress. Manning celebrates the inventiveness and initiative of the computer business with book covers based on the rich diversity of regional culture centuries ago, brought back to life by pictures from collections such as this one.

Part 1

Interpretability basics

This part will introduce you to the world of interpretable AI. In chapter 1, you will learn about different types of AI systems, interpretability and its importance, white-box and black-box models, and how to build interpretable AI systems.

In chapter 2, you will learn about characteristics that make white-box models inherently transparent and black-box models inherently opaque. You'll learn how to interpret simple white-box models, such as linear regression and decision trees and then switch gears to focus on generalized additive models (GAMs). You'll also learn about the properties that give GAMs high predictive power and how to interpret them. GAMs have very high predictive power and are highly interpretable too, so you get more bang for your buck by using GAMs.

Introduction 1

This chapter covers
- Different types of machine learning systems
- How machine learning systems are built
- What interpretability is and its importance
- How interpretable machine learning systems are built
- A summary of interpretability techniques covered in this book

Welcome to this book! I'm really happy that you are embarking on this journey through the world of Interpretable AI, and I look forward to being your guide. In the last five years alone, we have seen major breakthroughs in the field of artificial intelligence (AI), especially in areas such as image recognition, natural language understanding, and board games like Go. As AI augments critical human decisions in industries like healthcare and finance, it is becoming increasingly important that we build robust and unbiased machine learning models that drive these AI systems. In this book, I wish to give you a practical guide to interpretable AI systems and how to build them. Through a concrete example, this chapter will explain why interpretability is important and will lay the foundations for the rest of the book.

1.1   *Diagnostics+ AI—an example AI system*

Let's now look at a concrete example of a healthcare center called Diagnostics+ that provides a service to help diagnose different types of diseases. Doctors who work for Diagnostics+ analyze blood smear samples and provide their diagnoses, which can be either positive or negative. This current state of Diagnostics+ is shown in figure 1.1.

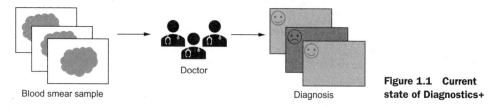

Blood smear sample   Doctor   Diagnosis

Figure 1.1   Current state of Diagnostics+

The problem with the current state is that the doctors are manually analyzing the blood smear samples. With a finite set of resources, diagnosis, therefore, takes a considerable amount of time. Diagnostics+ would like to automate this process using AI and diagnose more blood samples so that patients get the right treatment sooner. This future state is shown in figure 1.2.

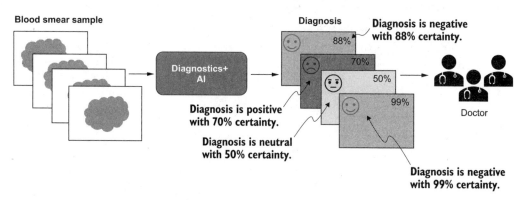

Figure 1.2   Future state of Diagnostics+

The goal for Diagnostics+ AI is to use images of blood smear samples with other patient metadata to provide diagnoses—positive, negative, or neutral—with a confidence measure. Diagnostics+ would also like to have doctors in the loop to review the diagnoses, especially the harder cases, thereby allowing the AI system to learn from mistakes.

1.2   *Types of machine learning systems*

We can use three broad classes of machine learning systems to drive Diagnostics+ AI: supervised learning, unsupervised learning, and reinforcement learning.

1.2.1 Representation of data

Let's first see how to represent the data that a machine learning system can understand. For Diagnostics+, we know that there's historical data of blood smear samples in the form of images and patient metadata.

How do we best represent the image data? This is shown in figure 1.3. Suppose the image of a blood smear sample is a colored image of size 256×256 pixels consisting of three primary channels: red (R), green (G), and blue (B). We can represent this RGB image in mathematical form as three matrices of pixel values, one for each channel and each of size 256×256. The three two-dimensional matrices can be combined into a multidimensional matrix of size $256 \times 256 \times 3$ to represent the RGB image. In general, the dimension of the matrix representing an image is of the following form: *{number of pixels vertically} × {number of pixels horizontally} × {number of channels}.*

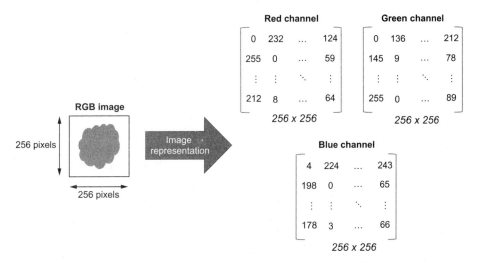

Figure 1.3   Representation of a blood smear sample image

Now, how do we best represent the patient metadata? Suppose that the metadata consists of information such as the patient identifier (ID), age, sex, and the final diagnosis. The metadata can be represented as a structured table, as shown in figure 1.4, with N columns and M rows. We can easily convert this tabular representation of the metadata into a matrix of dimension $M \times N$. In figure 1.4, you can see that the Patient Id, Sex, and Diagnosis columns are categorical and have to be encoded as integers. For instance, the patient ID "AAABBCC" is encoded as integer 0, sex "M" (for male) is encoded as integer 0, and diagnosis "Positive" is encoded as integer 1.

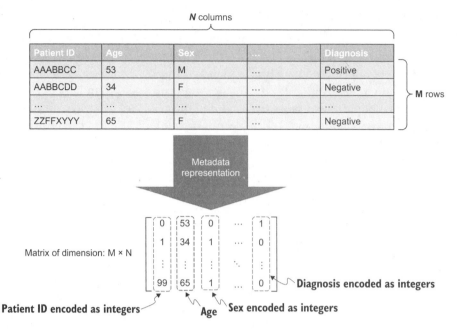

Figure 1.4   Representation of tabular patient metadata

1.2.2   *Supervised learning*

The objective of supervised learning is to learn a mapping from an input to an output based on example input-output pairs. It requires labeled training data where inputs (also known as *features*) have a corresponding label (also known as a *target*). How is this data represented? The input features are typically represented using a multidimensional array data structure or mathematically as a matrix X. The output or target is represented as a single-dimensional array data structure or mathematically as a vector y. The dimension of matrix X is typically $m \times n$, where m represents the number of examples or labeled data and n represents the number of features. The dimension of vector y is typically $m \times 1$ where m again represents the number of examples or labels. The objective is to learn a function f that maps from input features X to the target y. This is shown in figure 1.5.

In figure 1.5, you can see that with supervised learning, you are learning a function f that takes in multiple input features represented as X and provides an output that matches known labels or values, represented as the target variable y. The bottom half of the figure shows an example where a labeled dataset is given, and through supervised learning, you are learning how to map the input features to the output.

The model learns a mapping from the input features to the target variable.

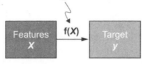

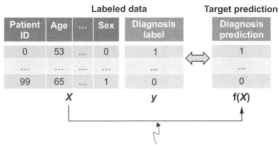

The model learns a mapping from the input patient features to the diagnosis based on the ground truth labels.

Figure 1.5 Illustration of supervised learning

The function *f* is a multivariate function—it maps from multiple input variables or features to a target. Two broad classes of supervised learning problems follow:

- *Regression*—The target vector *y* is continuous. For example, predicting the price of a house at a location in U.S. dollars is a regression type of learning problem.
- *Classification*—The target variable *y* is discrete and bounded. For example, predicting whether or not an email is spam is a classification type of learning problem.

1.2.3 *Unsupervised learning*

In unsupervised learning, the objective is to learn a representation of the data that best describes it. There is no labeled data, and the goal is to learn some unknown pattern from the raw data. The input features are represented as a matrix *X*, and the system learns a function *f* that maps from *X* to a pattern or representation of the input data. This is depicted in figure 1.6. An example of unsupervised learning is clustering, where the goal is to form groups or clusters of data points with similar properties or characteristics. This is shown in the bottom half of the figure. The unlabeled data consists of two features and the datapoints are shown in 2-D space. There are no known labels, and the objective of an unsupervised learning system is to learn latent patterns present in the data. In this illustration, the system learns how to map the raw data points into clusters based on their proximity or similarity to each other. These clusters are not known beforehand because the dataset is unlabeled and, hence the learning is entirely unsupervised.

The model learns a representation of the input data.

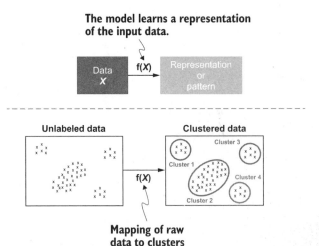

Mapping of raw
data to clusters

**Figure 1.6   Illustration of
unsupervised learning**

1.2.4   *Reinforcement learning*

Reinforcement learning consists of an agent that learns by interacting with an environment, as shown in figure 1.7. The learning agent takes an action within the environment and receives a reward or penalty, depending on the quality of the action. Based on the action taken, the agent moves from one state to another. The overall objective of the agent is to maximize the cumulative reward by learning a policy function *f* that maps from an input state to an action. Some examples of reinforcement learning are a robot vacuum cleaner learning the best path to take to clean a home and an artificial agent learning how to play board games like chess and Go.

The bottom half of figure 1.7 illustrates a reinforcement learning system. The system consists of a robot (agent) in a maze (environment). The objective of the learning

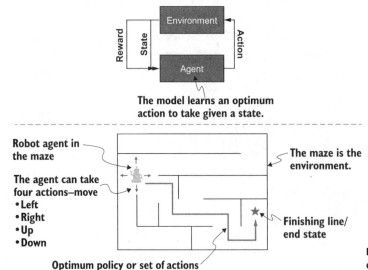

The model learns an optimum
action to take given a state.

Robot agent in
the maze

The maze is the
environment.

The agent can take
four actions–move
• Left
• Right
• Up
• Down

Finishing line/
end state

Optimum policy or set of actions

**Figure 1.7   An illustration
of reinforcement learning**

agent is to determine the optimum set of actions to take so that it can move from its current location to the finishing line (end state), indicated by the green star. The agent can take one of four actions: move left, right, up, or down.

1.2.5 Machine learning system for Diagnostics+ AI

Now that you know the three broad types of machine learning systems, which system is most applicable for Diagnostics+ AI? Given that the dataset is labeled, and you know from historical data what diagnosis was made for a patient and blood sample, the machine learning system that can be used to drive Diagnostics+ AI is *supervised learning.*

What class of supervised learning problem is it? The target for the supervised learning problem is the diagnosis, which can be either positive or negative. Because the target is discrete and bounded, it is a *classification* type of learning problem.

> **Primary focus of the book**
>
> This book primarily focuses on *supervised learning* systems where labeled data is present. I will teach you how to implement interpretability techniques for both regression and classification types of problems. Although this book does not explicitly cover unsupervised learning or reinforcement learning systems, the techniques learned in this book can be extended to them.

1.3 Building Diagnostics+ AI

Now that we've identified that Diagnostics+ AI is going to be a supervised learning system, how do we go about building it? The typical process goes through three main phases:

- Learning
- Testing
- Deploying

In the learning phase, illustrated in figure 1.8, we are in the development environment, where we use two subsets of the data called the training set and the dev set. As the name suggests, the training set is used to train a machine learning model to learn the mapping function f from the input features X (in this case, the image of the blood sample and metadata) to the target y (in this case, the diagnosis). Once we've trained the model, we use the dev set for validation purposes and tune the model based on the performance on that dev set. Tuning the model entails determining the optimum

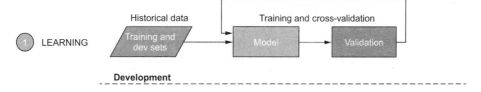

Figure 1.8 Process of building an AI system—learning phase

parameters for the model, called *hyperparameters*, that give the best performance. This is quite an iterative process, and we continue doing this until the model reaches an acceptable level of performance.

In the testing phase, illustrated in figure 1.9, we now switch over to the test environment where we use a subset of the data called the *test set*, which is different from the training set. The objective is to obtain an unbiased assessment of the accuracy of the model. Stakeholders and experts (in this case, doctors) would at this point evaluate the functionality of the system and performance of the model on the test set. This additional testing, called user acceptance testing (UAT), is the final stage in the development of any software system. If the performance is not acceptable, then we go back to phase 1 to train a better model. If the performance is acceptable, then we move on to phase 3, which is deploying.

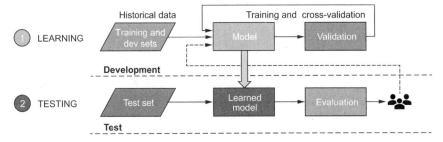

Figure 1.9   Process of building an AI system—testing phase

Finally, in the deploying phase, we now deploy the learned model into the production system where the model is now exposed to new data that it hasn't seen before. The complete process is illustrated in figure 1.10. In the case of Diagnostics+ AI, this data would be new blood samples and patient information that the model will use to predict whether the diagnosis is positive or negative with a confidence measure. This information is then consumed by the expert (the doctor) and in turn the end user (the patient).

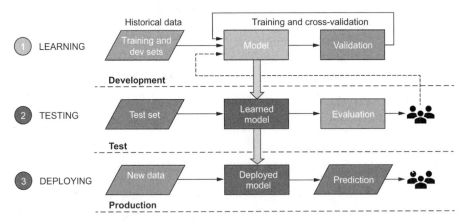

Figure 1.10   Process of building an AI system—complete

1.4   *Gaps in Diagnostics+ AI*

Figure 1.10 shows some major gaps in the Diagnostics+ AI system. This AI system does not safeguard against some common issues for which the deployed model does not behave as expected in the production environment. These issues could have a detrimental effect on the business of the diagnostics center. The common issues follow:

- Data leakage
- Bias
- Regulatory noncompliance
- Concept drift

1.4.1   *Data leakage*

Data leakage happens when features in the training, dev, and test sets unintentionally leak information that would otherwise not appear in the production environment when the model is scored on new data. For Diagnostics+, suppose we use notes made by the doctor about the diagnosis as a feature or input for our model. While evaluating the model using the test set, we could get inflated performance results, thereby tricking ourselves into thinking we've built a great model. The notes made by the doctor could contain information about the final diagnosis, which would leak information about the target variable. This problem, if not detected earlier, could be catastrophic once the model is deployed into production—the model is scored before the doctor has had a chance to review the diagnosis and add their notes. Therefore, the model would either crash in production because the feature is missing or would start to make poor diagnoses.

A classic case study of data leakage is the KDD Cup Challenge (https://www.kdd .org/kdd-cup/view/kdd-cup-2008) of 2008. The objective of this machine learning competition based on real data was to detect whether a breast cancer cell was benign or malignant based on X-ray images. A study (http://kdd.org/exploration_files/ KDDCup08-P1.pdf) showed that teams that scored the most on the test set for this competition used a feature called Patient ID, which was an identifier generated by the hospital for the patient. It turned out that some hospitals used the patient ID to indicate the severity of the condition of the patient when they were admitted to the hospital, which, therefore, leaked information about the target variable.

1.4.2   *Bias*

Bias is when the machine learning model makes an unfair prediction that favors one person or group over another. This unfair prediction could be caused by the data or the model itself. There may be sampling biases in which systematic differences exist between the data sample used for training and the population. Systemic social biases, which the model picks up on, may also be inherent in the data. The trained model could also be flawed—it may have some strong preconceptions despite evidence to the contrary. For the case of Diagnostics+ AI, if there is sampling bias, for instance, the model could make more accurate predictions for one group and not generalize well to the whole population. This is far from ideal because the diagnostics center wants the new AI system to be used for every patient, regardless of which group they belong to.

A classic case study of machine bias is the COMPAS AI system used by U.S. courts to predict future criminals. The study was conducted by ProPublica (http://mng .bz/7Ww4). (The webpage contains links to the analysis and dataset.) ProPublica obtained the COMPAS scores for 7,000 people who had been arrested in a county in Florida in 2013 and 2014. Using the scores, they found out that they could not accurately predict the recidivism rate (i.e., the rate at which a convicted person reoffends)—only 20% of the people who were predicted to commit violent crimes actually did so. More importantly, they uncovered serious racial biases in the model.

1.4.3 · Regulatory noncompliance

The General Data Protection Regulation (GDPR; https://gdpr.eu/) is a comprehensive set of regulations adopted by the European Parliament in 2016 that deals with how data is collected, stored, and processed by foreign companies. The regulation contains article 17 (https://gdpr-info.eu/art-17-gdpr/)—the "right to be forgotten"—where individuals can request a company collecting their data to erase all their personal data. The regulation also contains article 22 (https://gdpr-info.eu/art-22-gdpr/), under which individuals can challenge decisions made by an algorithm or AI system using their personal data. This regulation presses the need for providing an interpretation or explanation for why the algorithm made a particular decision. The current Diagnostics+ AI system does not comply with both sets of regulations. In this book, we are more concerned with article 22 because there are a lot of online resources on how to be compliant with article 17.

1.4.4   Concept drift

Concept drift happens when the properties or the distribution of the data in a production environment has changed when compared to the historical data used to train and evaluate the model. For Diagnostics+ AI, this could happen if new profiles of patients or diseases emerge that aren't captured in the historical data. When concept drift happens, we observe a dip in the performance of the machine learning model in production over time. The current Diagnostics+ AI system does not properly deal with concept drift.

1.5   Building a robust Diagnostics+ AI system

How do we address all the gaps highlighted in section 1.4 and build a robust Diagnostics+ AI system? We need to tweak the process. First, as shown in figure 1.11, we add a model understanding phase after the testing phase and before deploying.

The purpose of this new *understanding* phase is to answer the important *how* question—how did the model come up with a positive diagnosis for a given blood sample? This involves interpreting the important features for the model and how they interact

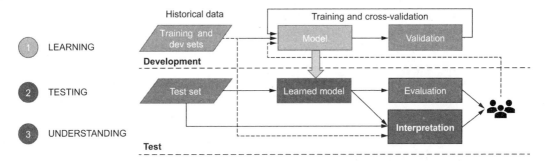

Figure 1.11   **Process of building a robust AI system—understanding phase**

with each other, interpreting what patterns the model learned, understanding the blind spots, checking for bias in the data, and ensuring those biases are not propagated by the model. This understanding phase should ensure that the AI system is safeguarded against the data leakage and bias issues highlighted in sections 1.4.1 and 1.4.2, respectively.

The second change is to add an *explaining* phase after deploying, as shown in figure 1.12. The purpose of the explaining phase is to interpret how the model came up with the prediction on new data in the production+ environment. Interpreting the prediction on new data allows us to expose that information, if needed, to expert users of the system who challenge the decision made by the deployed model. Another purpose is to come up with a human-readable explanation so that it can be exposed to wider end users of the AI system. By including the interpretation step, we will be able to address the regulatory noncompliance issue highlighted in section 1.4.3.

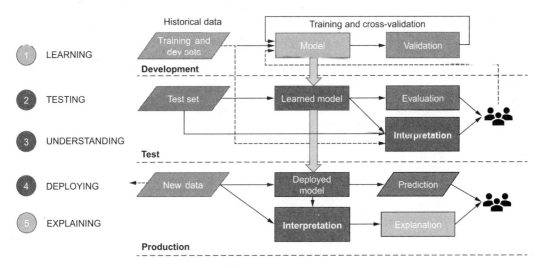

Figure 1.12   **Process of building a robust AI—explaining phase**

Finally, to address the concept drift issue highlighted in section 1.4.4, we need to add a *monitoring* phase in the production environment. This complete process is shown in figure 1.13. The purpose of the monitoring phase is to track the distribution of the data in the production environment as well as the performance of the deployed model. If any change occurs in data distribution or model performance dips, we will need to go back to the learning phase and incorporate the new data from the production environment to retrain the models.

Primary focus of the book

This book primarily focuses on the *interpretation* step in the understanding and explaining phases. I intend to teach you various interpretability techniques that you can apply to answer the important *how* question and address the data leakage, bias, and regulatory noncompliance issues. Although explainability and monitoring are important steps in the process, they are not the primary focus of this book. It is also important to distinguish between interpretability and explainability. This is addressed in the following section.

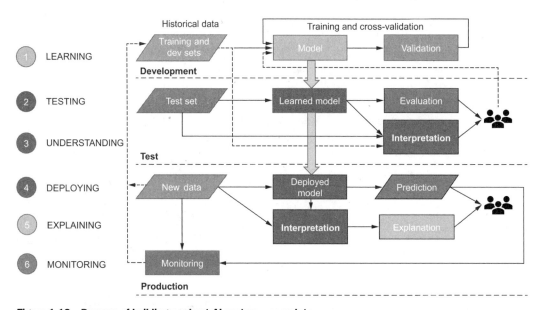

Figure 1.13   **Process of building a robust AI system—complete**

1.6   *Interpretability vs. explainability*

Interpretability and *explainability* are sometimes used interchangeably, but it is important to make a distinction between the two terms.

    Interpretability is all about understanding the cause and effect within an AI system. It is the degree to which we can consistently estimate what a model will predict given an input, understand how the model came up with the prediction, understand how the prediction changes with changes in the input or algorithmic parameters, and finally, understand when the model has made a mistake. Interpretability is mostly discernible by experts who are building, deploying, or using the AI system, and these techniques are building blocks that will help us get to explainability.

Explainability, on the other hand, goes beyond interpretability in that it helps us understand in a human-readable form how and why a model came up with a prediction. It explains the internal mechanics of the system in human terms, with the intent to reach a much wider audience. Explainability requires interpretability as a building block and also looks to other fields and areas, such as human-computer interaction (HCI), law, and ethics. In this book, I will focus more on interpretability and less on explainability. We have a lot to cover within interpretability itself, but it should give you a solid foundation to be able to later build an explainable AI system.

You should be aware of four different personas when you consider interpretability. They are the *data scientist* or *engineer* who is building the AI system, the *business stakeholder* who wants to deploy the AI system for their business, the *end user* of the AI system, and finally the *expert* or *regulator* who monitors or audits the health of the AI system. Note that interpretability means different things to these four personas, as described next:

- For a *data scientist* or *engineer*, it means gaining a deeper understanding of how the model made a particular prediction, which features are important, and how to debug issues by analyzing cases where the model did badly. This understanding helps the data scientist build more robust models.
- For a *business stakeholder*, it means understanding how the model made a decision so as to ensure fairness and protect the business's users and brand.
- For an *end user*, it means understanding how the model made a decision and allowing for meaningful challenge if the model made a mistake.
- For an *expert* or *regulator*, it means auditing the model and the AI system and following the decision trail, especially when things went wrong.

1.6.1   Types of interpretability techniques

Figure 1.14 summarizes various types of interpretability techniques. *Intrinsic* interpretability techniques are related to machine learning models with a simple structure, also called *white-box models*. White-box models are inherently transparent, and interpreting the internals of the model is straightforward. Interpretability comes right out of the box for such models. *Post hoc* interpretability techniques are usually applied after model training and are used to interpret and understand the importance of certain inputs for the model prediction. Post hoc interpretability techniques are suited for white-box and black-box models, that is, models that are not inherently transparent.

Interpretability techniques can also be model-specific or model-agnostic. *Model-specific* interpretability techniques, as the name suggests, can be applied only to certain types of models. Intrinsic interpretability techniques are model-specific by nature

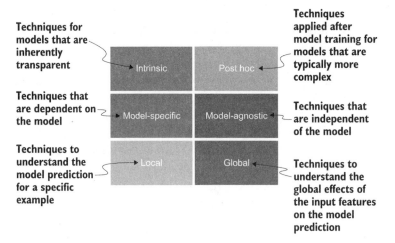

Figure 1.14   Types of interpretability techniques

because the technique is tied to the specific structure of the model being used. *Model-agnostic* interpretability techniques, however, are not dependent on the specific type of model being used. They can be applied to any model because they are independent of the internal structure of the model. Post-hoc interpretability techniques are mostly model-agnostic by nature.

Interpretability techniques can also be local or global in scope. *Local* interpretability techniques aim to give a better understanding of the model prediction for a specific instance or example. *Global* interpretability techniques, on the other hand, aim to give a better understanding of the model as a whole—the global effects of the input features on the model prediction. We cover all of these types of techniques in this book. Now let's take a look at what specifically you will learn.

1.7   *What will I learn in this book?*

Figure 1.15 depicts a map of all the interpretability techniques you will learn in this book. When interpreting supervised learning models, it is important to distinguish between white-box and black-box models. Examples of white-box models are linear regression, logistic regression, decision trees, and generalized additive models (GAMs). Examples of black-box models include tree ensembles, like random forest and boosted trees, and neural networks. White-box models are much easier to interpret than black-box models. On the other hand, black-box models have much higher predictive power than white-box models. So, we need to make a trade-off between predictive power and interpretability. It is important to understand the scenarios in which we can apply white-box and black-box models.

In chapter 2, you'll learn about characteristics that make white-box models inherently transparent and black-box models inherently opaque. You'll learn how to interpret simple white-box models, such as linear regression and decision trees, and then we'll switch gears to focus on GAMs. GAMs have high predictive power and are highly interpretable, too, so they offer more bang for the buck than GAMs. You'll learn about the properties that give GAMs power and how to interpret them. At the time of writing, there are not a lot of practical resources on GAMs to give a good understanding of the internals of the model and how to interpret them. To address this gap, we pay a lot of attention to GAMs in chapter 2. The rest of the chapters focus on black-box models.

We can interpret black-box models in two ways. One way is to interpret model processing, that is, to understand how the model processes the inputs and arrives at the final prediction. Chapters 3 to 5 focus on interpreting model processing. The other way is to interpret model representations, which is applicable only to deep neural networks. Chapters 6 and 7 focus on interpreting model representations with the goal of understanding what features or patterns have been learned by the neural network.

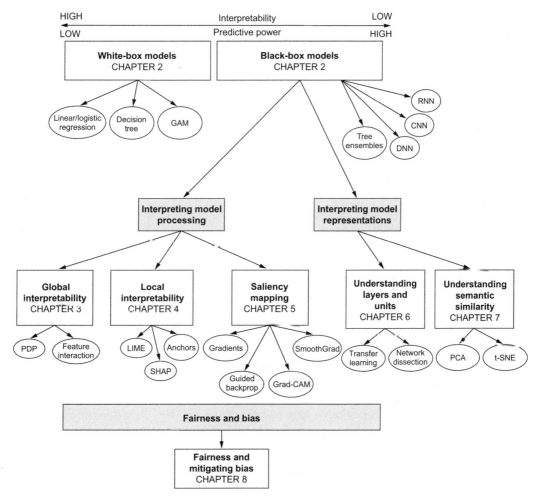

Figure 1.15 Map of interpretability techniques covered in this book

In chapter 3, we focus on a class of black-box models called tree ensembles. You'll learn about their characteristics and what makes them "black box." You will also learn how to interpret them using post hoc model-agnostic methods that are global in scope. We will focus specifically on partial dependence plots (PDPs), individual conditional expectation (ICE) plots, and feature interaction plots.

In chapter 4, we focus on deep neural networks, specifically the vanilla fully connected neural networks. You'll learn about characteristics that make these models black box and also how to interpret them using post hoc model-agnostic methods that are local in scope. You'll specifically learn about techniques such as local interpretable model-agnostic explanations (LIME), SHapley Additive exPlanations (SHAP), and anchors.

In chapter 5, we focus on convolutional neural networks, which is a more advanced form of architecture used mainly for visual tasks such as image classification and object detection. You'll learn how to visualize what the model is focusing on using saliency maps. You'll also learn techniques such as gradients, guided backpropagation (backprop for short), gradient-weighted class activation mapping (grad-CAM), guided grad-CAM, and smooth gradients (SmoothGrad).

In chapters 6 and 7, we focus on convolutional neural networks and neural networks used for language understanding. You'll learn how to dissect the neural networks and understand what representations of the data are learned by the intermediate or hidden layers in the neural network. You'll also learn how to visualize high-dimensional representations learned by the model using techniques like principal component analysis (PCA) and t-distributed stochastic neighbor embedding (t-SNE).

The book ends on the topic of building fair and unbiased models and learning what it takes to build explainable AI systems. In chapter 8, you'll learn about various definitions of fairness and how to check whether your model is biased. You'll also learn techniques to mitigate bias using a neutralizing technique. We discuss a standardizing approach to documenting datasets using datasheets that help improve transparency and accountability with the stakeholders and users of the system. In chapter 9, we pave the way for explainable AI by teaching how to build such systems, and you'll also learn about contrastive explanations using counterfactual examples. By the end of this book, you will have various interpretability techniques in your toolkit. When it comes to model understanding, there is, unfortunately, no silver bullet. No one interpretability technique is applicable for all scenarios. You, therefore, need to look at the model using a few different lenses by applying multiple interpretability techniques. In this book, I help you identify the right tools for the right scenarios.

1.7.1   *What tools will I be using in this book?*

In this book, we will implement the models and the interpretability techniques in the Python programming language. The main reason I chose Python is because most of the state-of-the-art interpretability techniques are created and actively developed in this language. Figure 1.16 gives an overview of the tools used in this book. For representing data, we will be using Python data structures and common data science libraries such as

Pandas and *NumPy*. To implement white-box models, we will use the *Scikit-Learn* library for simpler linear regression and decision trees, and *pyGAM* for GAMs. For black-box models, we will use *Scikit-Learn* for tree ensembles and *PyTorch* or *TensorFlow* for neural networks. For interpretability techniques used to understand model processing, we will use the *Matplotlib* library for visualization and open source libraries that implement techniques such as *PDP, LIME, SHAP, anchors, gradients, guided backprop, grad-CAM* and *SmoothGrad*. To interpret model representations, we will employ tools that implement *NetDissect* and *tSNE* and visualize them using the *Matplotlib* library. Finally, for mitigating bias, we will use *PyTorch and TensorFlow* to implement the bias-neutralizing technique and GANs for adversarial debiasing.

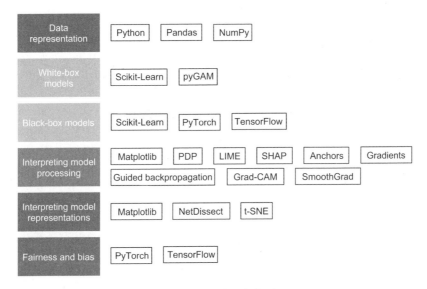

Figure 1.16   An overview of the tools used in this book

1.7.2   *What do I need to know before reading this book?*

This book is primarily focused on data scientists and engineers with experience programming in Python. A basic knowledge of common Python data science libraries such as NumPy, Pandas, Matplotlib, and Scikit-Learn will help, although this is not required. The book will show you how to use these libraries to load and represent data but will not give you an in-depth understanding of them, because it is beyond the scope of this book.

The reader must be familiar with linear algebra, specifically vectors and matrices, and operations on them, such as dot product, matrix multiplication, transpose, and inversion. The reader must also have a good foundation in probability theory and statistics, specifically on the topics of random variables, basic discrete and continuous probability distributions, conditional probability, and Bayes' theorem. Basic knowledge of calculus is also expected, specifically single-variable and multivariate functions and specific operations on them such as derivatives (gradients) and partial derivatives.

Although this book does not focus too much on the mathematics behind model interpretability, having this basic mathematical foundation is expected of data scientists and engineers interested in building machine learning models.

Basic knowledge of machine learning or practical experience training machine learning models is a plus, although this is not a hard requirement. This book does not cover machine learning in great depth because a lot of resources and books do justice to this topic. The book will, however, give you a basic understanding of the specific machine learning models being used and also show you how to train and evaluate them. The main focus is on the theory related to interpretability and how you can implement techniques to interpret the model after you have trained it.

Summary

- Three broad types of machine learning systems exist: supervised learning, unsupervised learning, and reinforcement learning. This book focuses on interpretability techniques for supervised learning systems that include both regression and classification types of problems.
- When building AI systems, it is important to add interpretability, model understanding, and monitoring to the process. If you don't, you could experience disastrous consequences such as data leakage, bias, concept drift, and a general lack of trust. Moreover, with the GDPR, we have legal reasons for including interpretability in our AI processes.
- It is important to understand the difference between interpretability and explainability.
- Interpretability is the degree to which we can consistently estimate what a model will predict, understand how the model came up with the prediction, and understand when the model has made a mistake. Interpretability techniques are building blocks that will help you get to explainability.
- Explainability goes beyond interpretability in that it helps us understand how and why a model came up with a prediction in a human-readable form. It makes use of interpretability techniques and also looks to other fields and areas, such as human-computer interaction (HCI), law, and ethics.
- You need to be mindful of different personas using or building the AI system, because interpretability means different things to different people.
- Interpretability techniques can be intrinsic or post hoc, model-specific or model-agnostic, local or global.
- Models that are inherently transparent are called white-box models, and models that are inherently opaque are called black-box models. White-box models are much easier to interpret but generally have lower predictive power than black-box models.
- Black-box models offer two broad classes of interpretability techniques: one that's focused on interpreting the model processing and another that's focused on interpreting the representation learned by the model.

White-box models

2

This chapter covers

- Characteristics that make white-box models inherently transparent and interpretable
- How to interpret simple white-box models such as linear regression and decision trees
- What generalized additive models (GAMs) are and their properties that give them high predictive power and high interpretability
- How to implement and interpret GAMs
- What black-box models are and their characteristics that make them inherently opaque

To build an interpretable AI system, we must understand the different types of models that we can use to drive the AI system and techniques that we can apply to interpret them. In this chapter, I cover three key white-box models—linear regression, decision trees, and generalized additive models (GAMs)—that are inherently transparent. You will learn how they can be implemented, when they can be applied, and how they can be interpreted. I also briefly introduce black-box models. You will learn when they can be applied and their characteristics that make them hard to interpret. This chapter focuses on interpreting white-box models, and the rest of the book will be dedicated to interpreting complex black-box models.

In chapter 1, you learned how to build a robust, interpretable AI system. The process is shown again in figure 2.1. The main focus of chapter 2 and the rest of the book will be on implementing interpretability techniques to gain a much better understanding of machine learning models that cover both white-box and black-box models. The relevant blocks are highlighted in figure 2.1. We will apply these interpretability techniques during model development and testing. We will also learn about model training and testing, especially the implementation aspects. Because the model learning, testing, and understanding stages are quite iterative, it is important to cover all three stages together. Readers who are already familiar with model training and testing are free to skip those sections and jump straight into interpretability.

When applying interpretability techniques in production, we also need to consider building an explanation-producing system to generate a human-readable explanation for the end users of your system. Explainability is, however, beyond the scope of this book, and the focus will be exclusively on interpretability during model development and testing.

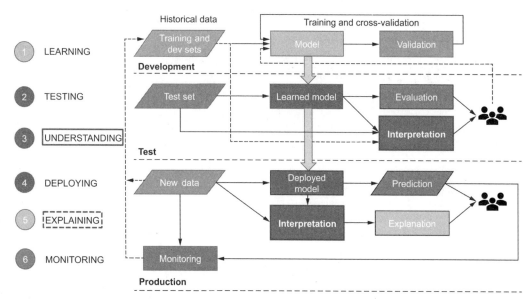

Figure 2.1   The process to build a robust AI system, focusing mainly on interpretation

2.1   *White-box models*

White-box models are inherently transparent, and the characteristics that make them transparent are

- The algorithm used for machine learning is straightforward to understand, and we can clearly interpret how the input features are transformed into the output or target variable.

- We can identify the most important features to predict the target variable, and those features are understandable.

Examples of white-box models include linear regression, logistic regression, decision trees, and generalized additive models (GAMs). Table 2.1 shows the machine learning tasks to which these models can be applied.

Table 2.1 Mapping of a white-box model to a machine learning task

White-box model	Machine learning task(s)
Linear regression	Regression
Logistic regression	Classification
Decision trees	Regression and classification
GAMs	Regression and classification

In this chapter, we focus on linear regression, decision trees, and GAMs. In figure 2.2, I have plotted these techniques on a 2-D plane with interpretability on the *x*-axis and predictive power on the *y*-axis. As you go from left to right on this plane, the models go from the low interpretability regime to the high interpretability regime. As you go from bottom to top on this plane, the models go from the low predictive power regime to the high predictive power regime. Linear regression and decision trees are highly interpretable but have low to medium predictive power. GAMs, on the other hand, have high predictive power and are highly interpretable as well. The figure also shows black-box models in gray and italic. We cover those in section 2.6.

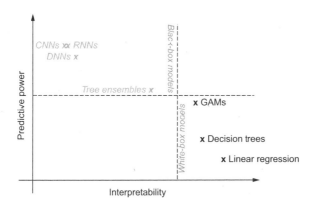

Figure 2.2 White-box models on the interpretability versus predictive power plane

We start off with interpreting the simpler linear regression and decision tree models and then go deep into the world of GAMs. For each of these white-box models, we learn how the algorithm works and the characteristics that make them inherently interpretable. For white-box models, it is important to understand the details of the algorithm because it will help us interpret how the input features are transformed into the final model output or prediction. It will also help us quantify the importance of each input feature. You'll learn how to train and evaluate all of the models in this book in Python first, before we dive into interpretability. As mentioned earlier, because the model learning, testing, and understanding stages are iterative, it is important to cover all three stages together.

2.2   *Diagnostics+—diabetes progression*

Let's look at white-box models in the context of a concrete example. Recall the Diagnostics+ AI example from chapter 1. The Diagnostics+ center would now like to determine the progression of diabetes in their patients one year after a baseline measurement is taken, as shown in figure 2.3. The center has tasked you, as a newly minted data scientist, to build a model for Diagnostics+ AI to predict diabetes progression one year out. This prediction will be used by doctors to determine a proper treatment plan for their patients. To gain the doctors' confidence in the model, it is important not just to provide an accurate prediction but also to be able to show how the model arrived at that prediction. How would you begin this task?

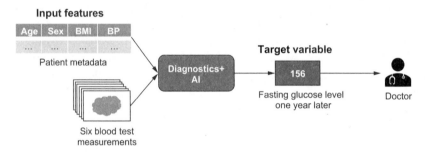

Figure 2.3   Diagnostics+ AI for diabetes

First, let's look at what data is available. The Diagnostics+ center has collected from around 440 patients data that consists of patient metadata such as age, sex, body mass index (BMI), and blood pressure (BP). Blood tests were also performed on these patients, and the following six measurements were collected:

- LDL (bad cholesterol)
- HDL (good cholesterol)
- Total cholesterol
- Thyroid-stimulating hormone
- Low-tension glaucoma
- Fasting blood glucose

The data also contains the fasting glucose levels for all patients one year after the baseline measurement was taken. This is the target for the model. How would you formulate this as a machine learning problem? Because labeled data is available, where you are given 10 input features and one target variable that you have to predict, you can formulate this problem as a supervised learning problem. The target variable is real valued or continuous, so it is a regression task. The objective is to learn a function *f* that will help predict the target variable *y* given the input features *x*.

Let's now load the data in Python and explore how correlated the input features are with each other and the target variable. If the input features are highly correlated with the target variable, then we can use them to train a model to make the prediction. If, however, they are not correlated with the target variable, then we will need to explore further to determine whether there is some noise in the data. The data can be loaded in Python as follows:

**Imports the scikit-learn function
to load the open diabetes dataset**

Loads the diabetes dataset

```
from sklearn.datasets import load_diabetes
diabetes = load_diabetes()
X, y = diabetes['data'], diabetes['target']
```

**Extracts the features
and the target variable**

We will now create a Pandas DataFrame, which is a two-dimensional data structure that contains all the features and the target variable. The diabetes dataset provided by Scikit-Learn comes with feature names that are not easy to understand. The six blood sample measurements are named s1, s2, s3, s4, s5, and s6, which makes it hard for us to understand what each feature is measuring. The documentation provides this mapping, however, and we use that to rename the columns to something that is more understandable, as shown here:

```
feature_rename = {'age': 'Age',
                  'sex': 'Sex',
                  'bmi': 'BMI',
                  'bp': 'BP',
                  's1': 'Total Cholesterol',
                  's2': 'LDL',
                  's3': 'HDL',
                  's4': 'Thyroid',
                  's5': 'Glaucoma',
                  's6': 'Glucose'}

df_data = pd.DataFrame(X,
                columns=diabetes['feature_names'])
df_data.rename(columns=feature_rename, inplace=True)
df_data['target'] = y
```

**Mapping the feature names
provided by Scikit-Learn to
a more readable form**

**Loads all the
features (x) into
a DataFrame**

**Uses the Scikit-Learn
feature names as
column names**

**Renames the Scikit-Learn
feature names to a more
readable form**

**Includes the target variable (y)
as a separate column**

Now let's compute the pairwise correlation of columns so that we can determine how correlated each of the input features is with each other and the target variable. This can be done easily in Pandas as follows:

```
corr = df_data.corr()
```

By default, the corr() function in pandas computes the Pearson or standard correlation coefficient. This coefficient measures the linear correlation between two variables and has a value between +1 and –1. If the magnitude of the coefficient is above 0.7, that means it's a really high correlation. If the magnitude of the coefficient is between 0.5 and 0.7, that indicates a moderately high correlation. If the magnitude of the coefficient is between 0.3 and 0.5, that means a low correlation, and a magnitude less than 0.3 means there is little to no correlation. We can now plot the correlation matrix in Python as follows:

```
import matplotlib.pyplot as plt
import seaborn as sns
sns.set(style='whitegrid')
sns.set_palette('bright')

f, ax = plt.subplots(figsize=(10, 10))
sns.heatmap(
    corr,
    vmin=-1, vmax=1, center=0,
    cmap="PiYG",
    square=True,
    ax=ax
)
ax.set_xticklabels(
    ax.get_xticklabels(),
    rotation=90,
    horizontalalignment='right'
);
```

Imports Matplotlib and Seaborn to plot the correlation matrix

Initializes a Matplotlib plot with a predefined size

Uses Seaborn to plot a heatmap of the correlation coefficients

Rotates the labels on the x-axis by 90 degrees

The resulting plot is shown in figure 2.4. Let's first focus on either the last row or the last column in the figure. This shows us the correlation of each of the inputs with the target variable. We can see that seven features—BMI, BP, Total Cholesterol, HDL, Thyroid, Glaucoma, and Glucose—have moderately high to high correlation with the target variable. We can also observe that the good cholesterol (HDL) also has a negative correlation with the progression of diabetes. This means that the higher the HDL value, the lower the fasting glucose level for the patient one year out. The features seem to have pretty good signal in being able to predict the disease progression, and we can go ahead and train a model using them. As an exercise, observe how each of the features is correlated with each other. Total cholesterol, for instance, seems very highly correlated with the bad cholesterol, LDL. We will come back to this when we start to interpret the linear regression model in section 2.3.1.

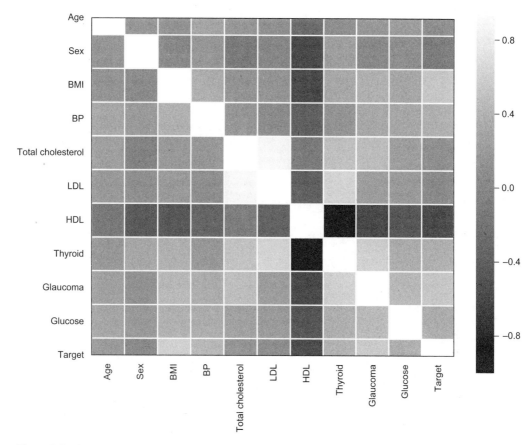

Figure 2.4 Correlation plot of the features and the target variable for the diabetes dataset

2.3   *Linear regression*

Linear regression is one of the simplest models you can train for regression tasks. In linear regression, the function f is represented as a linear combination of all the input features, as depicted in figure 2.5. The known variables are shown in gray, and the idea is to represent the target variable as a linear combination of the inputs. The unknown variables are the weights that must be learned by the learning algorithm.

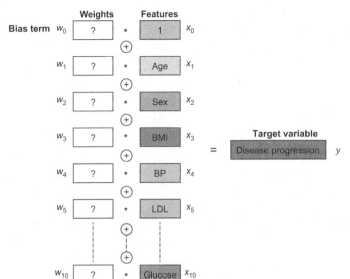

Figure 2.5   Disease progression represented as a linear combination of inputs

In general, the function f for linear regression is shown mathematically as follows, where n is the total number of features:

$$y = w_0 + w_1 x_1 + w_2 x_2 + \dots + w_n x_n$$

$$= w_0 + \sum_{i=1}^{n} w_i x_i$$

The objective of the linear regression learning algorithm is to determine the weights that accurately predict the target variable for all patients in the training set. We can apply the following techniques here:

- Gradient descent
- Closed-form solution (e.g., the Newton equation)

Gradient descent is commonly applied because it scales well to a large number of features and training examples. The general idea is to update the weights such that the squared error of the predicted target variable with respect to the actual target variable is minimized.

The objective of the gradient descent algorithm is to minimize the squared error or squared difference between the predicted target variable and the actual target variable across all the examples in the training set. This algorithm is guaranteed to find the optimum set of weights, and because the algorithm minimizes the squared error, it is said to be based on least squares. A linear regression model can be easily trained using the Scikit-Learn package in Python. The code to train the model is shown next. Note that the open diabetes dataset provided by Scikit-Learn is used here, and this dataset has been standardized, having zero mean and unit variance for all the input features. Feature standardization is a widely used form of preprocessing done on data-sets used in many machine learning models like linear regression, logistic regression, and more complex models based on neural networks. It allows the learning algo-rithms that drive these models to converge faster to an optimum solution:

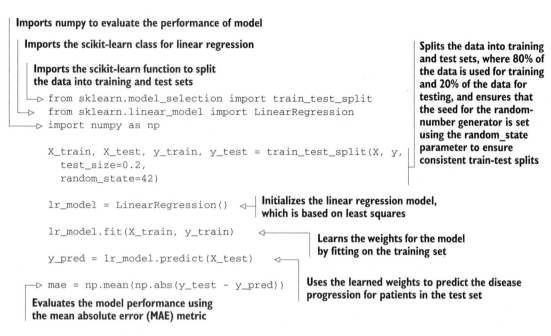

Imports numpy to evaluate the performance of model

Imports the scikit-learn class for linear regression

Imports the scikit-learn function to split the data into training and test sets

Splits the data into training and test sets, where 80% of the data is used for training and 20% of the data for testing, and ensures that the seed for the random-number generator is set using the random_state parameter to ensure consistent train-test splits

```
from sklearn.model_selection import train_test_split
from sklearn.linear_model import LinearRegression
import numpy as np

X_train, X_test, y_train, y_test = train_test_split(X, y,
    test_size=0.2,
    random_state=42)

lr_model = LinearRegression()

lr_model.fit(X_train, y_train)

y_pred = lr_model.predict(X_test)

mae = np.mean(np.abs(y_test - y_pred))
```

Initializes the linear regression model, which is based on least squares

Learns the weights for the model by fitting on the training set

Uses the learned weights to predict the disease progression for patients in the test set

Evaluates the model performance using the mean absolute error (MAE) metric

The performance of the trained linear regression model can be quantified by compar-ing the predictions with the actual values on the test set. We can use multiple metrics, such as root mean squared error (RMSE), mean absolute error (MAE), and mean absolute percentage error (MAPE). Each of these metrics offers pros and cons, and it helps to quantify the performance using multiple metrics to measure the goodness of a model. Both MAE and RMSE are in the same units as the target variable and are easy to understand in that regard. The magnitude of the error, however, cannot be easily understood using these two metrics. For example, an error of 10 may seem small at first, but if the actual value you are comparing with is, say, 100, then that error is not small in relation to that. This is where MAPE is useful for understanding these relative differences because the error is expressed in terms of percentage (%) error. The topic of measuring model goodness is important but is beyond the scope of this book. You can find a lot of resources online. I have written a comprehensive two-part blog post (http://mng.bz/ZzNP) to cover this topic.

The previous trained linear regression model was evaluated using the MAE metric, and the performance was determined to be 42.8. But is this performance good? To check whether the performance of a model is good, we need to compare it with a baseline. For Diagnostics+, the doctors have been using a baseline model that predicts the median diabetes progression across all patients. The MAE of this baseline model was determined to be 62.2. If we now compare this baseline with the linear regression model, we notice a drop in MAE by 19.4, which is a pretty good improvement. We have now trained a decent model, but it doesn't tell us how the model arrived at the prediction and which input features are most important. I cover this in the following section.

2.3.1 *Interpreting linear regression*

In the earlier section, we trained a linear regression model during model development and then evaluated the model performance during testing using the MAE metric. As a data scientist building Diagnostics+ AI, you now share these results with the doctors, and they are reasonably happy with the performance. But there is something missing. The doctors don't have a clear understanding of how the model arrived at the final prediction. Explaining the gradient descent algorithm does not help with this understanding because you are dealing with a pretty large feature space in this example—10 input features in total. It is impossible to visualize how the algorithm converges to the final prediction in a 10-dimensional space. In general, the ability to describe and explain a machine learning algorithm does not guarantee interpretability. So, what is the best way of interpreting a model?

For linear regression, because the final prediction is just a weighted sum of the input features, all we have to look at are the learned weights. This is what makes linear regression a white-box model. What do the weights tell us? If the weight of a feature is positive, a positive change in that input will result in a proportional positive change in the output, and a negative change in the input will result in a proportional negative change in the output. Similarly, if the weight is negative, a positive change in the input will result in a proportional negative change in the output, and a negative change in the input will result in a proportional positive change in the output. Such a learned function, shown in figure 2.6, is called a linear, monotonic function.

We can also look at the impact or importance of a feature in predicting the target variable by looking at the absolute value of the corresponding weight. The larger the

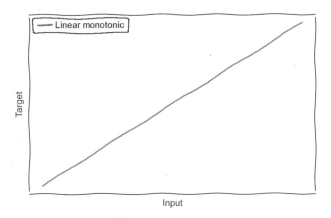

Figure 2.6   A representation of a linear, monotonic function

absolute value of the weight, the greater the importance. The weights for each of the 10 features are shown in descending order of importance in figure 2.7.

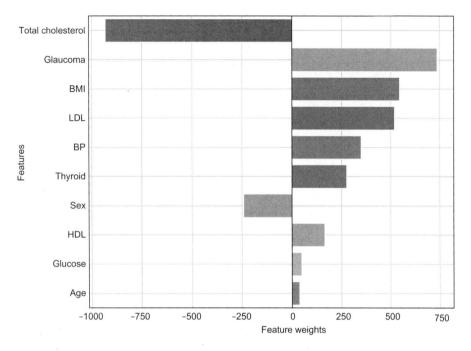

Figure 2.7 Feature importance for the diabetes linear regression model

The most important feature is the Total Cholesterol measurement. It has a large negative value for the weight. This means that a positive change in the cholesterol level has a large negative influence on predicting diabetes progression. This could be because Total Cholesterol also accounts for the good kind of cholesterol.

If we now look at the bad cholesterol, or LDL, feature, it has a large positive weight, and it is also the fourth most important feature in predicting the progression of diabetes. This means that a positive change in LDL cholesterol level results in a large positive influence in predicting diabetes one year out. The good cholesterol, or HDL, feature has a small positive weight and is the third least important feature. Why is that? Recall the exploratory analysis that we did in section 2.2 where we plotted the correlation matrix in figure 2.4. If we observe the correlation among total cholesterol, LDL, and HDL, we see a very high correlation between total cholesterol and LDL and moderately high correlation between total cholesterol and HDL. Because of this correlation, the HDL feature is deemed redundant by the model.

It also looks like the baseline Glucose measurement for the patient has a very small impact on predicting the progression of diabetes a year out. If we again go back to the correlation plot shown in figure 2.4, we can see that Glucose measurement is very highly correlated with the baseline Glaucoma measurement (the second most important feature for the model) and highly correlated with Total Cholesterol (the most important feature for the model). The model, therefore, treats Glucose as a redundant feature because a lot of the signal is obtained from the Total Cholesterol and Glaucoma features.

If an input feature is highly correlated with one or more other features, they are said to be multicollinear. *Multicollinearity* could be detrimental to the performance of a linear regression model based on least squares. Let's suppose we use two features, x_1 and x_2, to predict the target variable y. In a linear regression model, we are essentially estimating weights for each of the features that will help predict the target variable such that the squared error is minimized. Using least squares, the weight for feature x_1, or the effect of x_1 on the target variable y, is estimated by holding x_2 constant. Similarly, the weight for x_2 is estimated by holding x_1 constant. If x_1 and x_2 are collinear, then they vary together, and it becomes very difficult to accurately estimate their effects on the target variable. One of the features becomes completely redundant for the model. We saw the effects of collinearity on our diabetes model earlier where features such as HDL and Glucose that were pretty highly correlated with the target variable had very low importance in the final model. The problem of multicollinearity can be overcome by removing the redundant features for the model. As an exercise, I highly recommend doing that to see if you can improve the performance of the linear regression model.

In the process of training a machine learning model, it is important to explore the data first and determine how correlated features are with each other and with the target variable. The problem of multicollinearity must be uncovered early in the process, before training the model, but if it has been overlooked, interpreting the model will help expose such issues. The plot in figure 2.7 can be generated in Python using the following code snippet:

```
import numpy as np
import matplotlib.pyplot as plt
import seaborn as sns
sns.set(style='whitegrid')
sns.set_palette('bright')

weights = lr_model.coef_

feature_importance_idx = np.argsort(np.abs(weights))[::-1]
feature_importance = [feature_names[idx].upper() for idx in
   feature_importance_idx]
feature_importance_values = [weights[idx] for idx in
   feature_importance_idx]

f, ax = plt.subplots(figsize=(10, 8))
sns.barplot(x=feature_importance_values, y=feature_importance, ax=ax)
ax.grid(True)
ax.set_xlabel('Feature Weights')
ax.set_ylabel('Features')
```

Imports numpy to perform operation on vectors in an optimized way

Imports matplotlib and seaborn to plot the feature importance

Obtains the weights from the linear regression model trained earlier using the coef_ parameter

Sorts the weights in descending order of importance and gets their indices

Uses the ordered indices to get the feature names and the corresponding weight values

Generates the plot shown in figure 2.7

2.3.2 *Limitations of linear regression*

In the previous section, we saw how easy it is to interpret a linear regression model. It is highly transparent and easy to understand. However, it has poor predictive power, especially in cases where the relationship between the input features and target is nonlinear. Consider the example shown in figure 2.8.

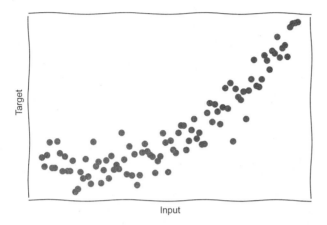

Figure 2.8 Illustration of a nonlinear dataset

If we were to fit a linear regression model to this dataset, we would get a straight-line linear fit, as shown in figure 2.9. As you can see, the model does not properly fit the data and does not capture the nonlinear relationship. This limitation of linear regression is called *underfitting*, and the model is said to have *high bias*. In the following sections, we will see how this problem can be overcome by using more complex models with higher predictive power.

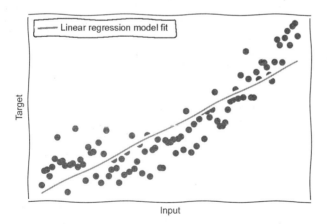

Figure 2.9 The problem of underfitting (high bias)

2.4 *Decision trees*

A decision tree is a great machine learning algorithm that can be used to model complex nonlinear relationships. It can be applied to both regression and classification tasks. It has relatively higher predictive power than linear regression and is highly interpretable, too. The basic idea behind a decision tree is to find optimum splits in the data that best predict the output or target variable. In figure 2.10, I have illustrated this by considering only two features, BMI and Age. The decision tree splits the dataset into five groups in total, three age groups and two BMI groups.

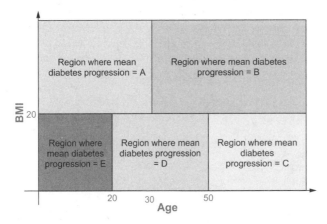

Figure 2.10 Decision tree splitting strategy

The algorithm that is commonly applied in determining the optimum splits is the classification and regression tree (CART) algorithm. This algorithm first chooses a feature and a threshold for that feature. Based on that feature and threshold, the algorithm splits the dataset into the following two subsets:

- Subset 1, where the value of the feature is less than or equal to the threshold
- Subset 2, where the value of the feature is greater than the threshold

The algorithm picks the feature and threshold that minimizes a cost function or criterion. For regression tasks, this criterion is typically the mean squared error (MSE), and for classification tasks, it is typically either Gini impurity or entropy. The algorithm then continues to recursively split the data until the criterion is reduced further or until a maximum depth is reached. The splitting strategy in figure 2.10 is shown as a binary tree in figure 2.11.

A decision tree model can be trained in Python using the Scikit-Learn package as follows. The code to learn the open diabetes dataset and to split it into the training and test sets is the same as the one used for linear regression in section 2.3, so, this code is not repeated here:

```
from sklearn.tree import DecisionTreeRegressor

dt_model = DecisionTreeRegressor(max_depth=None, random_state=42)

dt_model.fit(X_train, y_train)

y_pred = dt_model.predict(X_test)

mae = np.mean(np.abs(y_test - y_pred))
```

Trains the decision tree model ⊳ (points to dt_model.fit line)

Imports the scikit-learn class for the decision tree regressor ⊲ (points to import line)

Initializes the decision tree regressor. It is important to set the random_state to ensure that consistent, reproducible results can be obtained. (points to DecisionTreeRegressor line)

Uses the trained decision tree model to predict the disease progression for patients in the test set ⊲ (points to y_pred line)

Evaluates the model performance using the mean absolute error (MAE) metric ⊲ (points to mae line)

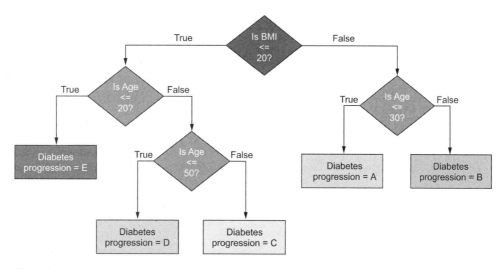

Figure 2.11   Decision tree data splitting visualized as a binary tree

The decision tree model trained here was evaluated using the MAE metric, and the performance was determined to be 54.7. If we tune the *max_depth* hyperparameter and set it to 3, we can improve the MAE performance further to 48.6. This performance, however, is poorer than the regression model trained in section 2.2. I will discuss the reasons for this in section 2.4.2, but first, let's look at how to interpret a decision tree in the following section.

> **Decision tree for classification tasks**
>
> As mentioned in this section, decision trees can also be used for classification tasks. In the CART algorithm, Gini impurity or entropy is used as the cost function. In Scikit-Learn, you can easily train a decision tree classifier as follows:
>
> ```
> from sklearn.tree import DecisionTreeClassifier
> dt_model = DecisionTreeClassifier(criterion='gini', max_depth=None)
> dt_model.fit(X_train, y_train)
> ```
>
> The `criterion` parameter in the `DecisionTreeClassifier` can be used to specify the cost function for the CART algorithm. By default, it is set to `gini`, but it can be changed to `entropy`.

2.4.1   *Interpreting decision trees*

Decision trees are great at modeling nonlinear relationships between the input and the output. By finding splits in the data across features, the model tends to learn a function that is nonlinear in nature. The function could be monotonic, where a change in the input results in a change in the output in the same direction, or nonmonotonic, where a change in the input could result in a change in the output in any direction and at a varying rate. This is illustrated in figure 2.12.

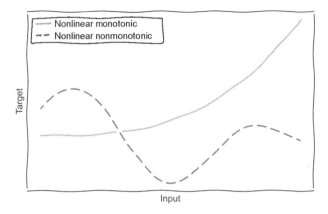

Figure 2.12 Representation of nonlinear, monotonic, and nonmonotonic functions

How do we interpret such a learned nonlinear function? As seen in the previous section, a decision tree can be visualized as a bunch of if-else conditions strung together, where each condition splits the data in two. Such a model can be easily visualized as a binary tree, as illustrated in figure 2.11. For the decision tree model trained for diabetes, the visualization of the binary tree is shown in figure 2.13. The tree can be interpreted as follows.

Starting at the root of the tree, check if the normalized BMI is <= 0. If true, go to the left part of the tree. If false, go to the right part of the tree. Because we are starting at the root of the tree, this node accounts for 100% of the data. This is why *samples* is equal to 100%. Also, if we were to set the *max_depth* to 0 and predict the disease progression, then we would use the average value of all the samples in the data, which is 153.7, represented as *value* in the tree. By predicting 153.7, we would get an MSE of 6076.4.

If the normalized BMI is <= 0, then we go to the left part of the tree and check if the normalized Glaucoma is <= 0. If BMI is <= 0, we would account for approximately 59% of the data, and the MSE would reduce from 6076.4 for the parent node to 3612.7. We can repeat this process until we have reached the leaf nodes in the tree. If we look at, say, the right-most leaf node, this corresponds to the following condition: if BMI > 0 and BMI > 0.1 and LDL > 0, then predict 225.8 for 2.3% of the data, resulting in an MSE of 2757.9.

Please note that the *max_depth* for the decision tree in figure 2.13 was set to 3. The complexity of this tree will increase as *max_depth* increases or as the number of input features increases.

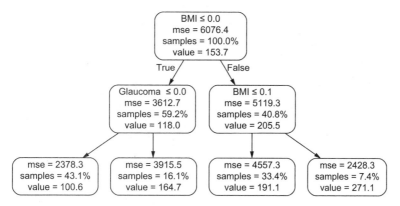

Figure 2.13   Visualization of the diabetes decision tree model

The visualization in figure 2.13 can be generated in Python using the following code snippet:

```
from sklearn.externals.six import StringIO
from IPython.display import Image
from sklearn.tree import export_graphviz
import pydotplus
```
Imports all the necessary libraries to generate and visualize the binary tree

```
diabetes_dt_dot_data = StringIO()                  ◄─────
export_graphviz(dt_model,
                out_file=diabetes_dt_dot_data,
                filled=False, rounded=True,
                feature_names=feature_names,
                proportion=True,
                precision=1,
                special_characters=True)    ◄──
dt_graph = pydotplus.graph_from_dot_data(diabetes_dt_dot_data.getvalue())  ◄─┐
Image(dt_graph.create_png())    ◄─┐
```
Initializes a string buffer to store the binary tree/graph in DOT format

Exports the decision tree model as a binary tree in DOT format

Visualizes the binary tree using the Image class

Generates an image of the binary tree using the DOT format string

Because decision trees learn a nonlinear relationship between the input features and the target, it is hard to understand what effects changes to each of the inputs have on the output. It is not as straightforward as linear regression. We can, however, compute the relative importance of each of the features in predicting the target at a global level. To compute the feature importance, we first need to compute the importance of a node in the binary tree. The importance of a node is computed as the decrease in the cost function or impurity measure for that node weighted by the probability of reaching that node in the tree. This is shown mathematically next:

$$I_k^{node} = \overbrace{p_k}^{\substack{\text{Proportion} \\ \text{of samples} \\ \text{to reach} \\ \text{node } k}} \cdot \underbrace{m_k}_{\substack{\text{Impurity} \\ \text{measure} \\ \text{of node } k}} - \overbrace{p_k^{(left)}}^{\substack{\text{Proportion} \\ \text{of samples} \\ \text{to reach} \\ \text{left subtree} \\ \text{of node } k}} \cdot \underbrace{m_k^{(left)}}_{\substack{\text{Impurity} \\ \text{measure} \\ \text{of left} \\ \text{subtree of} \\ \text{node } k}} - \overbrace{p_k^{(right)}}^{\substack{\text{Proportion} \\ \text{of samples} \\ \text{to reach} \\ \text{right subtree} \\ \text{of node } k}} \cdot \underbrace{m_k^{(right)}}_{\substack{\text{Impurity} \\ \text{measure} \\ \text{of right} \\ \text{subtree of} \\ \text{node } k}}$$

where I_k^{node} is the Importance of node k.

We can then compute the feature importance by summing up the importance of the nodes that split on that feature normalized by the importance of all the nodes in the tree. This is shown mathematically next. The feature importance for the decision tree is between 0 and 1, where a higher value implies greater importance:

$$\underbrace{I_i^{feature}}_{\substack{\text{Importance} \\ \text{of feature } i}} = \frac{\overbrace{\sum_{j \in \mathbb{J}} I_j^{node}}^{\substack{\text{Sum of importance} \\ \text{of all nodes } j \\ \text{that split on feature } i}}}{\underbrace{\sum_{k \in \mathbb{K}} I_k^{node}}_{\substack{\text{Sum of importance} \\ \text{of all nodes } k \\ \text{in the decision tree}}}}$$

In Python, the feature importance can be obtained from the Scikit-Learn decision tree model and plotted as follows:

Gets feature importance from the trained decision tree model

```
weights = dt_model.feature_importances_

feature_importance_idx = np.argsort(np.abs(weights))[::-1]
feature_importance = [feature_names[idx].upper() for idx in
    feature_importance_idx]
feature_importance_values = [weights[idx] for idx in
    feature_importance_idx]

f, ax = plt.subplots(figsize=(10, 8))
sns.barplot(x=feature_importance_values, y=feature_importance, ax=ax)
ax.grid(True)
ax.set_xlabel('Feature Weights')
ax.set_ylabel('Features')
```

Sorts indices of feature weights in descending order of importance

Gets the feature names and feature weights in descending order of importance

Generates the plot shown in figure 2.14

The features ordered in descending order of importance and their corresponding weights are shown in figure 2.14. As can be seen from the figure, the order of important features is different from linear regression. The most important feature is BMI, accounting for roughly 42% of the overall model importance. The Glaucoma measurement is the next most important feature, accounting for roughly 15% of the model importance. These importance values are useful in determining what features have the most signal in predicting the target variable. Decision trees are immune to the problem of multicollinearity because the algorithm picks the feature that is highly correlated with the target and that most reduces the cost function or impurity. As a data scientist, it is important to visualize the learned decision tree, as shown in figure 2.13, because this will help you understand how the model arrived at the final prediction. You could reduce the complexity of the tree by setting the *max_depth* hyperparameter or by pruning the number of features you feed into the model. You can determine what features to prune by visualizing the global feature importance, as shown in figure 2.14.

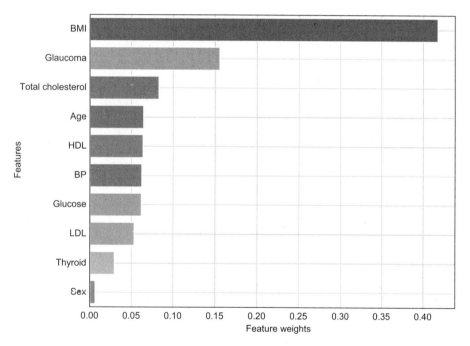

Figure 2.14 Diabetes feature importance for decision tree

2.4.2 *Limitations of decision trees*

Decision trees are quite versatile because they can be applied to both regression and classification tasks, and they also have the ability to model nonlinear relationships. The algorithm, however, is prone to the problem of *overfitting* and the model is said to have *high variance*.

The problem of overfitting occurs when the model fits the training data almost perfectly and, therefore, does not generalize well to data that it hasn't seen before,

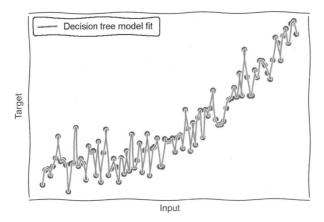

Figure 2.15   The problem of overfitting (high variance)

such as the test set. This is illustrated in figure 2.15. When a model overfits, you will notice really good performance on the training set but poor performance on the test set. This could explain why the decision tree model trained on the diabetes dataset performed poorer than the linear regression model.

The problem of overfitting can be overcome by tuning certain hyperparameters in the decision tree, like *max_depth*, and the minimum number of samples required for the leaf nodes. As shown in the visualization of the decision tree model in figure 2.13, one leaf node accounts for only 0.8% of the samples. This means that the prediction for this node is based on the data from roughly only three patients. By increasing the minimum number of samples required to 5 or 10, we could improve the performance of the model on the test set.

2.5   *Generalized additive models (GAMs)*

Diagnostics+ and the doctors are reasonably happy with the two models built so far, but the performance is not that good. By interpreting the models, we have also uncovered some shortcomings. The linear regression model does not seem to handle features that are highly correlated with each other, such as Total Cholesterol, LDL, and HDL. The decision tree model performs worse than linear regression, and it seems to have overfit on the training data.

Let's look at one specific feature from the diabetes data. Figure 2.16 shows a contrived example of a nonlinear relationship between age and the target variable, where both variables are normalized. How would you best model this relationship without overfitting? One possible approach is to extend the linear regression model where the target variable is modeled as an nth degree polynomial of the feature set. This form of regression is called *polynomial regression.*

Polynomial regression for various-degree polynomials is shown in the following equations. In these equations, we are considering only one feature, x_1, to model the target variable y. The degree 1 polynomial is the same as linear regression. For the degree 2 polynomial, we would add an additional feature, which is the square of x_1.

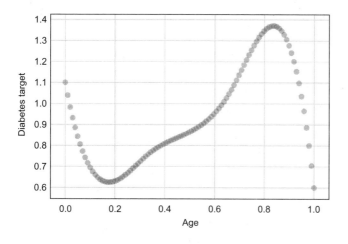

Figure 2.16   An illustration of a nonlinear relationship for Diagnostics+ AI

For the degree 3 polynomial, we would add two additional features—one that is the square of x_1 and the other that is the cube of x_1:

$$y = w_0 + w_1 x_1 \ (\text{Degree 1})$$
$$y = w_0 + w_1 x_1 + w_2 x_1^2 \ (\text{Degree 2})$$
$$y = w_0 + w_1 x_1 + w_2 x_1^2 + w_3 x_1^3 \ (\text{Degree 3})$$

The weights for the polynomial regression model can be obtained using the same algorithm as linear regression, that is, the method of least squares using gradient descent. The best fit learned by each of the three polynomials is shown in figure 2.17.

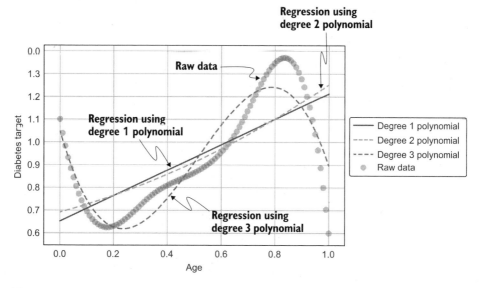

Figure 2.17   Polynomial regression for modeling a nonlinear relationship

We can see that the degree 3 polynomial fits the raw data better than degrees 2 and 1. We can interpret a polynomial regression model the same way as we would a linear regression because the model is essentially a linear combination of the features including the higher degree features.

Polynomial regression has some limitations, however. The complexity of the model increases as the number of features or the dimension of the feature space increases. It, therefore, has a tendency to overfit on the data. It is also hard to determine the degree for each feature in the polynomial, especially in a higher-dimensional feature space.

So, what model can be applied to overcome all these limitations and is also interpretable? Enter generalized additive models (GAMs)! GAMs are models with medium to high predictive power and are highly interpretable. Nonlinear relationships are modeled by using smoothing functions for each feature and adding all of them, as shown in the following equation:

$$y = w_0 + \underbrace{f_1(x_1)}_{\substack{\text{Smoothing Function} \\ \text{for Feature } x_1}} + \underbrace{f_2(x_2)}_{\substack{\text{Smoothing Function} \\ \text{for Feature } x_2}} + \ldots + \underbrace{f_n(x_n)}_{\substack{\text{Smoothing Function} \\ \text{for Feature } x_n}}$$

In this equation, each feature has its own associated smoothing function that best models the relationship between that feature and the target. You can choose from many types of smoothing functions, but a widely used smoothing function is called *regression splines* because it is practical and computationally efficient. I will focus on regression splines in this book. Let's now go deep into the world of GAMs using regression splines!

2.5.1 *Regression splines*

Regression splines are represented as a weighted sum of basis functions. This is shown mathematically in the next equation. In this equation, f_j is the function that models the relationship between the feature x_j and the target variable. This function is represented as a weighted sum of basis functions where the weight is represented as w_k and the basis function is represented as b_k. In the context of GAMs, the function f_j is called a smoothing function.

$$f_j(x_j) = \underbrace{\sum_{k=1}^{K} w_k b_k(x_j)}_{\substack{\text{Smoothing Function} \\ \text{represented as a} \\ \text{weighted sum of basis functions}}}$$

Now, what is a basis function? A basis function is a family of transformations that can be used to capture a general shape or nonlinear relationship. For regression splines, as the name suggests, splines are used as the basis function. A spline is a polynomial of degree n with $n-1$ derivatives. It will be much easier to understand splines using an illustration. Figure 2.18 shows splines of various degrees. The top-left graph shows the simplest spline of degree 0, from which higher degree splines can be generated. As you can see from the top-left graph, six splines have been placed on a grid. The idea is to split the distribution of the data into portions and fit a spline on each of those portions. So, in this illustration, the data has been split into six portions, and we are modeling each portion as a degree 0 spline.

A degree 1 spline, shown in the top-right graph, can be generated by convolving a degree 0 spline with itself. Convolution is a mathematical operation that takes in two functions and creates a third function that represents the correlation of the first function and a delayed copy of the second function. When we convolve a function with itself, we are essentially looking at the correlation of the function with a delayed copy of itself. There is a nice blog post by Christopher Olah on convolutions (http://mng.bz/5Kdq). By convolving a degree 0 spline with itself, we get a degree 1 spline, which is triangular, and this has a continuous 0th-order derivative.

If we now convolve a degree 1 spline with itself, we will get a degree 2 spline, shown in the bottom-left graph. This degree 2 spline has a first-order derivative. Similarly, we can get a degree 3 spline by convolving a degree 2 spline, and this has a second-order derivative. In general, a degree n spline has an $n-1$ derivative. In the limit, as n

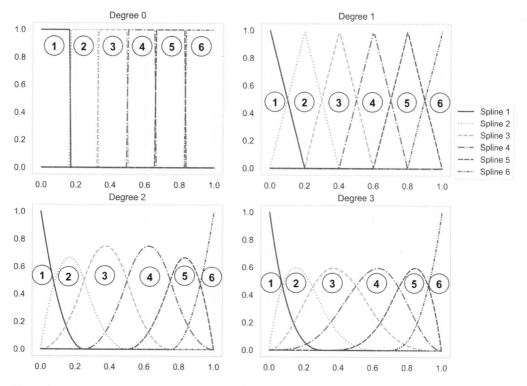

Figure 2.18 **An illustration of degree 0, degree 1, degree 2, and degree 3 splines**

approaches infinity, we will obtain a spline that has the shape of a Gaussian distribution. In practice, a *degree 3 spline*, or *cubic spline*, is used because it can capture most general shapes.

As mentioned earlier, in figure 2.18, we have divided the distribution of data into six portions and have placed six splines on the grid. In the earlier mathematical equation, the number of portions or splines was represented as variable *K*. The idea behind regression splines is to learn the weights for each of the splines so that you can model the distribution of the data in each of the portions. The number of portions or splines in the grid, *K*, is also called *degrees of freedom*. In general, if we place these *K* splines on a grid, we will have *K* + 3 points of division, also known as *knots*.

Let's now zoom in on cubic splines, as shown in figure 2.19. We can see that there are six splines, or six degrees of freedom, resulting in nine points of division or knots.

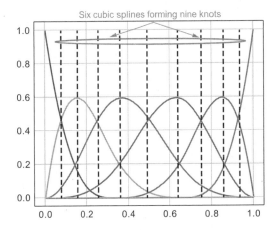

Figure 2.19   An illustration of splines and knots

To capture a general shape, we need to take a weighted sum of the splines. We will use cubic splines here. In figure 2.20, we are using the same six splines overlaid to create nine knots. For the graph on the left, I have set the same weights for all six splines. As you can imagine, if we take an equally weighted sum of all six splines, we will get a horizontal straight line. This is an illustration of a poor fit to the raw data. For the graph on the right, however, I have taken an unequal weighted sum of the six splines generating a shape that perfectly fits the raw data. This shows the power of regression splines and GAMs. By increasing the number of splines or by dividing the data into more portions, we can model more complex nonlinear relationships. In GAMs based on regression splines, we individually model nonlinear relationships of each feature with the target variable and then add them all up to come up with the final prediction.

In figure 2.20, the weights were determined using trial and error to best describe the raw data. But, how do you algorithmically determine the weights for a regression spline that best captures the relationship between the features and the target? Recall from the start of this section that a regression spline is a weighted sum of basis functions or splines. This is essentially a linear regression problem, and you can learn the

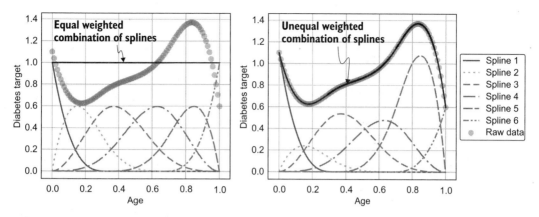

Figure 2.20   Splines for modeling a nonlinear relationship

weights using the method of least squares and gradient descent. We would, however, need to specify the number of knots, or degrees of freedom. We can treat this as a hyperparameter and determine it using a technique called *cross-validation*. Using cross-validation, we would remove a portion of the data and fit a regression spline with a certain number of predetermined knots on the remaining data. This regression spline is then evaluated on the held-out set. The optimum number of knots is the one that results in the best performance on the held-out set.

In GAMs, you can easily overfit by increasing the number of splines or degrees of freedom. If the number of splines is high, the resulting smoothing function, which is a weighted sum of the splines, would be quite "wiggly"—it would start to fit some of the noise in the data. How can we control this wiggliness or prevent overfitting? We can use a technique called *regularization*. In regularization, we would add a term to the least square cost function that quantifies the wiggliness. We could then quantify the wiggliness of a smoothing function by taking the integral of the square of the second-order derivative of the function. Then, using a hyperparameter (also called regularization parameter) represented by λ, we could adjust the intensity of wiggliness. A high value for λ penalizes wiggliness heavily. We can determine λ the same way we determine other hyperparameters using cross-validation.

Summary of GAMs

A GAM is a powerful model where the target variable is represented as a sum of smoothing functions representing the relationship of each of the features and the target. We can use the smoothing function to capture any nonlinear relationship. This is shown mathematically here:

$$y = w_0 + f_1(x_1) + f_2(x_2) + \ldots + f_n(x_n)$$

(continued)
This is a white-box model—we can easily see how each feature is transformed to the output using the smoothing function. A common way of representing the smoothing function is by using regression splines. A regression spline is represented as a simple weighted sum of basis functions. A basis function that is widely used for GAMs is the cubic spline. By increasing the number of splines or degrees of freedom, we can divide the distribution of data into small portions and model each portion piecewise. This way, we can capture very complex nonlinear relationships. The learning algorithm essentially has to determine the weights for the regression spline. We can do this the same way as for linear regression, using the method of least squares and gradient descent. We can determine the number of splines using the cross-validation technique. As the number of splines increases, GAMs have a tendency to overfit on the data. We can safeguard against this by using the regularization technique. Using a regularization parameter λ, we can control the amount of wiggliness. A higher λ ensures a smoother function. The parameter λ can also be determined using cross-validation.

GAMs can also be used to model interactions between variables. GA2M, shown mathematically next, is a type of GAM that models pairwise interactions:

$$y = w_0 + f_1(x_1) + f_2(x_2) + \underbrace{f_3(x_1, x_2)}_{\substack{\text{Modeling interaction} \\ \text{between } x_1 \text{ and } x_2}} + f_4(x_4) + \ldots + f_n(x_n)$$

With the help of subject matter experts (SMEs)—the doctors in the Diagnostics+ example—you can determine what feature interactions need to be modeled. You could also look at the correlation between features to understand what features need to be modeled together.

In Python, you can use a package called pyGAM to build and train GAMs. It is inspired by the GAM implementation in the popular mgcv package in R. You can install pyGAM in your Python environment using the pip package as follows:

```
pip install pygam
```

2.5.2 *GAM for Diagnostics+ diabetes*

Let's now go back to the Diagnostics+ example to train a GAM to predict diabetes progression using all 10 features. Note that the Sex of the patient is a categorical or discrete feature. It does not make sense to model this feature using a smoothing function. We can treat such categorical features in GAMs as factor terms. We can train the GAM using the pyGAM package as follows. As with decision trees, I'm not going to repeat the code that loads the diabetes dataset and splits it into the train and test sets. Please refer to section 2.2 for that snippet of code:

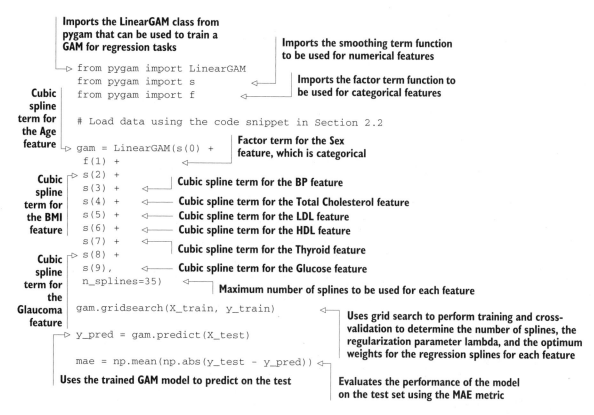

Imports the LinearGAM class from pygam that can be used to train a GAM for regression tasks

Imports the smoothing term function to be used for numerical features

Imports the factor term function to be used for categorical features

Cubic spline term for the Age feature

Factor term for the Sex feature, which is categorical

Cubic spline term for the BMI feature

Cubic spline term for the BP feature

Cubic spline term for the Total Cholesterol feature

Cubic spline term for the LDL feature

Cubic spline term for the HDL feature

Cubic spline term for the Thyroid feature

Cubic spline term for the Glaucoma feature

Cubic spline term for the Glucose feature

Maximum number of splines to be used for each feature

Uses grid search to perform training and cross-validation to determine the number of splines, the regularization parameter lambda, and the optimum weights for the regression splines for each feature

Uses the trained GAM model to predict on the test

Evaluates the performance of the model on the test set using the MAE metric

```python
from pygam import LinearGAM
from pygam import s
from pygam import f

# Load data using the code snippet in Section 2.2

gam = LinearGAM(s(0) +
    f(1) +
    s(2) +
    s(3) +
    s(4) +
    s(5) +
    s(6) +
    s(7) +
    s(8) +
    s(9),
    n_splines=35)

gam.gridsearch(X_train, y_train)

y_pred = gam.predict(X_test)

mae = np.mean(np.abs(y_test - y_pred))
```

Now for the moment of truth! How did the GAM perform? The MAE performance of the GAM is 41.4—a pretty good improvement when compared to the linear regression and decision tree models. A comparison of the performance of all three models is summarized in table 2.2. I have also included the performance of a baseline model that Diagnostics+ and the doctors have been using where they look at the median diabetes progression across all patients. All models are compared against the baseline to show how much of an improvement the models give to the doctors. It looks like GAM is the best model across all performance metrics.

Table 2.2 Performance comparison of linear regression, decision tree, and GAM against a baseline for Diagnostics+ A

	MAE	RMSE	MAPE
Baseline	62.2	74.7	51.6
Linear regression	42.8 (–19.4)	53.8 (–20.9)	37.5 (–14.1)
Decision tree	48.6 (–13.6)	60.5 (–14.2)	44.4 (–7.2)
GAM	41.4 (–20.8)	52.2 (–22.5)	35.7 (–15.9)

We have now seen the predictive power of GAMs. We could potentially get further improvement in the performance by modeling feature interactions, especially the cholesterol features with each other and with other features that are potentially highly correlated, like BMI. As an exercise, I encourage you to try modeling feature interactions using GAMs.

GAMs are white box and can be easily interpreted. In the following section, we will see how GAMs can be interpreted.

GAMs for classification tasks

GAMs can also be used to train a binary classifier by using the logistic link function where the response *y* can be either 0 or 1. In the pyGAM package, you can make use of the logistic GAM for binary classification problems as follows:

```
from pygam import LogisticGAM
gam = LogisticGAM()
gam.gridsearch(X_train, y_train)
```

2.5.3 *Interpreting GAMs*

Although each smoothing function is obtained as a linear combination of basis functions, the final smoothing function for each feature is nonlinear, and, therefore, we cannot interpret the weights the same way as we do for linear regression. We can, however, easily visualize the effects of each feature on the target using partial dependence or partial effects plots. Partial dependence looks at the effect of each feature by marginalizing on the rest. It is highly interpretable because we can see the average effect of each feature value on the target variable. We can see whether the target response to the feature is linear, nonlinear, monotonic, or nonmonotonic. Figure 2.21 shows the effect of each of the patient features on the target variable. The 95% confidence interval around them have also been plotted. This will help us determine the sensitivity of the model to data points with a low sample size.

Let's now look at a couple of features in figure 2.21, namely, BMI and BP. The effect of BMI on the target variable is shown in the bottom-left graph. On the *x*-axis, we see the normalized values of BMI, and on the *y*-axis, we see the effect that BMI has on the progression of diabetes for the patient. We see that as BMI increases, the effect on the progression of diabetes also increases. We see a similar trend for BP shown by the bottom-right graph. We see that the higher the BP, the higher the impact on the progression of diabetes. If we look at the 95% confidence interval lines (the dashed lines in figure 2.21), we see a wider confidence interval around the lower and higher ends of BMI and BP. This is because fewer samples of patients exist at this range of values, resulting in higher uncertainty in understanding the effects of these features at those ranges.

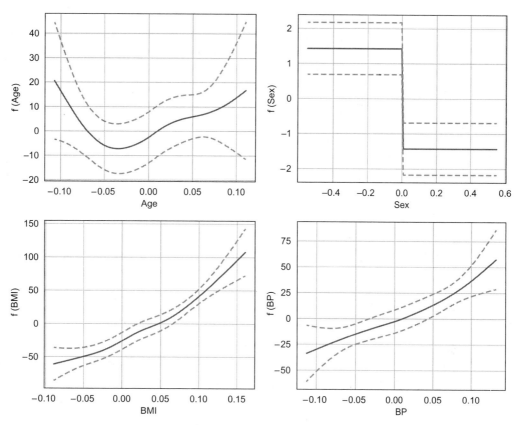

Figure 2.21 The effect of each of the patient features on the target variable

The code to generate figure 2.21 follows:

```
Locations of the four graphs                                    Iterates
in the 2x2 Matplotlib grid                                      through the      Generates the
    grid_locs1 = [(0, 0), (0, 1),                               four patient     partial dependence
                  (1, 0), (1, 1)]                               metadata         of the feature values
    fig, ax = plt.subplots(2, 2, figsize=(10, 8))               features         with the target
    for i, feature in enumerate(feature_names[:4]):                              marginalizing on
Creates a   gl = grid_locs1[i]        Gets the location of feature in the 2x2 grid   the other features
2x2 grid of XX = gam.generate_X_grid(term=i)
Matplotlib  ax[gl[0], gl[1]].plot(XX[:, i], gam.partial_dependence(term=i, X=XX))
graphs      ax[gl[0], gl[1]].plot(XX[:, i], gam.partial_dependence(term=i, X=XX,
            width=.95)[1], c='r', ls='--')
            ax[gl[0], gl[1]].set_xlabel('%s' % feature)            Plots the partial
            ax[gl[0], gl[1]].set_ylabel('f ( %s )' % feature)      dependence values
                                                                   as a solid line
    Plots the 95% confidence interval around the
    partial dependence values as a dashed line         Adds labels for the x- and y-axes
```

Figure 2.22 shows the effect of each of the six blood test measurements on the target. As an exercise, observe the effects that features like Total Cholesterol, LDL, HDL, and Glaucoma have on the progression of diabetes. What can you say about the impact of higher LDL values (or bad cholesterol) on the target variable? Why does higher Total Cholesterol have a lower impact on the target variable? To answer these questions, let's look at a few patient cases with very high cholesterol values. The following code snippet will help you zoom in on those patients:

```
print(df_data[(df_data['Total Cholesterol'] > 0.15) &
              (df_data['LDL'] > 0.19)])
```

If you execute this code, you will see only one patient out of 442 that has a Total Cholesterol reading greater than 0.15 and an LDL reading greater than 0.19. The fasting glucose level for this patient one year out (the target variable) seems to be 84, which is in the normal range. This could explain why in figure 2.22 we are seeing a very large negative effect for Total Cholesterol on the target variable for a range that is greater

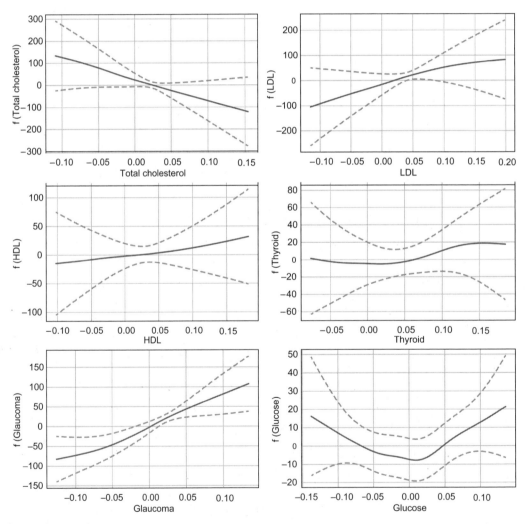

Figure 2.22   The effect of each of the blood test measurements on the target variable

than 0.15. The negative effect of Total Cholesterol seems to be greater than the positive effect the bad LDL cholesterol seems to have on the target. The confidence interval seems much wider in these range of values. The model may have overfit on this one outlier patient record, and so, we should not read too much into these effects. By observing these effects, we can identify cases or a range of values where the model is sure of the prediction and cases where there is high uncertainty. For high uncertainty cases, we can go back to the diagnostics center to collect more patient data so that we have a representative sample.

The code to generate figure 2.22 follows:

Iterates through the six blood test measurement features

Creates a 3 × 2 grid of Matplotlib graphs

```
grid_locs2 = [(0, 0), (0, 1),
              (1, 0), (1, 1),
              (2, 0), (2, 1)]
fig2, ax2 = plt.subplots(3, 2, figsize=(12, 12))
for i, feature in enumerate(feature_names[4:]):
    idx = i + 4
    gl = grid_locs2[i]
    XX = gam.generate_X_grid(term=idx)
    ax2[gl[0], gl[1]].plot(XX[:, idx], gam.partial_dependence(term=idx,
       X=XX))
    ax2[gl[0], gl[1]].plot(XX[:, idx], gam.partial_dependence(term=idx, X=XX,
       width=.95)[1], c='r', ls='--')
    ax2[gl[0], gl[1]].set_xlabel('%s' % feature)
    ax2[gl[0], gl[1]].set_ylabel('f ( %s )' % feature)
```

Locations of the six graphs in the 3 × 2 Matplotlib grid

Generates the partial dependence of the feature values with the target marginalizing on the other features grid of Matplotlib graphs

Plots the partial dependence values as a solid line

Gets the location of the feature in the 3 × 2 grid

Plots the 95% confidence interval around the partial dependence values as a dashed line

Adds labels for the x- and y-axes

Through figures 2.21 and 2.22, we can gain a much deeper understanding of the marginal effect of each of the feature values on the target. The partial dependence plots are useful for debugging any issues with the model. By plotting the 95% confidence interval around the partial dependence values, we can also see data points with low sample sizes. If a feature value with a low sample size has a dramatic effect on the target, then there could be an overfitting problem. We can also visualize the wiggliness of the smoothing function to determine whether the model has fit on the noise in the data. We can fix these overfitting problems by increasing the value of the regularization parameter. These partial dependence plots can also be shared with the SME—doctors, in this case—for validation which will help gain their trust.

2.5.4 Limitations of GAMs

We have so far seen the advantages of GAMs in terms of predictive power and interpretability. GAMs have a tendency to overfit, although this can be overcome with regularization. You do need to be aware of the following other limitations, however:

- GAMs are sensitive to feature values outside of the range in the training set and tend to lose predictive power when exposed to outlier values.
- For mission-critical tasks, GAMs may sometimes have limited predictive power, in which case you may need to consider more powerful black-box models.

2.6   *Looking ahead to black-box models*

Black-box models are models with really high predictive power and are typically applied in tasks for which model performance (such as accuracy) is extremely important. They are, however, inherently opaque, and the characteristics that make them opaque include the following:

- The machine learning process is complicated, and you can't easily understand how the input features are transformed into the output or target variable.
- You can't easily identify the most important features to predict the target variable.

Examples of black-box models are tree ensembles such as random forest and gradient-boosted trees, deep neural networks (DNNs), convolutional neural networks (CNNs), and recurrent neural networks (RNNs). Table 2.3 shows the machine learning tasks for which these models are typically applied.

Table 2.3   Mapping of black-box model to machine learning tasks

Black-box model	Machine learning tasks
Tree ensembles (random forest, gradient-boosted trees)	Regression and classification
Deep neural networks (DNNs)	Regression and classification
Convolutional neural networks (CNNs)	Image classification, object detection
Recurrent neural networks (RNNs)	Sequence modeling, language understanding

I have now plotted in the black-box models in the same predictive power versus interpretability plane as introduced in section 2.1, shown in figure 2.23.

The black-box models are clustered in the top left of the plane because they have high predictive power but low interpretability. For mission-critical tasks, it is important not to trade off model performance (such as accuracy) for interpretability by applying white-box models. We will need to apply black-box models for such tasks and will need to find ways to interpret them. We can interpret black-box models in multiple ways, and doing so is the main focus of the remaining chapters in this book. In the next

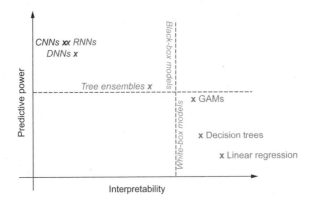

Figure 2.23   Black-box models on the interpretability versus predictive power plane

chapter, we will specifically focus on tree ensembles and how to interpret them using global, model-agnostic techniques.

Summary

- White-box models are inherently transparent. The machine learning process is straightforward to understand, and you can clearly interpret how the input features are transformed into the output. Using white-box models, you can identify the most important features, and those features are understandable.

- Linear regression is one of the simplest white-box models, where the target variable is modeled as a linear combination of the input features. You can determine the weights using the method of least squares and gradient descent.

- We can implement linear regression in Python using the `LinearRegression` class in the Scikit-Learn package. You can interpret the model by inspecting the coefficients or learned weights. The weights can also be used to determine the importance of each of the features. Linear regression, however, suffers from the problems of multicollinearity and underfitting.

- A decision tree is a slightly more advanced white-box model that can be used for both regression and classification tasks. You can predict the target variable by splitting the data across all features to minimize a cost function. You have learned the CART algorithm to learn the splits.

- A decision tree for regression tasks can be implemented in Python using the `DecisionTreeRegressor` class in Scikit-Learn. You can implement a decision tree for classification tasks using the `DecisionTreeClassifier` class in Scikit-Learn. You can interpret a decision tree learned using CART by visualizing it as a binary tree. The Scikit-Learn implementation also computes the feature importance for you. A decision tree can be used to model nonlinear relationships but tends to suffer from overfitting.

- GAMs are a powerful white-box model where the target variable is represented as a sum of smoothing functions representing the relationship of each of the features and the target. You know that regression splines and cubic splines are widely used to represent the smoothing function.

- Regression splines and GAMs can be implemented using the pyGAM package in Python. We can use the `LinearGAM` class for regression tasks and the `LogisticGAM` class for classification tasks. You can interpret a GAM by plotting the partial dependence of each of the features on the target. GAMs have a tendency to overfit, but this problem can be mitigated through regularization.

- Black-box models are models with really high predictive power and are typically applied to tasks for which model performance (such as accuracy) is extremely important. They are, however, inherently opaque. The machine learning process is complicated, and you can't easily understand how the input features are transformed into the output or target variable. As a result, you can't easily identify the most important features to predict the target variable.

Part 2

Interpreting model processing

This part of the book focuses on black-box models and understanding how the model processes the inputs and arrives at the final prediction.

In chapter 3, you'll learn about a class of black-box models called tree ensembles. You will learn about their characteristics and what makes them black-box. You'll also learn how to interpret them using post hoc model-agnostic methods that are global in scope, such as partial dependence plots (PDPs) and feature interaction plots.

In chapter 4, you'll learn about deep neural networks, specifically the vanilla fully connected neural networks. You will learn about characteristics that make these models black-box and how to interpret them using post hoc model-agnostic methods that are local in scope, such as local interpretable model-agnostic explanations (LIME), SHapley Additive exPlanations (SHAP), and anchors.

In chapter 5, you'll learn about convolutional neural networks, which are a more advanced form of architecture used mainly for visual tasks, such as image classification and object detection. You'll learn how to visualize what the model is focusing on using saliency maps. You will also learn about techniques such as gradients, guided backpropagation (*backprop* for short), gradient-weighted class activation mapping (Grad-CAM), guided Grad-CAM, and smooth gradients (SmoothGrad).

Model-agnostic methods: Global interpretability

This chapter covers

- Characteristics of model-agnostic methods and global interpretability
- How to implement tree ensembles, specifically random forest—a black-box model
- How to interpret random forest models
- How to interpret black-box models using a model-agnostic method called partial dependence plots (PDPs)
- How to uncover bias by looking at feature interactions

In the previous chapter, we saw two different types of machine learning models—white box and black box—and focused most of our attention on how to interpret white-box models. Black-box models have a high predictive power and, as the name suggests, are hard to interpret. In this chapter, we will focus on interpreting black-box models, and you'll learn specifically about techniques that are *model agnostic* and (*global*) in scope. Recall from chapter 1 that model-agnostic interpretability techniques are not dependent on the specific type of model being used. They can be applied to any model because they are independent of the internal structure of the model. Also, interpretability techniques that are global in scope can help us understand the entire model as a whole. We will also focus on tree ensembles, specifically random forest. Although we focus on random forest, you can apply the model-agnostic techniques that you will learn in this chapter to any model. We will switch our attention to more complex black-box models, like neural networks, in the following chapter. In chapter 4, you will also learn about model-agnostic techniques that are local in scope, such as LIME, SHAP, and anchors.

The structure of chapter 3 is similar to that of chapter 2. We will start off by looking at a concrete example. In this chapter, we will take a break from Diagnostics+ and focus on another problem related to education. I've chosen this problem because the dataset has some interesting characteristics and we can expose some issues in this dataset through the interpretability techniques that you will learn in this chapter. As in chapter 2, the main focus of this chapter is on implementing interpretability techniques to gain a better understanding of black-box models (specifically tree ensembles). We will apply these interpretability techniques during model development and testing. You will also learn about model training and testing, especially the implementation aspects. Because the model learning, testing, and understanding stages are iterative, it is important to cover all three stages together. Readers who are already familiar with training and testing tree ensembles are free to skip those sections and jump straight into interpretability.

3.1   *High school student performance predictor*

Let's begin by looking at a concrete example. We will switch from Diagnostic+ and the healthcare sector to education. A superintendent of a school district in the United States has approached you to help her with a data science problem. The superintendent would like to understand how students are performing in three key subject areas—math, reading, and writing—to determine the level of funding required for various schools and also to ensure that every student succeeds as part of the Every Student Succeeds Act (ESSA).

The superintendent is specifically looking for help in predicting the grades of a high school student in her district in math, reading, and writing subjects. The grade can be A, B, C, or F. Given this information, how would you formulate this as a machine learning problem? Because the target of the model is to predict the grade, which can be one of four discrete values, the problem can be formulated as a *classification* problem. In terms of data, the superintendent has collected the data of 1,000 students in her district representing various schools and backgrounds. The following five data points are collected for each student:

- Gender
- Ethnicity
- Parent Level of Education
- Type of Lunch purchased by the student
- Test Preparation level

Given this data, you will, therefore, need to train three separate classifiers, one for each subject area. This is illustrated in figure 3.1.

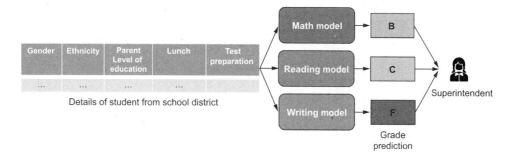

Figure 3.1 An illustration of student performance models required by the superintendent of the school district

Protected attributes and fairness

Protected attributes are attributes associated with an individual related to social bias, including gender, age, race, ethnicity, sexual orientation, and so on. Laws in certain regions like the United States and Europe prohibit discriminating against individuals on the basis of these protected attributes, especially in domains like housing, employment, and credit lending. It is important to be aware of these legal frameworks and nondiscrimination laws when building machine learning models that may use these protected attributes as features. We want to ensure that machine learning models do not embed bias and discriminate against certain individuals on the basis of protected attributes. In this chapter, our dataset contains a couple of protected attributes that we use as features for the model primarily to learn how to expose, through interpretability techniques, possible issues with the model pertaining to bias. We will cover the legal frameworks around protected attributes and various fairness criteria in more depth in chapter 8. Moreover, the dataset used in this chapter is contrived and does not reflect actual student performance in a school district. The race/ethnicity feature is also anonymized.

3.1.1 *Exploratory data analysis*

We are dealing with a new dataset here, so before we train the model, let's first understand the different features and possible values for them. The dataset contains five features: the student's Gender, their Ethnicity, Parent Level of Education, the Type of Lunch that they purchase, and their Test Preparation level. All of these features are *categorical* features where the possible values are discrete and finite. There are three target variables for each student: math grade, reading grade, and writing grade. The grades can be A, B, C, or F.

There are two gender categories—male and female—and the female population (52%) of students is slightly higher than the male population (48%). Let's now focus on two other features—the student's Ethnicity and Parent Level of Education. Figure 3.2 shows the different categories for each of those features and the proportion of students who fall under those categories. Five groups or ethnicities are in the population, and groups C and D are the most represented, accounting for about 58% of the student population. Six different levels of parent education occur. In ascending order, they are some high school, (recognized) high school, some college, associate degree, bachelor's degree, and master's degree. It looks like there are a lot more students in the population whose parents have lower levels of education. Roughly 82% of the students have parents with a high school or college level of education or an associate degree. Only 18% of the students have parents with a bachelor's or master's degree.

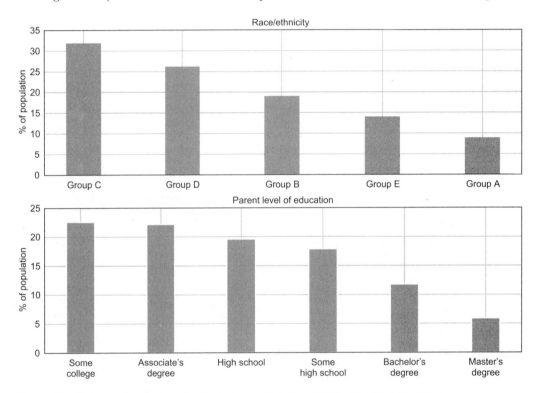

Figure 3.2   Values and proportions for the features Ethnicity and Parent Level of Education

Now for the remaining two features—Type of Lunch purchased and the Test Preparation level. The majority (roughly 65%) purchase a standard lunch and the rest purchase free/reduced lunches. In terms of test preparation, only 36% of the students completed their preparation for the tests, whereas for the remaining, it is either not completed or unknown.

Let's now look at the proportion of students who earn grades A, B, C, or F for the three subject areas. This is shown in figure 3.3. We can see that the majority of the students (48–50%) get grade B and a very small proportion of the students (3–4%) get grade F. About 18–25% of the students get grade A, and 22–28% of the students get grade C across all the three subject areas. It is important to note that the data is quite *imbalanced* before we train our models. Why is that important, and how do we deal with imbalanced data? In a classification type of problem, we say that the data is imbalanced when a disproportionate number of examples or data points exist for a given class. It is important to note this because most machine learning algorithms work best when the proportion of samples for each class is roughly the same. Most algorithms are designed to minimize error or maximize accuracy, and these algorithms tend to naturally bias toward the majority class. We can deal with imbalanced classes in a few ways, including these common approaches:

- Use the right performance metrics when we test and evaluate the models.
- Resample the training data such that the majority class is either undersampled or the minority class is oversampled.

You will learn more about these methods in section 3.2.

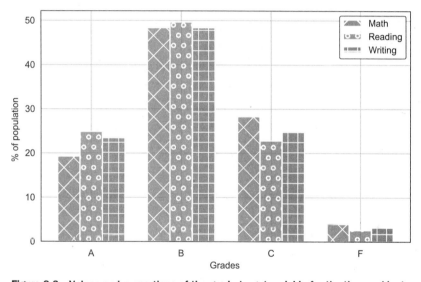

Figure 3.3   Values and proportions of the grade target variable for the three subject areas

Let's dissect the data a bit more. The insights that follow will be useful in section 3.4 when we have to interpret and validate what the model has learned. How do students generally perform when their parents have the lowest and highest levels of education? Let's compare the grade distributions for students whose parents have the lowest level of education (i.e., high school) with students whose parents have the highest level of education (i.e., master's degree). Figure 3.4 shows this comparison across all three subject areas.

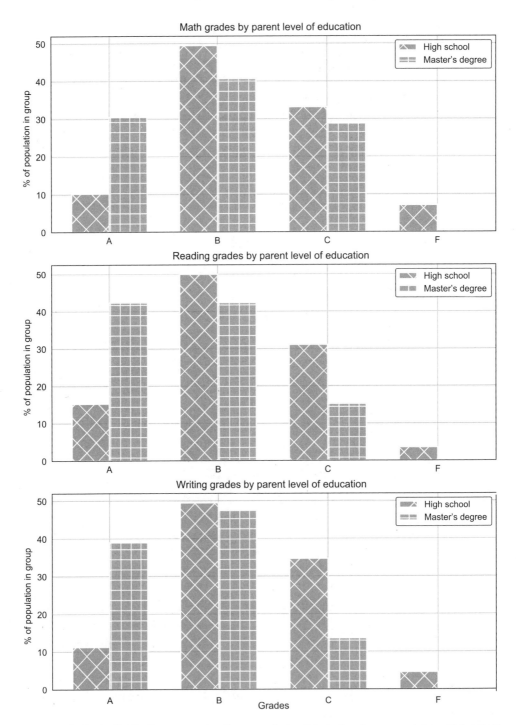

Figure 3.4   **Grade distributions comparing the percentage of students whose parents have high school education vs. a master's degree**

Let's focus on the students whose parents have high school education. Across all three subject areas, it looks like, in general, fewer students get grade A and more students get grade F than the overall population. For the math subject area, for instance, only 10% of the students whose parents have a high school education get grade A, whereas in the overall population (as we saw in figure 3.3), roughly 20% of the students get grade A. Let's now focus on students whose parents have a master's degree. It looks like, in general, more students get grade A and zero students get grade F when compared to the overall population. For the math subject area, for instance, roughly 30% of the students whose parents have a master's degree get grade A. If we now compare the two bars in figure 3.4, we can see a lot more students get a higher grade (A or B) when their parents have a higher level of education across all three subject areas.

How about ethnicity? How does the performance of a student belonging to the most represented group compare with one from the least represented group? From figure 3.2, we know that the most represented group is C and the least represented group is A. Figure 3.5 compares the grade distributions of students belonging to group C with students belonging to group A.

It looks like, in general, students from group C perform better than those from group A—a larger proportion of students seem to get a higher grade (A or B) and a smaller proportion of students get a lower grade (C or F). As mentioned earlier, the insights in this section will come in handy in section 3.4 when we interpret and validate what the model has learned.

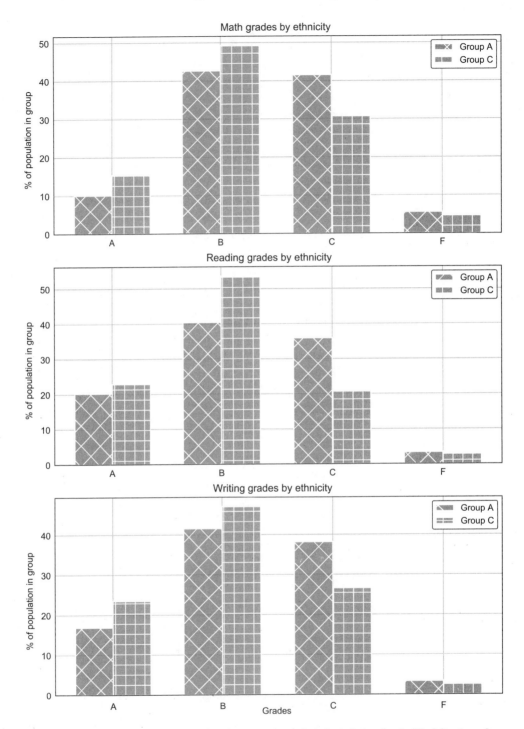

Figure 3.5   **Grade distributions comparing the percentage of students belonging to Ethnicity group A vs. group C**

3.2 *Tree ensembles*

In chapter 2, you learned about decision trees, a powerful way of modeling nonlinear relationships. Decision trees are white-box models and are easy to interpret. We saw, however, that more complex decision trees suffer from the problem of overfitting where the model heavily fits the noise or variance in the data. To overcome the problem of overfitting, we can reduce the complexity of decision trees by pruning them in terms of depth and the minimum number of samples required for the leaf nodes. This results in low predictive power, however.

By combining several decision trees, we can circumvent the overfitting problem without compromising on predictive power. This is the principle behind tree ensembles. We can combine, or ensemble, decision trees in the following two broad ways:

- *Bagging*—Multiple decision trees are trained in parallel on separate random subsets of the training data. We can use these individual decision trees to make predictions and combine them by taking an average to come up with the final prediction. Random forest is a tree ensemble using the bagging technique. In addition to training individual decision trees on random subsets of the data, the random forest algorithm also takes a random subset of the features to split the data on.
- *Boosting*—Like in bagging, the boosting technique also trains multiple decision trees but in sequence. The first decision tree is typically a shallow tree and is trained on the training set. The objective of the second decision tree is to learn from the errors made by the first tree and to further improve the performance. Using this technique, we string together multiple decision trees, and they iteratively try to optimize and reduce the errors made by the previous one. Adaptive boosting and gradient boosting are two common boosting algorithms.

In this chapter, we will be focusing on the bagging technique, specifically the *random forest* algorithm, which is illustrated in figure 3.6. First, we take random subsets of the

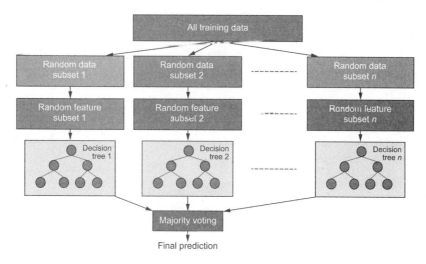

Figure 3.6 An illustration of the random forest algorithm

training data and train separate decision trees on them. Each decision tree is then split on random subsets of the features. We obtain the final prediction by taking the majority vote across all decision trees. As you can see, a random forest model is much more complex than a decision tree. As the number of trees in the ensemble increases, the complexity increases. Moreover, it is much harder to visualize and interpret how features are split across all decision trees because random subsets of the data and features are taken for each of them. This makes random forest a black-box model and much harder to interpret. Being able to explain the algorithm does not guarantee interpretability in this case.

For completeness, let's also discuss how the adaptive-boosting and gradient-boosting algorithms work. *Adaptive boosting*, usually shortened as *AdaBoost*, is illustrated in figure 3.7. The algorithm works as follows. First, we train a decision tree using all the training data. Each data point is given equal weight for the first decision tree. Once the first decision tree is trained, calculate the error rate of the tree by taking a weighted sum of the error for each data point. We then use this weighted error rate to determine the weight of the decision tree. If the error rate of the tree is high, then a lower weight is given for the tree because its predictive power is low. If the error rate is low, then a higher weight is given for the tree because it has a higher predictive power. We then use the weight of the first decision tree to determine the weights for each data point for the second decision tree. The wrongly classified data points will be given a higher weight so that the second decision tree can try to reduce the error rate. We repeat this process in sequence until the number of trees we set during training is

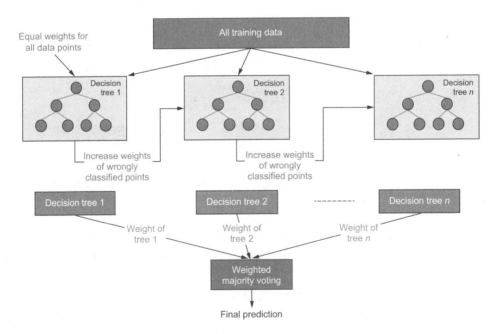

Figure 3.7   An illustration of the AdaBoost algorithm

reached. After all the trees have been trained, we come up with the final prediction by taking a weighted majority vote. Because a decision tree with a higher weight has higher predictive power, it is given more influence in the final prediction.

The *gradient-boosting* algorithm works slightly differently and is illustrated in figure 3.8. As with AdaBoost, the first decision tree is trained on all of the training data, but unlike AdaBoost, no weights are associated with the data points. After training the first decision tree, we calculate a residual error metric, which is the difference between the actual target and the predicted target. We then train the second decision tree to predict the residual error made by the first decision tree. So, rather than updating the weights for each data point like in AdaBoost, gradient boosting predicts the residual error directly. The objective for each tree is to fix the errors of the previous tree. This process is repeated in sequence until the number of trees we set during training is reached. After all the trees have been trained, we come up with the final prediction by summing the predictions of all the trees.

As mentioned earlier, we will focus on the random forest algorithm, but the methods used to train, evaluate, and interpret the algorithm can be extended to the boosting techniques as well.

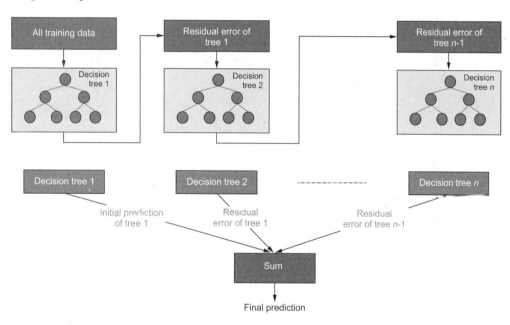

Figure 3.8   An illustration of the gradient-boosting algorithm

3.2.1   *Training a random forest*

Let's now train our random forest model to predict high school student performance. The following code snippet shows how to prepare the data before training the model. Note that when splitting the data into the training and test sets, 20% of the data is used for testing. The rest of the data is used for training and validation. Also, we take a stratified sample on the math target variable so that the distribution of the grades is the same for both the training and test sets. You can easily create similar splits using the reading and writing grades as well:

```
import pandas as pd
from sklearn.preprocessing import LabelEncoder

# Load the data
df = pd.read_csv('data/StudentsPerformance.csv')
```

Loads the data into a Pandas DataFrame

```
# First, encode the input features
gender_le = LabelEncoder()
race_le = LabelEncoder()
parent_le = LabelEncoder()
lunch_le = LabelEncoder()
test_prep_le = LabelEncoder()
df['gender_le'] = gender_le.fit_transform(df['gender'])
df['race_le'] = race_le.fit_transform(df['race/ethnicity'])
df['parent_le'] = parent_le.fit_transform(df['parental level of education'])
df['lunch_le'] = lunch_le.fit_transform(df['lunch'])
df['test_prep_le'] = test_prep_le.fit_transform(df['test preparation
➥ course']);
```

Because the input features are textual and categorical, we need to encode them into a numerical value.

Fits and transforms the input features into numerical values

```
# Next, encode the target variables
math_grade_le = LabelEncoder()
reading_grade_le = LabelEncoder()
writing_grade_le = LabelEncoder()
df['math_grade_le'] = math_grade_le.fit_transform(df['math grade'])
df['reading_grade_le'] = reading_grade_le.fit_transform(df['reading grade'])
df['writing_grade_le'] = writing_grade_le.fit_transform(df['writing grade'])
```

Initializes the LabelEncoders for the target variables as well because letter grades have to be converted to a numerical value

Fits and transforms the target variables into numerical values

```
# Creating training/val/test sets
df_train_val, df_test = train_test_split(df, test_size=0.2,
stratify=df['math_grade_le'], #F shuffle=True, random_state=42)
feature_cols = ['gender_le', 'race_le',
 'parent_le', 'lunch_le',[CA] 'test_prep_le']
X_train_val = df_train_val[feature_cols]
X_test = df_test[feature_cols]
y_math_train_val = df_train_val['math_grade_le']
y_reading_train_val = df_train_val['reading_grade_le']
y_writing_train_val = df_train_val['writing_grade_le']
y_math_test = df_test['math_grade_le']
y_reading_test = df_test['reading_grade_le']
y_writing_test = df_test['writing_grade_le']
```

Splits the data into training/validation and test sets

Extracts the target vectors for math, reading, and writing for both the train/validation and test sets

Extracts the feature matrix for the train/validation and test sets

Once you have prepared the data, you are now ready to train the three random forest models for math, reading, and writing, as shown in the next code sample. Note that we can determine the optimum parameters for the random forest classifier using cross-validation. Also note that the random forest algorithm first takes random subsets of the training data to train each decision tree, and for each decision tree, the model takes random subsets of the feature on which to split the data. For both of these random elements in the algorithm, it is important to set the seed for the random-number generator, using the `random_state` parameter. If this seed is not set, you will not be able to achieve reproducible and consistent results. First, let's use a helper function to create a random forest model with predefined parameters:

Sets the number of decision trees in the random forest

```
from sklearn.ensemble import RandomForestClassifier

def create_random_forest_model(n_estimators,
                               max_depth=10,
                               criterion='gini',
                               random_state=42,
                               n_jobs=4):
    return RandomForestClassifier(n_estimators=n_estimators,
                                  max_depth=max_depth,
                                  criterion=criterion,
                                  random_state=random_state,
                                  n_jobs=n_jobs)
```

The maximum depth parameter for the decision tree

Gini impurity is used as the cost function on which to optimize each decision tree.

For reproducibility, sets the seed for the random-number generator

Sets n_jobs to train the individual decision trees in parallel, using all available cores in your computer

Now let's use this helper function to initialize and train the three random forest models for the math, reading, and writing subject areas, as shown here:

Fits the math student performance classifier on the training data using the math grade as the target

Initializes the math model random forest classifier with 50 decision trees

```
math_model = create_random_forest_model(50)
math_model.fit(X_train_val, y_math_train_val)
y_math_model_test = math_model.predict(X_test)

reading_model = create_random_forest_model(25)
    reading_model.fit(X_train_val, y_reading_train_val)
y_reading_model_test = reading_model.predict(X_test)

writing_model = create_random_forest_model(40)
writing_model.fit(X_train_val, y_writing_train_val)
y_writing_model_test = writing_model.predict(X_test)
```

Predicts the math grade for all the students in the test set using the pretrained model

Initializes and trains the random forest classifier with 25 decision trees to predict the reading grade

Initializes and trains the random forest classifier with 40 decision trees to predict the writing grade

Now that we've trained the three random forest models for math, reading, and writing, let's evaluate them and compare them with a baseline model that always predicts the majority grade (in this case, B) for all the subjects. A metric that is typically used for classification problems is accuracy. This metric, however, is not suitable for situations where the classes are imbalanced. In our case, we've seen the student grades are pretty imbalanced, as depicted earlier in figure 3.3. If, for instance, 98% of the students obtain grade B in math, you can trick yourself into building a highly accurate model with 98% accuracy by always predicting grade B for all students. To gauge the performance of the model across all classes, we can use better metrics like precision, recall, and F1. *Precision* is a metric that measures the proportion of predicted classes that are accurate. *Recall* is a metric that measures the proportion of actual classes that the model predicted accurately. The formulas for precision and recall are shown next:

$$\text{Precision} = \frac{\text{True Positives}}{\text{True Positives} + \text{False Positives}}$$

$$\text{Recall} = \frac{\text{True Positives}}{\text{True Positives} + \text{False Negatives}}$$

The perfect classifier has a precision score of 1 and a recall score of 1 because the number of false positives and false negatives will be 0. But in practice, these two metrics are at odds with each other—there is always a trade-off that you need to make between false positives and false negatives. As you reduce the false positives and increase precision, the cost will be increased false negatives and lower recall. To find the right balance between precision and recall, we can combine the two metrics into a score called F1. The *F1 score* is the harmonic mean of precision and recall, as shown here:

$$F1 = 2 \cdot \frac{\text{Precision} \cdot \text{Recall}}{\text{Precision} + \text{Recall}}$$

Table 3.1 shows the performance of all three models . They are compared against baselines for each subject to see how much of an improvement in performance the new models provide. A reasonable baseline used by the superintendent is to predict the majority grade (in this case, B) for each subject.

Table 3.1   Performance of math, reading, and writing models

	Precision (%)	Recall (%)	F1 Score (%)
Math baseline	23	49	32
Math model	39	41	39
Reading baseline	24	49	32
Reading model	39	43	41
Writing baseline	18	43	25
Writing model	44	45	41

In terms of performance, we can see that the math and reading random forest models perform better than the baseline in terms of precision and F1. The baseline math and reading models, however, perform better than the random forest models in terms of recall. Because the baseline models always predict the majority class, it gets all the majority class predictions right. But the precision metric and F1 give us a better measure of the accuracy of all the predictions. The random forest model for the writing subject area does better than the baseline for all three metrics. The superintendent is happy with this improvement in performance but would like to now understand how the model came up with the prediction. In sections 3.3 and 3.4, we will see how to interpret a random forest model.

Training AdaBoost and gradient-boosting trees

We can train the AdaBoost classifier by using the `AdaBoostClassifier` class provided by Scikit-Learn. We initialize an AdaBoost classifier in Python as follows:

```
from sklearn.ensemble import AdaBoostClassifier
math_adaboost_model = AdaBoostClassifier(n_estimators=50)
```

We train a gradient-boosting tree classifier by using the `GradientBoostingClassifier` class provided by Scikit-Learn as shown next:

```
from sklearn.ensemble import GradientBoostingClassifier
math_gbt_model = GradientBoostingClassifier(n_estimators=50)
```

We train the models the same way as we do the random forest classifier. Variants of gradient-boosting trees are available that are faster and scalable, such as CatBoost and XGBoost. As an exercise, try training AdaBoost and gradient-boosting classifiers for all three subject areas and compare your results with the random forest models.

3.3 Interpreting a random forest

Random forest is an ensemble of multiple decision trees, so we could look at the global relative importance of each feature by averaging the normalized feature importance across all decision trees. In chapter 2, we saw how to compute the importance of features for a decision tree. This is shown next for a given decision tree t:

$$\underbrace{I_{i,t}^{feature}}_{\substack{\text{Importance} \\ \text{of feature } i \\ \text{in decision tree } t}} = \frac{\overbrace{\sum_{j \in \mathbb{J}} I_{j,t}^{node}}^{\substack{\text{Sum of importance} \\ \text{of all nodes } j \\ \text{that split on feature } i \\ \text{in decision tree } t}}}{\underbrace{\sum_{k \in \mathbb{K}} I_{k,t}^{node}}_{\substack{\text{Sum of importance} \\ \text{of all nodes } k \\ \text{in decision tree } t}}}$$

To compute the relative importance, we need to normalize the feature importance shown previously by dividing it by the sum of all feature importance values, as shown next:

$$
\underbrace{I_{i,t}^{\text{feature}}}_{\substack{\text{Importance} \\ \text{of feature } i \\ \text{in decision tree } t}} = \frac{\overbrace{\displaystyle\sum_{j\in\mathbb{J}} I_{j,t}^{\text{node}}}^{\substack{\text{Sum of importance} \\ \text{of all nodes } j \\ \text{that split on feature } i \\ \text{in decision tree } t}}}{\underbrace{\displaystyle\sum_{k\in\mathbb{K}} I_{k,t}^{\text{node}}}_{\substack{\text{Sum of importance} \\ \text{of all nodes } k \\ \text{in decision tree } t}}}
$$

You can now easily compute the global relative importance of each feature for the random forest by averaging the normalized feature importance for that feature across all decision trees, as shown next. Note that feature importance is computed the same way for AdaBoost and gradient-boosting trees:

$$
\underbrace{I_i^{\text{feature}}}_{\substack{\text{Relative Importance} \\ \text{of feature } i}} = \frac{\overbrace{\displaystyle\sum_{t\in\text{all trees}} \bar{I}_{i,t}^{\text{feature}}}^{\substack{\text{Sum of normalized importance} \\ \text{of feature } i \\ \text{across all decision trees}}}}{\underbrace{T}_{\substack{\text{Total number of trees}}}}
$$

In Python, we can obtain feature importance from the Scikit-Learn random forest model and plot it as follows:

Gets the feature importance of the math random forest model

Gets the feature importance of the reading random forest model

Gets the feature importance of the writing random forest model

Initializes the list of feature names

```python
math_fi = math_model.feature_importances_ * 100
reading_fi = reading_model.feature_importances_ * 100
writing_fi = writing_model.feature_importances_ * 100

feature_names = ['Gender', 'Ethnicity', 'Parent Level of Education',
                 'Lunch', 'Test Preparation']

# Code below plots the relative feature importance
# of the math, reading and writing random forest models
fig, ax = plt.subplots()
index = np.arange(len(feature_names))
bar_width = 0.2
opacity = 0.9
error_config = {'ecolor': '0.3'}
ax.bar(index, math_fi, bar_width,
       alpha=opacity, color='r',
       label='Math Grade Model')
ax.bar(index + bar_width, reading_fi, bar_width,
       alpha=opacity, color='g',
       label='Reading Grade Model')
```

```
ax.bar(index + bar_width * 2, writing_fi, bar_width,
        alpha=opacity, color='b',
        label='Writing Grade Model')
ax.set_xlabel('')
ax.set_ylabel('Feature Importance (%)')
ax.set_xticks(index + bar_width)
ax.set_xticklabels(feature_names)
for tick in ax.get_xticklabels():
    tick.set_rotation(90)
ax.legend(loc='center left', bbox_to_anchor=(1, 0.5))
ax.grid(True);
```

The features and their importance values are shown in figure 3.9. As can be seen in the figure, the two most important features for the three subjects are Parent Level of Education and the Ethnicity of the student. This is useful information, but it does not tell us anything about how the grade is influenced by different levels of education and how race and education interact with each other.

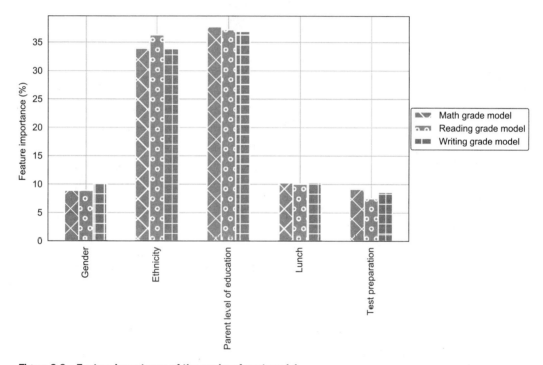

Figure 3.9   Feature importance of the random forest model

Moreover, we can easily compute and visualize feature importance for tree ensembles, but this becomes a lot harder when we look at neural networks and more complex black-box models, as will be more apparent in chapter 4. We, therefore, need to look at interpretability techniques that are agnostic to the type of black-box model. These model-agnostic methods are introduced in the following section.

3.4   *Model-agnostic methods: Global interpretability*

So far, we have been looking at interpretability techniques that are model-specific or dependent. For white-box models, we saw how to interpret linear regression models using the weights learned by the method of least squares. We interpreted decision trees by visualizing them as binary trees where each node splits the data using a feature determined using the CART algorithm. We were also able to visualize the global importance of features, the computation of which was specific to the model. We interpreted GAMs by visualizing the average effect of the basis splines for an individual feature on the target and then marginalizing the rest of the features. These visualizations were called partial dependence, or partial effect plots.

For black-box models like tree ensembles, we can compute the global relative importance of features, but we cannot extend this computation to other black-box models like neural networks. To better interpret black-box models, we will now explore model-agnostic methods that can be applied to any type of model. We will also focus our attention in this chapter on interpretability techniques that are global in scope. Global interpretability techniques aim to give a better understanding of the model as a whole, that is, the global effects of the features on the target variable. One globally interpretable model-agnostic method is partial dependence plots (PDPs). You will see in the following section how to extend the PDPs that you learned for GAMs in chapter 2 to black-box models like random forest. We will formalize the definition of PDPs and also see how to extend PDPs to visualize interactions between any two features to validate whether the model has picked up on any dependence between them.

Model-agnostic interpretability techniques can also be local in scope. We can use these techniques to interpret a model for a given local instance or prediction. Techniques such as LIME, SHAP, and anchors are model-agnostic and local in scope, and you will learn more about them in chapter 4.

3.4.1   *Partial dependence plots*

As we saw with GAMs in chapter 2, the idea behind partial dependence plots (PDPs) is to show the marginal or average effects of different feature values on the model prediction. Let f be the function learned by the model. For the high school student prediction problem, let f_{math}, $f_{reading}$, and $f_{writing}$ be the functions learned by the random forest models trained for the math, reading, and writing subject areas, respectively. For each subject, the function returns the probability of receiving a certain grade given the input features. Let's now focus on the math random forest model for ease of understanding. You can easily extend the theory that you will learn now to the other subject areas.

Suppose that for the math random forest model, we want to understand what effect different parent levels of education have on predicting a given grade. To achieve this, we will need to do the following:

- Use the same values for the rest of the features as were used in the dataset.
- Create an artificial dataset by setting Parent Level of Education to be the value of interest for all data points—if you are interested in looking at the average effects of high school education on the student's grade, then set Parent Level of Education to be high school for all data points.
- Run through the model, and obtain the predictions for all data points in this artificial set.
- Take the average of the predictions to determine the overall average effect for that Parent Level of Education.

More formally, if we want to plot the partial dependence of feature *S*, we marginalize on the rest of the features represented as set *C*, set feature *S* to be the value of interest, and then look at the average effect of the math model for feature *S*, assuming values of all the features in set *C* are known. Let's look at a concrete example. Suppose we are interested in understanding the marginal effects of Parent Level of Education on students' math grades. In this case, feature *S* is Parent Level of Education, and the rest of the features are represented as *C*. To understand the effect of, say, a high school level of education, we set feature *S* to the value corresponding to high school education (the value of interest) and take the average of the math model's output, assuming we know the values of the rest of the features. Mathematically, this is shown by the following equation:

$$\hat{f}_{math, \, x_S}\left(x_S \,|\, \mathbf{X}_C\right) = \frac{1}{n}\sum_{i=1}^{n} f_{math}\left(x_S, x_C^{(i)}\right)$$

In this equation, the partial function for feature *S* is obtained by computing the average of the learned function f_{math}, assuming the values for features in set *C* are known for all the examples in the training set, represented as *n*.

It is important to note that the PDP cannot be trusted if feature *S* is correlated with features in set *C*. Why is that? To determine the average effects of a given value for feature *S*, we are creating an artificial dataset where we use the actual feature values for all the other features in set *C* but change the value of feature *S* to be the one of interest. If feature *S* is highly correlated with any feature in set *C*, we could be creating an artificial dataset that is highly unlikely. Let's look at a concrete example. Suppose we are interested in understanding the average effects of a high school level of education for a student's parent on their grade. We will be setting Parent Level of Education as high school for all the instances in our training set. Now, if Parent Level of Education is highly correlated with Ethnicity, where we know Parent Level of Education given the Ethnicity, we could have an instance where it is highly unlikely for parents belonging to a certain ethnicity to have just a high school education. We are, therefore, creating an artificial dataset whose distribution does not match the original training data. Because the model has not been exposed to that distribution of the data, the predictions from that model may be way off, resulting in untrustworthy PDPs. We will come back to this limitation in section 3.4.2.

Let's now see how to implement PDPs. In Python, you can use the implementation provided by Scikit-Learn, but this limits you to gradient-boosted regressors or classifiers. A better implementation in Python that is truly model-agnostic is PDPBox, developed by Jiangchun Lee. You can install this library as follows:

```
pip install pdpbox
```

Now let's see PDPs in action. We will first focus on the most important feature, which you learned in section 3.3 is Parent Level of Education (see figure 3.9). We can look at the influence of different levels of education on predicting grades A, B, C, and F for math as follows:

Extracts only the label-encoded feature columns

Imports the PDP function from PDPBox

Obtains the partial dependence function for each level of education by passing in the learned math random forest model

Uses the preloaded dataset

Marginalizes on all the other features except Parent Level of Education

Initializes the labels for the xticks starting from the lowest level of education until the highest

```
from pdpbox import pdp

feature_cols = ['gender_le', 'race_le', 'parent_le', 'lunch_le',
    'test_prep_le']

pdp_education = pdp.pdp_isolate(model=math_model,
                dataset=df,
                model_features=feature_cols,
                feature='parent_le')
ple_xticklabels = ['High School',
                   'Some High School',
                   'Some College',
                   "Associate\'s Degree",
                   "Bachelor\'s Degree",
                   "Master\'s Degree"]
# Parameters for the PDP Plot
plot_params = {
    # plot title and subtitle
    'title': 'PDP for Parent Level Educations - Math Grade',
    'subtitle': 'Parent Level Education (Legend): \n%s' % (parent_title),
    'title_fontsize': 15,
    'subtitle_fontsize': 12,
```

```
    # color for contour line
    'contour_color':  'white',
    'font_family': 'Arial',
    # matplotlib color map for interact plot
    'cmap': 'viridis',
    # fill alpha for interact plot
    'inter_fill_alpha': 0.8,
    # fontsize for interact plot text
    'inter_fontsize': 9,
}
# Plot PDP of parent level of education in matplotlib
fig, axes = pdp.pdp_plot(pdp_isolate_out=pdp_education,
    feature_name='Parent Level Education',
                            center=True, x_quantile=False, ncols=2,
    plot_lines=False, frac_to_plot=100,
                            plot_params=plot_params, figsize=(18, 25))
axes['pdp_ax'][0].set_xlabel('Parent Level Education')
axes['pdp_ax'][1].set_xlabel('Parent Level Education')
axes['pdp_ax'][2].set_xlabel('Parent Level Education')
axes['pdp_ax'][3].set_xlabel('Parent Level Education')
axes['pdp_ax'][0].set_title('Grade A')
axes['pdp_ax'][1].set_title('Grade B')
axes['pdp_ax'][2].set_title('Grade C')
axes['pdp_ax'][3].set_title('Grade F')
axes['pdp_ax'][0].set_xticks(parent_codes)
axes['pdp_ax'][1].set_xticks(parent_codes)
axes['pdp_ax'][2].set_xticks(parent_codes)
axes['pdp_ax'][3].set_xticks(parent_codes)
axes['pdp_ax'][0].set_xticklabels(ple_xticklabels)
axes['pdp_ax'][1].set_xticklabels(ple_xticklabels)
axes['pdp_ax'][2].set_xticklabels(ple_xticklabels)
axes['pdp_ax'][3].set_xticklabels(ple_xticklabels)
for tick in axes['pdp_ax'][0].get_xticklabels():
    tick.set_rotation(45)
for tick in axes['pdp_ax'][1].get_xticklabels():
    tick.set_rotation(45)
for tick in axes['pdp_ax'][2].get_xticklabels():
    tick.set_rotation(45)
for tick in axes['pdp_ax'][3].get_xticklabels():
    tick.set_rotation(45)
```

The plot generated by this code snippet is shown in figure 3.10. The partial dependence of Parent Level of Education is shown separately for each grade—A, B, C, and F. The range of values for the partial dependence function is between 0 and 1 because the learned math model function for this classifier is a probability measure that ranges from 0 to 1. Let's now zoom in on a couple of grades to analyze the impact of Parent Level of Education on the student's grade.

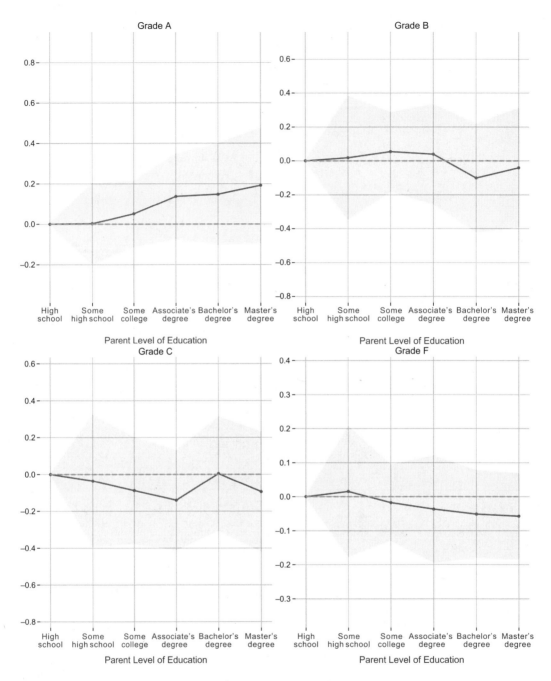

Figure 3.10   PDP of various Parent Level of Education features for math grades A, B, C, and F

In figure 3.11, we have zoomed in on the PDP for math grade A. We saw in section 3.1.1 that the proportion of students getting grade A in math is higher when the parent has a master's degree than when the parent has a high school degree (see figure 3.4). Has the random forest model learned this pattern? We can see from figure 3.11 that the impact on getting grade A increases as the Parent Level of Education increases. For a parent with a high school education, the effect on predicting grade A in math is negligible—close to 0. This means that having a high school education does not change anything for the model, and other features besides Parent Level of Education come into play when predicting grade A. We can, however, see a high positive impact of roughly +0.2 when the parent has a master's degree. This means that on average, a master's degree pushes the probability of a student getting grade A by roughly 0.2.

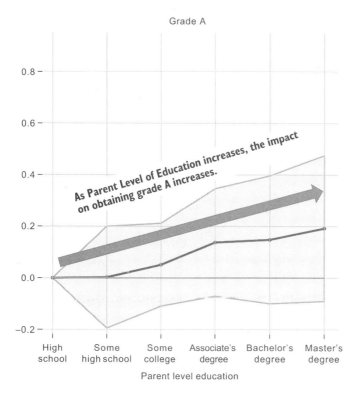

Figure 3.11 Interpreting the Parent Level of Education PDP for math grade A

In figure 3.12, we have zoomed in on the PDP of math grade F. We can notice a downward trend for grade F—the more educated the parent is, the more of a negative impact on predicting grade F. We can see that a student whose parent has a master's degree has a negative impact of roughly –0.05 on average in predicting grade F. This means that the parent having a master's degree decreases the likelihood of the student getting grade F and, therefore, increases the likelihood of the student getting grade A. This insight is great and would not have been possible by just looking at the feature importance. The end user of this system (i.e., the superintendent) will have more trust in the model that she is using.

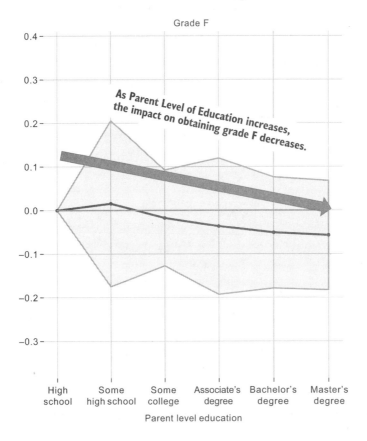

Figure 3.12
Interpreting the Parent Level of Education PDP for math grade F

As an exercise, I encourage you to extend the PDP code for math grade and Parent Level of Education to the other subject areas—reading and writing. You can check whether the patterns observed in section 3.1.1 (see figure 3.4) are learned by the random forest models. You can also extend the code to other features. As an exercise, pick the second most important feature, which is Race or Ethnicity of the student, and generate the PDP for that feature.

3.4.2   *Feature interactions*

We can extend PDPs to understand feature interactions. Returning to the equation in section 3.4.1, we will now look at two features in set *S* and marginalize on the rest. Let's examine the interactions between the two most important features—Parent Level of Education and student Ethnicity—in predicting grades A, B, C, and F in math. Using PDPBox, we can easily visualize pairwise feature interactions as shown in the following code snippet:

**Obtains the feature interactions between two features
for the learned math random forest model**

```
pdp_race_parent = pdp.pdp_interact(model=math_model,
                                   dataset=df,
                                   model_features=feature_cols,
                                   features=['race_le', 'parent_le'])
```

Uses the preloaded dataset

**Sets the feature
column names**

**List of the features for
which to obtain the
feature interactions**

```
# Parameters for the Feature Interaction plot
plot_params = {
    # plot title and subtitle
    'title': 'PDP Interaction - Math Grade',
    'subtitle': 'Race/Ethnicity (Legend): \n%s\nParent Level of Education
➥ (Legend): \n%s' % (race_title, parent_title),
    'title_fontsize': 15,
    'subtitle_fontsize': 12,
    # color for contour line
    'contour_color':  'white',
    'font_family': 'Arial',
    # matplotlib color map for interact plot
    'cmap': 'viridis',
    # fill alpha for interact plot
    'inter_fill_alpha': 0.8,
    # fontsize for interact plot text
    'inter_fontsize': 9,
}


# Plot feature interaction in matplotlib
fig, axes = pdp.pdp_interact_plot(pdp_race_parent, [CA]['Race/Ethnicity',
➥ 'Parent Level of Education'],
                                  plot_type='grid', plot_pdp=True,
                                  ➥ plot_params=plot_params)
axes['pdp_inter_ax'][0]['_pdp_x_ax'].set_xlabel('Race/Ethnicity (Grade A)')
axes['pdp_inter_ax'][1]['_pdp_x_ax'].set_xlabel('Race/Ethnicity (Grade B)')
axes['pdp_inter_ax'][2]['_pdp_x_ax'].set_xlabel('Race/Ethnicity (Grade C)')
axes['pdp_inter_ax'][3]['_pdp_x_ax'].set_xlabel('Race/Ethnicity (Grade F)')
axes['pdp_inter_ax'][0]['_pdp_x_ax'].grid(False)
```

The plot generated by this code is shown in figure 3.13. There are four plots generated, one for each grade. Feature interactions are visualized in a 2-D grid where the six Parent Level of Education features are on the *y*-axis and the five Ethnicity features are on the *x*-axis. I'll zoom in on grade A to decompose and explain this plot further.

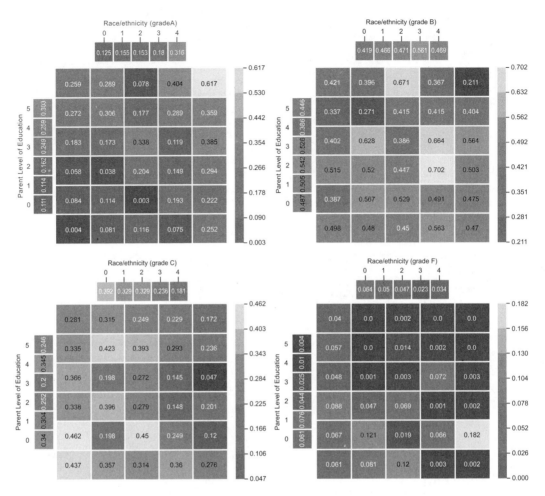

Figure 3.13   Interaction between Parent Level of Education and Ethnicity for all math grades A, B, C, and F

Figure 3.14 shows the feature interaction plot for math grade A. Parent Level of Education is on the *y*-axis, and the anonymized Ethnicity of the student is on the *x*-axis. As you go from the bottom to the top of the *y*-axis, Parent Level of Education increases from high school all the way to a master's degree. High school education is represented by a value of 0, and a master's degree is represented by a value of 5. The *x*-axis shows the five distinct ethnicity groups—A, B, C, D, and E. Ethnicity group A is represented by a value of 0, group B is represented by a value of 1, group C by a value of 2, and so on. The number in each cell represents the impact of a given Parent Level of Education and student Ethnicity on getting grade A.

For instance, the cell in the bottom-most row and the left-most column represents the average impact of a student belonging to ethnicity group A and having a parent who has a high school education on getting grade A. Please also note the numerical values in each cell of the grid—a lower number represents lower impact, and a higher number represents a higher impact in predicting grade A.

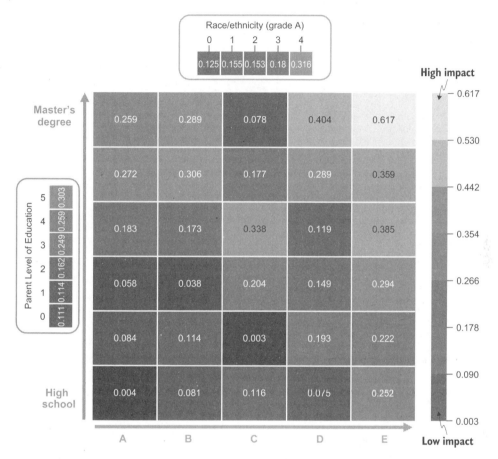

Figure 3.14 Zooming in on math grade A and decomposing the feature interaction plot

Now let's focus on ethnicity group A, which is the left-most column in the grid, highlighted in figure 3.15. You can see that as Parent Level of Education increases, the impact on predicting grade A also increases. This makes sense because it shows that Parent Level of Education has more influence on the grade than Ethnicity. This is validated by the feature importance plot shown in figure 3.9 as well. The model has, therefore, learned this pattern well.

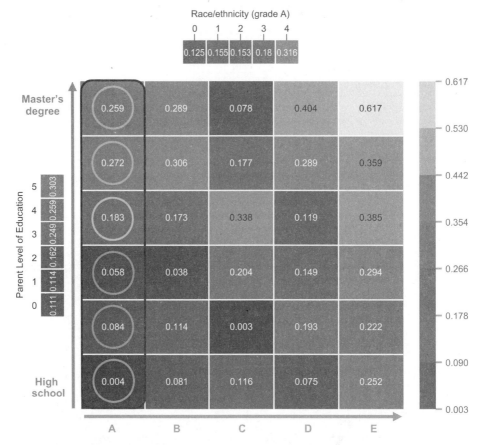

Figure 3.15   Impact of predicting grade A by conditioning on Ethnicity group A

But what is going on with ethnicity group C, the third column, highlighted in figure 3.16? It looks like a student whose parent has a high school degree has a higher positive impact in predicting grade A than a student whose parent has a master's degree (compare the bottom-most cell with the top-most cell of the highlighted column). It also looks like a student whose parent has an associate degree has the highest positive impact in predicting grade A than any other level of education (see the third cell from the top in the highlighted column).

This is a bit concerning because it may expose one or more of the following problems:

- Parent Level of Education might be correlated with the Ethnicity feature and, therefore, results in untrustworthy feature interaction plots.
- The dataset does not properly represent the population, especially Ethnicity group C. This is called sampling bias.
- The model is biased and has not learned the interaction between Parent Level of Education and Ethnicity well.
- The dataset exposes a bias that is systemic in society.

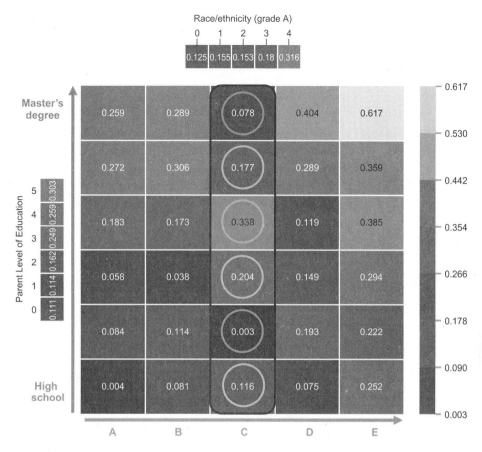

Figure 3.16 Impact of predicting grade A by conditioning on Ethnicity group C

The first problem exposes the limitation of PDPs, and we will discuss this limitation in the following paragraph. The second problem can be solved by collecting more data that is representative of the population. You will learn about other forms of bias and how to mitigate them in chapter 8. The third problem can be solved by adding or engineering more features or by training a better, more complex model. The last problem is much harder to solve, requiring better policies and laws, and this is beyond the scope of this book.

To check whether the first problem exists, let's look at the correlation between Parent Level of Education and Ethnicity. We saw in chapter 2 how to compute and visualize the correlation matrix. We used the Pearson correlation coefficient to quantify the correlation between the features for that problem. This coefficient can be used only for numerical features and not for categorical features. Because we are dealing with categorical features in this example, we have to use a different metric. We can use the *Cramer's V statistic* here because it measures the association between two categorical variables. This statistic can be between 0 and 1, where 0 signifies no correlation/association and 1 signifies maximum correlation/association. The following helper function can be used to compute this statistic:

```
import scipy.stats as ss

def cramers_corrected_stat(confusion_matrix):
    """ Calculate Cramers V statistic for categorial-categorial association.
        uses correction from Bergsma and Wicher,
        Journal of the Korean Statistical Society 42 (2013): 323-328
    """
    chi2 = ss.chi2_contingency(confusion_matrix)[0]
    n = confusion_matrix.sum().sum()
    phi2 = chi2/n
    r,k = confusion_matrix.shape
    phi2corr = max(0, phi2 - ((k-1)*(r-1))/(n-1))
    rcorr = r - ((r-1)**2)/(n-1)
    kcorr = k - ((k-1)**2)/(n-1)
    return np.sqrt(phi2corr / min( (kcorr-1), (rcorr-1)))
```

We can compute the correlation between Parent Level of Education and Ethnicity as follows:

```
confusion_matrix = pd.crosstab(df['parental level of education'],
                               df['race/ethnicity'])
print(cramers_corrected_stat(confusion_matrix))
```

By executing these lines of code, we can see that the correlation or association between Parent Level of Education and Ethnicity is *0.0486*. This is quite low, and we can, therefore, rule out the issue of the feature interaction plot or PDP being untrustworthy.

We saw in figure 3.5 that students belonging to group C perform better in general than students belonging to group A. It could be the case that the model has learned this pattern. We can validate it by looking at the top-most legend in figures 3.14, 3.15, and 3.16. If the student belongs to group C, it has a positive impact of +0.153 on predicting grade A, which is greater than the impact that student has when belonging to group A, which is +0.125. Let us now look at the difference in the distributions of Parent Level of Education between Ethnicity groups A and C, shown in figure 3.17.

In figure 3.17, we can see that parents of students belonging to Ethnicity group A are much more likely to have high school or some high school education than the overall population and students belonging to group C. It also looks like group C has a higher proportion of students whose parents have an associate degree than the overall population and group A. The differences in distributions are quite striking. We are not sure if the dataset represents the overall population and each Ethnicity group accurately. As a data scientist, it is important to highlight this problem to the stakeholder (the superintendent, in this example) and ensure that the dataset is legitimate and that there is no sampling bias.

The important point to take away from this section is that interpretability techniques, especially PDPs and feature interactions, are great tools for exposing potential

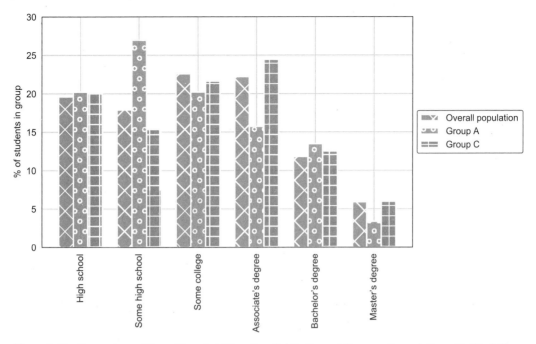

Figure 3.17 **Comparison of Parent Level of Education distributions of the overall population with Ethnicity groups A and C**

problems with the model or the data before the model is deployed into production. None of the insights in this section would have been possible by just looking at the feature importance. As an exercise, I encourage you to use the PDPBox package on other black-box models, such as gradient-boosting trees.

> **Accumulated local effects (ALE)**
>
> We have seen in this chapter that PDPs and feature interaction plots based on them are not trustworthy if the features are correlated with each other. An interpretability technique that is unbiased and overcomes the limitation of PDPs is accumulated local effects (ALE). This technique was proposed in 2016 by Daniel W. Apley and Jingyu Zhu. At the time of writing, ALE is implemented only in the R programming language. A Python implementation is still a work in progress and does not support categorical features yet. Because the implementation of ALE is not mature yet, we will cover this technique in greater depth in a later release of this book.

In the next chapter, we will enter the world of black-box neural networks. This may seem like a pretty big jump because neural networks are inherently complex and, therefore, require more sophisticated interpretability techniques to understand them. We will specifically focus on model-agnostic techniques that are local in scope, such as LIME, SHAP, and anchors.

Summary

- Model-agnostic interpretability techniques are not dependent on the specific type of model being used. They can be applied to any model because they are independent of the internal structure of the model.

- Interpretability techniques that are global in scope will help us understand the entire model as a whole.

- To overcome the problem of overfitting, we can combine or ensemble decision trees in two broad ways: bagging and boosting.

- Using the bagging technique, we train multiple decision trees in parallel on separate random subsets of the training data. We use these individual decision trees to make predictions and combine them by taking an average to come up with the final prediction. Random forest is a tree ensemble that uses the bagging technique.

- Like in bagging, the boosting technique also trains multiple decision trees, but in sequence. The first decision tree is typically a shallow tree and is trained on the training set. The objective of the second decision tree is to learn from the errors made by the first tree and to further improve the performance. Using this technique, we string multiple decision trees together, and they iteratively try to optimize and reduce the errors made by the previous one. Adaptive boosting and gradient boosting are two common boosting algorithms.

- We can train a random forest model for classification tasks in Python using the `RandomForestClassifier` class provided by the Scikit-Learn package. This implementation will also help you easily compute the global relative importance of features.

- We can train the Scikit-Learn adaptive-boosting and gradient-boosting classifiers by using the Scikit-Learn `AdaBoostClassifier` and `GradientBoostingClassifier` classes, respectively. Variants of gradient-boosting trees are available that are faster and scalable, such as `CatBoost` and `XGBoost`.

- For tree ensembles, we can compute the global relative importance of features, but we cannot extend this computation to other black-box models like neural networks.

- Partial dependence plot (PDP) is a global, model-agnostic interpretability technique that we can use to understand the marginal or average effects of different feature values on the model prediction. PDPs cannot be trusted if features are correlated with each other. We can implement PDPs using the `PDPBox` Python package.

- PDPs can be extended to understand feature interactions as well. PDPs and feature interaction plots can be used to expose possible issues such as sampling bias and model bias.

Model-agnostic methods:
Local interpretability

In the previous chapter, we looked at tree ensembles, especially random forest models, and learned how to interpret them using model-agnostic methods that are global in scope, such as partial dependence plots (PDPs) and feature interaction plots. We saw that PDPs are a great way of understanding how individual feature values impact the final model prediction at a global scale. We were also able to see how features interact with each other using the feature interaction plots and how they can be used to expose potential issues such as bias. PDPs are easy and intuitive to understand, but their major drawback is that they assume features are independent of each other. In addition, higher-order feature interactions cannot be visualized using feature interaction plots.

In this chapter, we will look at black-box neural networks, specifically focusing on deep neural networks (DNNs). These models are inherently complex and require more sophisticated interpretability techniques to understand them. We will specifically focus on techniques such as local interpretable model-agnostic explanations (LIME), SHapley Additive exPlanations (SHAP), and anchors. Unlike PDPs and feature interaction plots, these techniques are local in scope. This means that we can use them to interpret only a single instance or prediction.

We will follow a similar structure as the previous chapters. We start off with a concrete example where the objective is to build a model for breast cancer diagnosis. We will explore this new dataset and learn how to train and evaluate DNNs in PyTorch. We then learn how to interpret them. It is worth reiterating that although the main focus of this chapter is on interpreting DNNs, we will also cover basic concepts of DNNs and how to train and test them. Because the learning, testing, and understanding stages are iterative, it is important to cover all three together. We also cover some key insights and concepts in the earlier sections that will be useful during model interpretation. Readers who are already familiar with DNNs and how to train and test them are free to skip the earlier sections and jump straight to section 4.4, in which we cover model interpretability.

4.1   *Diagnostics+ AI: Breast cancer diagnosis*

Let's look at a concrete example. We'll go back to Diagnostics+, introduced in chapters 1 and 2. The center would like to extend its AI capabilities to diagnose breast cancer and has digitized the images of a fine needle aspiration of breast masses from around 570 patients. Features were computed from these digitized images that described the characteristics of cell nuclei present in the images. For each cell nucleus, the following 10 features are used to describe its characteristics:

- Radius
- Texture
- Perimeter
- Area
- Smoothness
- Compactness
- Concavity
- Concave points
- Symmetry
- Fractal dimension

For all the nuclei present in an image for a patient, the mean, standard error, and the largest or worst values are computed for each of these 10 features. Each patient, therefore, has 30 features in total. Given these input features, the goal of the AI system is to predict whether the cell is benign or malignant and to provide a confidence score for the doctor to help with their diagnosis. This is summarized in figure 4.1.

Figure 4.1   Diagnostics+ AI for breast cancer diagnosis

Given this information, how would you formulate this as a machine learning problem? Because the target of the model is to predict whether a given breast mass is benign or malignant, we can formulate this problem as a *binary classification* problem.

4.2   *Exploratory data analysis*

Let's now try to understand this dataset a bit better. Exploratory data analysis is an important step in the process of model development. We will specifically be looking at the volume of the data, the target class distribution, and whether features like the cell's Area, Radius, and Perimeter can be used to differentiate between benign and malignant cases. We will use a lot of the insights gleaned in this section to determine what features should be used for model training, what metrics should be used for model evaluation, and how to validate the model interpretations obtained using the techniques that we will cover later in this chapter.

The dataset contains 569 patient cases and 30 features in total. The features are all continuous. Figure 4.2 shows the proportion of cases that are benign and malignant. Out of the 569 cases, 357 of them (roughly 62.7%) are benign and 212 (roughly 37.3%) are malignant. This shows that the dataset is skewed, or imbalanced. As we saw

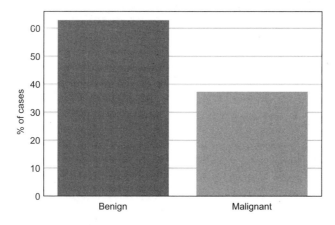

Figure 4.2   Distribution of benign and malignant cases

in chapter 3, we say that the data is imbalanced when a disproportionate number of examples or data points exist for a given class. Most machine learning algorithms work best when the proportion of samples for each class is roughly the same. This is because most algorithms are designed to minimize error or maximize accuracy, and these algorithms tend to be naturally biased toward the majority class. To recapitulate, you should note the following two things when dealing with imbalanced datasets:

- Use the right performance metrics (like precision, recall, and F1) when testing and evaluating the models.
- Resample the training data such that the majority class is either undersampled or the minority class is oversampled.

We will discuss this further in section 4.3.2. Let's now look at the distributions of the cell's Area, Radius, and Perimeter and see if there are any major differences between the benign and malignant cases. Figure 4.3 shows the distributions of the mean cell area and worst or largest cell area.

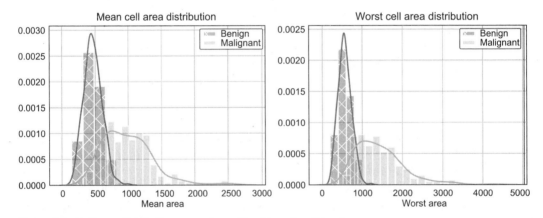

Figure 4.3   Cell area distribution comparison of benign and malignant cases

In figure 4.3, we can see that if the mean cell area is greater than 750, then the case is much more likely to be malignant than benign. Also, if the worst or largest cell area is greater than 1,000, then the case is much more likely to be malignant. There seems to be a good but weak separation between the malignant and benign cases by looking at just two features related to the cell area.

How about the cell's Radius and Perimeter? Figures 4.4 and 4.5 show the distributions of the Radius and Perimeter, respectively. We see a similar separation between the benign and malignant cases. For instance, a case with a mean radius that is greater than 15 is much more likely to be malignant than benign. Also, a case with worst or largest cell perimeter of 100 is much more likely to be malignant.

The purpose of this analysis is to get a sense of how good the features are in predicting the target variable, that is, whether a given case is benign or malignant. By looking at the distributions in figures 4.3, 4.4, and 4.5, we can see pretty good signal in

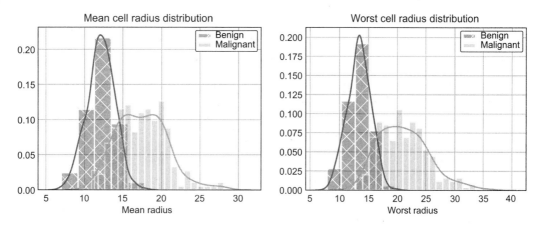

Figure 4.4 Cell radius distribution comparison of benign and malignant cases

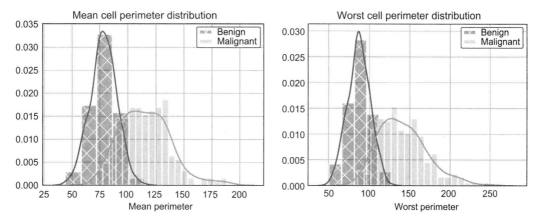

Figure 4.5 Cell perimeter distribution comparison of benign and malignant cases

the six features that we've considered where there's good separation between the benign and malignant cases. We will also use these insights to validate the interpretations obtained through LIME, SHAP, and anchors later in this chapter.

Let's finally look at how correlated each of the input features are with each other and the target variable. We know that the input features are continuous, but the target variable is discrete and binary. In the dataset, a malignant case is encoded as 0 and a benign case is encoded as 1. Because the input features and the target are all numerical values, we can use the Pearson, or standard, correlation coefficient to measure correlation. As we saw in chapter 2, the Pearson correlation coefficient measures the linear correlation between two variables and has a value between +1 and –1. If the magnitude of the coefficient is above 0.7, that means really high correlation. If the magnitude of the coefficient is between 0.5 and 0.7, that means moderately high correlation. If the magnitude of the coefficient is between 0.3 and 0.5, that means low correlation, and a magnitude less than 0.3 means little to no correlation. You can easily compute the pairwise correlations using the `corr()` function provided by Pandas. As an exercise, please reuse the code learned in section 2.2 to compute and plot the correlation matrix. The code to load the dataset can be found in section 4.3.1. The resulting plot for the breast cancer dataset is shown in figure 4.6.

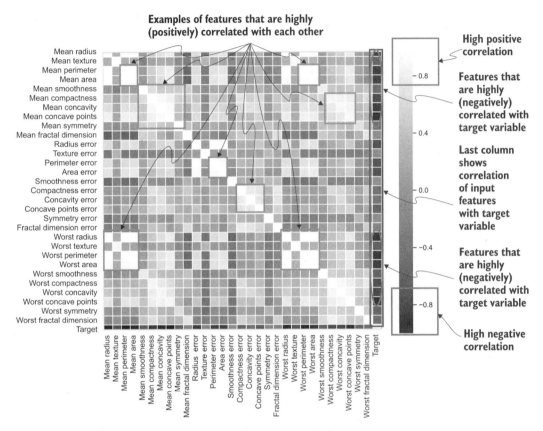

Figure 4.6   Correlation plot of input features and the target variable

In figure 4.6, let's first focus on the last column, which shows the correlation of all the input features with the target variable. We can see that features like mean cell Area, Radius, and Perimeter are highly correlated with the target class. The correlation coefficient is negative, however, which means that the larger the value for the features, the smaller the value for the target variable. This makes sense because the target class has a smaller value (i.e., 0) for the malignant class and a higher value (i.e., 1) for the benign class. As we saw in figures 4.3, 4.4, and 4.5, the larger the value for these features, the more likely that the case is malignant. We can also see that quite a few features are highly correlated with each other. For instance, features like mean cell Radius, Area, and Perimeter are highly correlated with worst cell Radius, Area, and Perimeter. As we discussed in chapter 2, features that are correlated with each other are said to be multicollinear, or redundant. One way of dealing with multicollinearity is to remove redundant features for the model. We will discuss this further in the following section.

4.3 *Deep neural networks*

An artificial neural network (ANN) is a system designed to loosely model a biological brain. It belongs to a broad class of machine learning methods called *deep learning*. The central idea of deep learning based on ANNs is to build complex concepts or representations from simpler concepts or features. An ANN learns a complex function by mapping the input to the output and is composed of many simpler functions. In this chapter, we will focus on ANNs consisting of multiple layers of units, or neurons, that are fully interconnected with each other. These are also called *deep neural networks (DNNs)*, *fully connected neural networks* (*FCNNs*), or *multilayer perceptrons* (*MLPs*). In subsequent chapters, we will cover *convolutional neural networks* (*CNNs*) and *recurrent neural networks* (*RNNs*), which are more advanced structures of neural networks used for complex computer vision and language understanding tasks.

Figure 4.7 illustrates a simple ANN consisting of three types of layers: the input layer, the hidden layer, and the output layer. The input layer acts as the input for your data. The number of units in the input layer is equal to the number of features in your dataset. In figure 4.7, we consider only two features from the breast cancer dataset, namely, mean cell Radius and mean cell Area. This is why two units exist in the input layer.

The input layer is then connected to all the units in the first hidden layer. The hidden layer transforms the inputs based on the activation function used for its units. In figure 4.7, the function f is used to represent the activation function for all the units in the hidden layer. The units in one layer are connected with units in another layer using edges. Each edge is associated with a weight, which defines the strength of the connection between the units that it connects. Note that a bias term also connects to

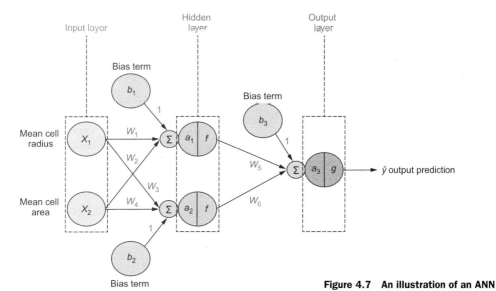

Figure 4.7   An illustration of an ANN

each of the units in the hidden layer, with an edge weight of 1. A weighted sum of the inputs and the bias term is taken before it is transformed by the activation function. If more than one hidden layer is present, then the ANN is said to be "deep." Hence, an ANN with two or more hidden layers is called a *DNN*.

The units in the final hidden layer are then connected to units in the output layer. In figure 4.7, one unit exists in the output layer because for the breast cancer detection task, we have binary output where the given cell is either malignant or benign. The unit in the output layer also has an activation function g, which transforms the inputs to that unit to an output prediction. One of the challenges in creating neural networks is determining the structure of the neural network—how deep (number of hidden layers) and how wide (number of units in each layer) the network should be. We will briefly talk about how to determine and interpret the structure of the neural network in section 4.4 and cover it in more detail in subsequent chapters when we look at CNNs and RNNs.

Let's now see how the input data is transformed into the output as it passes through the ANN. This is called forward propagation and is illustrated in figure 4.8. The input data is fed through the units in the input layer. The values of the input units for the two features are represented as *x1* and *x2*. These values are then propagated through the network in the forward direction through the hidden layers. At each unit in the hidden layer, a weighted sum of the inputs is computed and passed through an activation function. In figure 4.8, the first unit in the hidden layer computes the weighted sum of the inputs *x1* and *x2* and the bias term *b1* to obtain the pre-activation value *a1*. This is then passed through the activation function *f* to obtain *f(a1)*. A similar set of operations happens at the second unit in the hidden layer. Note that the same activation function is used for both units in the hidden layer. We will discuss activation functions in more depth later in this section.

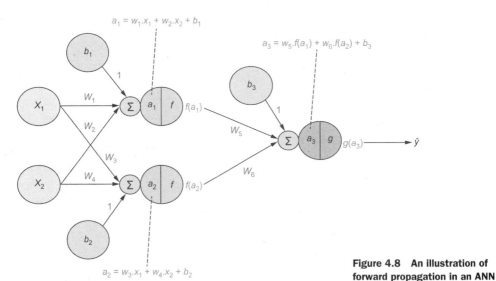

Figure 4.8   **An illustration of forward propagation in an ANN**

Once we have computed the outputs for the units on the hidden layer, these outputs are then fed as inputs to the units in the subsequent layer. In the next illustration, the outputs from the two units at the hidden layer are fed as inputs to the one unit in the output layer. Just as before, first a weighted sum of the inputs together with the bias term is determined to obtain the preactivation value *a3*. This is then passed through the activation function *g* to obtain the output of the unit as *g(a3)*. The output of this final unit is meant to be an estimate of the target variable *y*, represented as $\hat{y}$. The weights for all the edges in the network will be randomly initialized at the start.

Now the objective of the learning algorithm is to determine the weights of the edges, or the strength of the connections between the units, such that the output prediction is as close to the actual value for the target variable. How do you learn these weights? We will apply the same technique that we learned in chapter 2 to determine the weights for a linear regression model—gradient descent. An optimum set of weights are those that minimize a cost or loss function. For regression problems, a common cost function is the squared error or squared difference between the predicted output and the actual output. For binary classification problems, a common cost function is the log loss or the binary cross-entropy (BCE) loss function.

The squared error cost function and its corresponding derivative with respect to the predicted output are shown in the following equations:

$$J(\hat{y}|y) = \frac{(\hat{y} - y)^2}{2}$$

$$J'(\hat{y}|y) = \hat{y} - y$$

The log loss or BCE loss function and its corresponding derivative with respect to the predicted output are shown next:

$$J(\hat{y}|y) = \begin{cases} -\log(\hat{y}), & \text{if } y = 1 \\ -\log(1 - \hat{y}), & \text{if } y = 0 \end{cases}$$

$$J'(\hat{y}|y) = \begin{cases} -\frac{1}{\hat{y}}, & \text{if } y = 1 \\ \frac{1}{1-\hat{y}}, & \text{if } y = 0 \end{cases}$$

The cost function is said to be at a minimum (global or local) when the gradient of the cost function is 0 or close to 0. We can easily determine the weights for a linear regression or logistic regression type of problem because the number of weights is equal to the number of input features (plus an additional bias term). For a DNN, on the other hand, the number of weights depends on the structure of the network. The number of weights can easily explode as we add more units and layers to the network. Applying the gradient descent algorithm directly is not computationally feasible. An efficient algorithm to determine these weights in a DNN is backpropagation.

The backpropagation algorithm for the simple ANN structure seen earlier is illustrated in figure 4.9. Once we have evaluated the output of the network after forward propagation, the next step is to compute the cost or loss function and the gradient of the cost function with respect to the predicted output. Then visit the nodes in reverse order and propagate an error signal that we can use to compute the gradient with respect to the weights for all the edges in the network. Let's go through it step by step by parsing figure 4.9 from right to left.

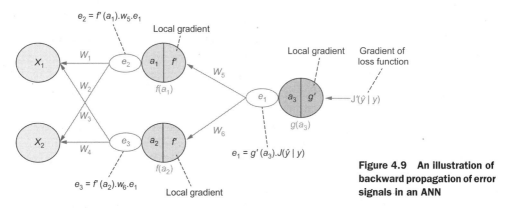

Figure 4.9   An illustration of backward propagation of error signals in an ANN

We first compute the gradient of the cost function with respect to the predicted output variable. This is represented as *J*'in figure 4.9. This gradient is then passed in the reverse direction through the unit in the output layer. Within the output layer, the local gradient of the activation function *g* is stored. This is represented as *g*'. The preactivation value *a3* evaluated during forward propagation is also stored. These values are used to compute the output error signal of the unit, represented as *e1*. The computed value, shown in figure 4.9, is the gradient of the loss function multiplied by the local gradient of the activation function. Using terminology from calculus, we are applying the chain rule here to compute the gradient of the loss function with respect to the input to the unit in the output layer. This error signal *e1* is then propagated to the two units in the hidden layer. The process is then repeated to compute the output error signals of the hidden units. Once the error signals have been propagated through the network and we have reached the input layer, we can compute the gradient, with respect to each edge weight, by multiplying the error signal flowing through it during backward propagation by the value that flowed through it during forward propagation. Multiple online resources and books explain backpropagation and the mathematical concepts in great depth. We will, therefore, not cover these concepts in more depth in this chapter.

The activation function is an important feature within a neural network. It decides whether a neuron should be activated and by how much. The properties of an activation function are that it is differentiable (i.e., the first derivative exists) and monotonic (i.e., it is either entirely nondecreasing or nonincreasing). Common activation functions used in neural networks include the sigmoid function, hyperbolic tangent (tanh), and the rectified linear unit (ReLU), which are defined in table 4.1.

Table 4.1   Common activation functions used in neural networks

Activation Function	Description
Sigmoid	The sigmoid function is defined as follows: $$sigmoid(x) = 1 \, / \, (1 + exp(-x))$$ 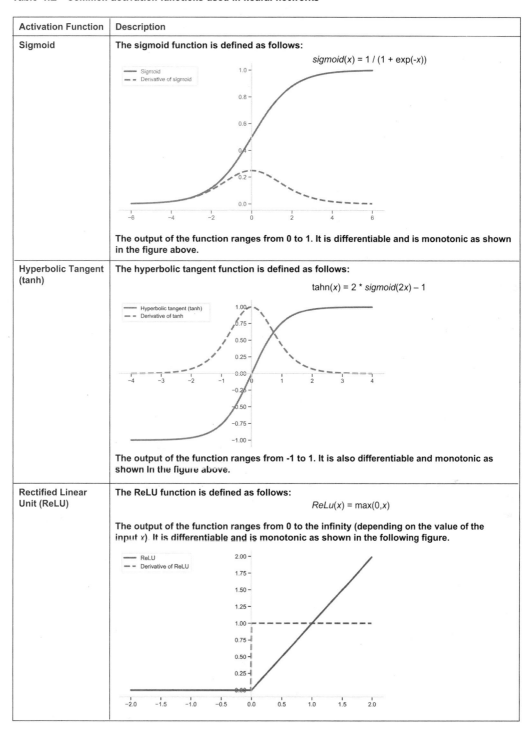 The output of the function ranges from 0 to 1. It is differentiable and is monotonic as shown in the figure above.
Hyperbolic Tangent (tanh)	The hyperbolic tangent function is defined as follows: $$tahn(x) = 2 * sigmoid(2x) - 1$$ The output of the function ranges from -1 to 1. It is also differentiable and monotonic as shown in the figure above.
Rectified Linear Unit (ReLU)	The ReLU function is defined as follows: $$ReLu(x) = max(0,x)$$ The output of the function ranges from 0 to the infinity (depending on the value of the input *x*). It is differentiable and is monotonic as shown in the following figure.

The sigmoid activation function is typically used for classifiers because the output of the function ranges from 0 to 1. For the breast cancer detection problem in this chapter, we will use the sigmoid function as the activation function g in the output layer. The hyperbolic tangent function has similar properties as the sigmoid, but the output ranges from –1 to 1. Both the sigmoid and hyperbolic tangent activation functions suffer from the problem of vanishing gradients. This is because the gradients for both functions are 0 (also said to be saturated) for very large or small values of the input, as seen in table 4.1.

ReLUs are the most widely used activation functions in neural networks because they handle the vanishing gradient problem well. We can see that the value of the ReLU is 0 if the input is negative. This means that if the input to a neuron with a ReLU activation function is negative, then the output of that neuron is 0 and is, therefore, not activated. Only neurons with non-negative inputs are activated. Because not all neurons are activated at the same time, the ReLU activation function is more computationally efficient. In practice, for simplicity, the same activation function is used for all the units in the hidden layers of the neural network.

4.3.1 Data preparation

Let's now train a DNN for the breast cancer detection problem. We will use PyTorch to build and train the network. PyTorch is a library that facilitates building neural networks in Python. PyTorch is gaining popularity among researchers and machine learning practitioners in the industry due to its ease of use. We can use other libraries, such as TensorFlow and Keras, to build neural networks as well, but we will focus on PyTorch in this book. Because the library is pythonic, it will be easier for data scientists and engineers who are already familiar with Python to use it. To learn more about PyTorch, please see appendix B.

The first step before training the DNN is to prepare the data. The following code shows how to load the data—split it into training, validation, and test sets, and then transform them into inputs for the PyTorch implementation of the network:

Imports PyTorch and the Variable data structure to store the input dataset as tensors

Imports NumPy, which is used for loading the dataset as vectors and matrices

Imports the breast cancer dataset available in Scikit-Learn

Imports the train_test_split function available in Scikit-Learn

```
import numpy as np

from sklearn.datasets import load_breast_cancer
from sklearn.model_selection import import train_test_split

import torch
from torch.autograd import Variable
```

Loads the breast cancer dataset and extracts the features and target

Splits the data into train and validation/test sets

```
data = load_breast_cancer()
X = data['data']
y = data['target']

X_train, X_val, y_train, y_val = train_test_split(X, y, test_size=0.3,
    random_state=24)
```

```
X_val, X_test, y_val, y_test = train_test_split(X_val, y_val, test_size=0.5,
    random_state=24)                          ◁──────────    Splits the validation/test set into
                                                             two equal sets: validation and test
X_train = Variable(torch.from_numpy(X_train))
X_val = Variable(torch.from_numpy(X_val))
y_train = Variable(torch.from_numpy(y_train))    Initializes the train, validation, and
y_val = Variable(torch.from_numpy(y_val))        test sets into PyTorch tensors
X_test = Variable(torch.from_numpy(X_test))
y_test = Variable(torch.from_numpy(y_test))
```

Note that 70% of the data is used for training, 15% for validation, and the remaining 15% as the held-out test set. Let's now check to see if the distribution of the target variable, shown in figure 4.10, is similar across the three sets. We can see that roughly 60–62% of the cases are benign (where the target variable = 1) and 38–40% of the cases are malignant (where the target variable = 0) in all three sets.

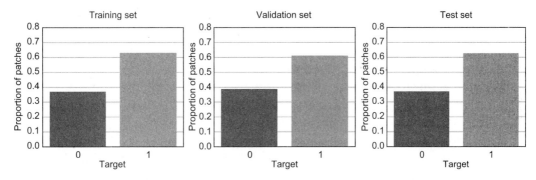

Figure 4.10 Target variable distribution across the training, validation, and test sets

4.3.2 *Training and evaluating DNNs*

Now that we've prepared the data, the next step is to define the DNN. We will create a class where the number of layers and units can be passed in as attributes, as shown here:

Creates a Model class that inherits from the PyTorch Sequential class

Passes the number of layers and units for each layer as an array to the constructor

```
class Model(torch.nn.Sequential):
    def __init__(self, layer_dims):            ◁──
        super(Model, self).__init__()
        for idx, dim in enumerate(layer_dims):    ◁──
            if (idx < len(layer_dims) - 1): #E
                module = torch.nn.Linear(dim, layer_dims[idx + 1])
                self.add_module("linear" + str(idx), module)
            else:
                self.add_module("sig" + str(idx), torch.nn.Sigmoid())
            if (idx < len(layer_dims) - 2):
                self.add_module("relu" + str(idx), torch.nn.ReLU())
```

Initializes the PyTorch Sequential super class

For each element in the array, extracts the index and the number of units for that layer

Creates a layer module containing all linear units until the final output layer

Uses the ReLU activation function for all the units in the hidden layers

Uses the sigmoid activation function for the unit in the output layer

Note that the DNN Model class inherits from the PyTorch Sequential class, which layers modules in the sequential order that they are initialized. For the input layer and hidden layers, Linear units are used to compute a weighted sum of all the inputs to that unit. For the hidden layers, we use the ReLU activation function. The final output layer consists of a single unit where we use the sigmoid activation function. The output of a sigmoid activation function is a score between 0 and 1. This output acts as a proxy for a probability measure for the positive class in the classification task. In this case, the positive class is benign. Now that we have the Model class, let's initialize it as follows:

The number of units for the input layer is equal to the number of features in the training set.

The number of units in the output layer is 1 because we are dealing with a binary classification problem.

```
dim_in = X_train.shape[1]
dim_out = 1
layer_dims = [dim_in, 20, 10, 5, dim_out]
model = Model(layer_dims)
```

Initializes the layer dimensions array to define the structure for the DNN

Initializes the DNN model with the predefined structure

If you print the model, using the command print(model), you will get the following output, which summarizes the structure of the DNN:

```
Model(
  (linear0): Linear(in_features=30, out_features=20, bias=True)
  (relu0): ReLU()
  (linear1): Linear(in_features=20, out_features=10, bias=True)
  (relu1): ReLU()
  (linear2): Linear(in_features=10, out_features=5, bias=True)
  (relu2): ReLU()
  (linear3): Linear(in_features=5, out_features=1, bias=True)
  (sig4): Sigmoid()
)
```

In this output, you can see that the DNN consists of one input layer, three hidden layers, and one output layer. The input layer consists of 30 units because the dataset contains 30 input features. The first hidden layer consists of 20 units, the second hidden layer consists of 10 units, and the third hidden layer consists of 5 units. The ReLU activation function is used for all the units in the hidden layers. Finally, the output layer consists of a single unit with a sigmoid activation function. The number of units in the input and output layers must be 30 and 1, respectively, for this dataset, because the number of features is 30 and only a single output is required for the binary classification task. You are, however, free to tune the number of hidden layers and the number of units in each hidden layer, depending on which structure gives the best performance. You can use the validation set to determine these hyperparameters.

With the model in place, let's now define the loss function and the optimizer that will be used to determine the weights during backpropagation as follows:

Initializes the binary cross-entropy (BCE)
loss as the criterion for optimization

Uses the Adam optimizer with a
learning rate of 0.001 to determine
the weights during backpropagation

```
criterion = torch.nn.BCELoss(reduction='sum')
optimizer = torch.optim.Adam(model.parameters(), lr=0.001)
```

As mentioned in the previous section, the BCE loss is used as the criterion of optimization for binary classification problems. We are also using the Adam optimizer here with a predefined initial learning rate to determine the edge weights during backpropagation. The Adam optimizer is a technique that adaptively determines the learning rate for the gradient descent algorithm. You can find more details on the Adam optimization technique in this blog post: http://mng.bz/zQzX. Finally, train the model as follows:

Initializes the number
of epochs to 300

In each epoch, obtains
the output of the DNN
for the training set

Computes the
BCE loss for the
training set

Updates
the weights
based on
the current
gradients

```
num_epochs = 300
for epoch in range(num_epochs):
    y_pred = model(X_train.float())
    loss = criterion(y_pred, y_train.view(-1, 1).float())

    optimizer.zero_grad()
    loss.backward()
    optimizer.step()
```

Zeroes out the gradients before backpropagating

Computes the gradient with respect
to every parameter/edge weight

Note that we are training the model over 300 epochs. An epoch is a hyperparameter that defines the number of times we propagate the entire training set in the forward and backward directions through the neural network. During each epoch, we first obtain the output of the DNN by propagating the training set through the network in the forward direction. We then compute the gradient with respect to every parameter or edge weight and update the weights during backpropagation. Note that the gradients are set to 0 in each epoch before starting backpropagation because PyTorch accumulates gradients during backward passes by default. If we do not set the gradients to 0, the weights will not be updated correctly.

The next step is to evaluate the model performance using the test set. Because this is a classification problem, we will use the same metrics that we used in chapter 3 for the student grade-prediction problem. The metrics we will use are precision, recall, and the F1 score. We will compare the performance of the trained DNN model with a reasonable baseline model. As seen in section 4.2, the majority of the cases in the dataset are benign. We will, therefore, consider a baseline model that always predicts benign. This is not ideal because we will get all the malignant cases wrong. In a real-life situation, the baseline model will typically be predictions made by a human or expert or an existing model that the business is using. For this example, unfortunately, we do not have access to that information, and so we will compare the model with a baseline that always predicts benign.

Table 4.2 shows the three key performance metrics used to benchmark the models—precision, recall, and F1. If we look at the recall metric, the baseline model does better than the DNN. This is expected because the baseline model is predicting the positive class all the time and will, therefore, get all the positive cases right. The recall with respect to the negative class, however, will be 0 for the baseline model. Overall, though, the DNN model does much better than the baseline, achieving a precision of 98.1% (+35.4% better than the baseline) and an F1 score of 96.2% (+19.1% better than the baseline).

As an exercise, I highly encourage you to tune the hyperparameters of the model and see if you can improve the performance of this model. You can tune the structure of the network by changing the number of hidden layers and units in each layer, and also the number of epochs used for training. In section 4.2 (figure 4.6), we also saw that some of the input features are highly correlated with each other. The performance of the model could be further improved by removing some of the redundant features. As another exercise, perform feature selection, and determine the best subset of features that maximizes the performance of the model.

Table 4.2   Performance comparison of the baseline model with the DNN model

	Precision (%)	Recall (%)	F1 score (%)
Baseline model 1	62.7	100	77.1
DNN model	98.1 (+35.4)	94.4 (–5.6)	96.2 (+19.1)

With the DNN model performing better than the baseline, let's now interpret it and understand how the black-box model arrived at the final prediction.

4.4   *Interpreting DNNs*

As we saw in the previous section, to make a prediction with a DNN, we pass data through multiple layers, with each layer consisting of multiple units. The inputs to each layer go through a nonlinear transformation based on the weights and the activation function used for the units. A single prediction can involve a lot of mathematical operations, depending on the structure of the neural network. For the relatively simple architecture used in the previous section for breast cancer detection, a single prediction involved roughly 890 mathematical operations based on the number of training parameters or weights, as shown next:

```
+----------------+------------+
|    Modules     | Parameters |
+----------------+------------+
| linear0.weight |    600     |
|  linear0.bias  |     20     |
| linear1.weight |    200     |
|  linear1.bias  |     10     |
| linear2.weight |     50     |
|  linear2.bias  |      5     |
| linear3.weight |      5     |
|  linear3.bias  |      1     |
+----------------+------------+
Total Trainable Parameters: 891
```

This example can very easily explode into millions of operations as we add more hidden layers and units per hidden layer. This is what makes DNNs black boxes—it becomes really difficult to understand what transformations each layer is doing and how the model arrives at the final prediction. We will see in later chapters that it becomes even more difficult with more complex structures like CNNs and RNNs.

One way we can interpret DNNs is by looking at the weights or the strengths of the edges connected to the units in the input layer. This could be seen as a proxy to determine the overall influence of the input features on the output prediction. It will not, however, give us an accurate measure of the feature importance as we saw for white-box models and tree ensembles in the previous chapters. The main reason is the neural network learns a representation of the input at the hidden layers. The initial input features are transformed into intermediate features and concepts. Therefore, the importance of those input features is not just dictated by the edges connected to the units in the input layer. So how do we interpret DNNs?

We have multiple ways of interpreting DNNs. We can use the model-agnostic methods we learned in the previous chapter that are global in scope. We learned about PDPs and feature interaction plots—model-agnostic techniques, meaning they are interpretability techniques that could work with any machine learning model. They are also global in scope, in that they look at the overall influence of the model on the final prediction. PDPs and feature interaction plots are easy and intuitive to use, and they are great tools for shedding light into how specific feature values influence the model output. We also learned how they can be used to uncover potential issues like data and model bias. We could very easily apply these techniques to the DNN model trained for breast cancer detection. For PDPs and feature interaction plots to work, however, the input features for the model have to be independent, and we saw in section 4.2 that they are not.

In the subsequent sections, we will learn about more advanced model-agnostic techniques, specifically focusing on LIME, SHAP, and anchors. These interpretability techniques are local in scope, that is, they focus on a specific instance or example to interpret. In later chapters, we will learn about feature attribution methods that aim to quantify the contribution of each input feature on the final prediction and also learn how to dissect the neural network and visualize the features learned by the intermediate hidden layers and units.

4.5   *LIME*

LIME, an acronym for local interpretable model-agnostic explanations, was proposed in 2016 by Marco Tulio Ribeiro and team. Let's break down this technique. In the previous section, we trained a DNN that learned how to separate the benign cases from the malignant cases using 30 features. Let's simplify this by collapsing the feature space into 2-D space, as shown in figure 4.11. The figure illustrates the complex decision function learned by the DNN where the model separates the benign cases from the malignant cases. The decision boundary is intentionally exaggerated in figure 4.11 to illustrate a complex function that is harder to explain globally and possibly easier to explain locally using a technique such as LIME.

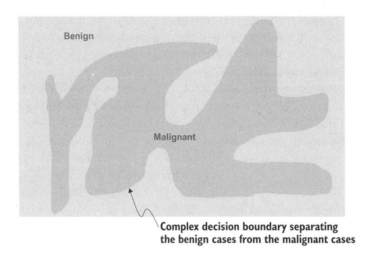

Benign

Malignant

Complex decision boundary separating
the benign cases from the malignant cases

**Figure 4.11   A 2-D
illustration of a complex
decision boundary learned by
the DNN (or any black-box
model) to separate the
benign cases from the
malignant cases**

LIME first picks an example to interpret. This is shown in figure 4.12 where we have picked one malignant case to interpret. The aim is to probe the model as often as needed to interpret how the model comes up with the prediction for that picked example. You can probe the model by *perturbing* the dataset to get the model predictions for that new dataset.

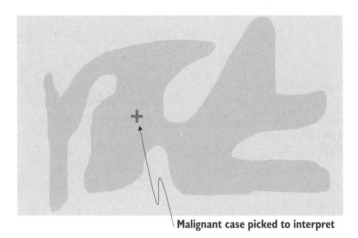

Malignant case picked to interpret

**Figure 4.12   An illustration
of an instance picked to
interpret using LIME**

How do we create this new *perturbed dataset*? Given the training data, we calculate the key summary statistics for each feature. For numerical or continuous features, we calculate the mean and standard deviation. For categorical features, we compute the frequency of each value. Then we create a new dataset by sampling based on these summary statistics. For numerical features, we sample data from a Gaussian distribution, given the mean and standard deviation for that feature. For categorical features, we sample based on the frequency distribution or probability mass function. Once we've created this dataset, we probe the model by getting predictions for them, as shown in figure 4.13.

The picked instance is shown as the big plus sign. The malignant and benign predictions on the perturbed dataset are shown as small plus signs and circles, respectively.

Model predictions for a perturbed dataset

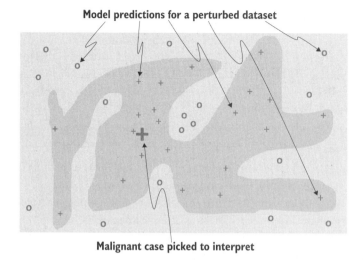

Malignant case picked to interpret

Figure 4.13 An illustration of a generated or perturbed dataset and the corresponding model predictions

Once we have created the perturbed dataset and obtained the model predictions for them, we weight these new samples by their proximity to the picked instance to interpret the picked instance by looking at cases similar to it in terms of features. The locality of the interpretation is captured by this weighting—hence, the "local" in the acronym LIME. Figure 4.14 shows the perturbed samples that are close to the picked instance given a higher weight.

Instances close to picked malignant case are given a higher weight.

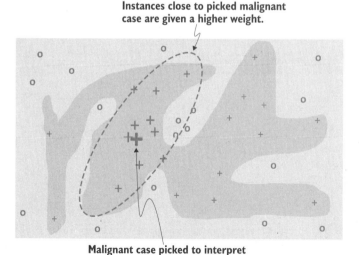

Malignant case picked to interpret

Figure 4.14 An illustration of weighted instances in close proximity to the picked instance to interpret

Now, how do we weight the samples based on their proximity to the picked instance? In the original paper, the authors use the exponential kernel function. The *exponential kernel function* takes two parameters as inputs:

- *Distance of perturbed sample from picked instance*—For the breast cancer dataset (or tabular data in general), we use Euclidean distance to measure the distance of the perturbed sample from the picked instance in the feature space. Euclidean distance is also used for images. For text, the cosine distance measure is used.
- *Kernel width*—This is a hyperparameter that can be tuned. If the width is small, only samples that are close to the picked instance will influence the interpretation. If the width is large, however, samples that are further away can influence the interpretation. This is an important hyperparameter, and we will study its impact on the interpretation in greater depth later. By default, the kernel width is set to $0.75 \times \sqrt{}$ *Number of features*. So, for the model with 30 input features, the default kernel width is 4.1. The value of the kernel width can range from zero to infinity.

Using the exponential kernel function, samples closer to the picked instance in terms of distance will have a larger weight than samples further away.

The final step is to fit a white-box model that is easily interpretable on the weighted samples. In LIME, linear regression is used, and as we've seen in chapter 2, we can use the weights of the linear regression model to interpret the importance of features for that picked instance—hence the "interpretable" in the acronym LIME. We get an interpretation that is locally faithful, and because we're fitting a linear surrogate model, LIME is totally agnostic of the DNN or black-box model—hence, the "model-agnostic" in the acronym LIME. Figure 4.15 illustrates the linear surrogate model (shown by the dashed gray line) that is faithful to the region near and around the instance picked to interpret.

Let's now get our hands dirty and see LIME in action for the breast cancer diagnostics DNN model that we trained earlier. First, install the LIME library using `pip` as follows:

```
pip install lime
```

Interpretable linear model that is locally faithful to the picked malignant case

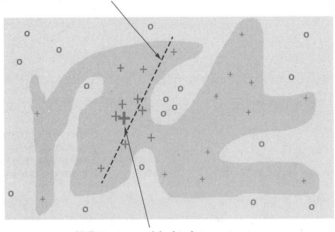

Malignant case picked to interpret

Figure 4.15 An illustration of a linear model that is used to interpret the picked instance using the weighted samples around it

After installing, the first step is to initialize a LIME explainer object. Because the dataset is tabular, we use the `LimeTabularExplainer` class. Other explainer classes are `Lime-ImageExplainer` to explain models that use images as inputs and `LimeTextExplainer` for text. We will make use of the `LimeImageExplainer` class in the next chapter when we deal with images:

```
import lime                          Imports the library and
import lime.lime_tabular              the relevant modules            Initializes the explainer
                                                                      using the training dataset
explainer = lime.lime_tabular.LimeTabularExplainer(X_train.numpy(),
Provides the feature names ┌──→  feature_names=data.feature_names,
                           ├──→  class_names=data.target_names,
    Provides the target class      discretize_continuous=True)    Discretizes the continuous
    names (benign/malignant)                                      variables to reduce
                                                                  computational complexity
```

Let's now pick two cases to interpret—one benign and one malignant. We will use the test set here where we pick the first benign and malignant cases, as shown in the following code:

```
benign_idx = np.where(y_test.numpy() == 1)[0][0]
malignant_idx = np.where(y_test.numpy() == 0)[0][0]
```

We need to create a helper function to provide the predictions of the DNN model for the perturbed dataset, as shown here:

```
def prob(data):
    return model.forward(Variable(torch.from_numpy(data)).float()).\
      detach().\
      numpy().\
      reshape(-1, 1)
```

We also need to create another function to plot the LIME interpretation in Matplotlib. We can create this plot using the library, but it doesn't allow customizations. This is why we've created this helper function so that we can add titles and labels, change the colors, and even create our own plots using the LIME interpretation:

```
def lime_exp_as_pyplot(exp, label=0, figsize=(8,5)):
    exp_list = exp.as_list(label=label)
    fig, ax = plt.subplots(figsize=figsize)
    vals = [x[1] for x in exp_list]
    names = [x[0] for x in exp_list]
    vals.reverse()
    names.reverse()
    colors = ['green' if x > 0 else 'red' for x in vals]
    pos = np.arange(len(exp_list)) + .5
    ax.barh(pos, vals, align='center', color=colors)
    plt.yticks(pos, names)
    return fig, ax
```

Let's now interpret the first benign case. This is shown next, where we pass the picked benign case to the LIME explainer:

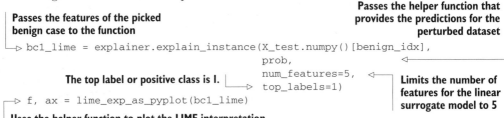

Passes the features of the picked benign case to the function

Passes the helper function that provides the predictions for the perturbed dataset

```
bc1_lime = explainer.explain_instance(X_test.numpy()[benign_idx],
                                      prob,
                                      num_features=5,
                                      top_labels=1)
f, ax = lime_exp_as_pyplot(bc1_lime)
```

The top label or positive class is I.

Limits the number of features for the linear surrogate model to 5

Uses the helper function to plot the LIME interpretation

Note that we are limiting the number of features for the linear surrogate model to 5. LIME uses a ridge regression model as the surrogate model by default. Ridge regression is a variant of the linear regression model that allows for variable selection or parameter elimination through regularization. By using a high regularization parameter, we can create sparse models that pick only a few top features for prediction. We can use a low regularization parameter for less sparsity. Figure 4.16 shows the resulting LIME interpretation for the benign case.

For the benign case used to interpret with LIME, the DNN model predicted that it was benign with a probability of 0.99, or a confidence of 99%. To understand how it arrived at that prediction, figure 4.16 shows the top five most important features for the linear surrogate model and their corresponding weights or importance. It looks like the most important feature was the worst area with a large positive weight. According to LIME, the reason the model predicted benign was because the worst area value was between 511 and 683.95. How did LIME get this range of values? It is based on the standard deviation of the weighted perturbed dataset used by the linear surrogate model.

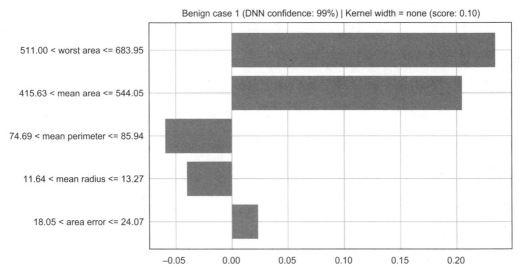

Figure 4.16   LIME interpretation of benign case 1 where the DNN model predicted benign with a confidence of 99%

Now, does this interpretation make sense? To validate this, we must go back to the exploratory data analysis that we did in section 4.2. We saw in figure 4.3 that when the worst or largest cell area is less than 700, a lot more cases are benign than malignant. If we now look at the second most important feature identified by LIME, we can see that if the mean area is between 415.63 and 544.05, it is much more likely for the case to be benign. This is further validated by our observation made in figure 4.3. We can also make a similar observation for the third most important feature—mean perimeter. You might have observed the kernel width and a score in the title in figure 4.16. We will come to this in a bit.

Let's now look at the first malignant case in the test set to interpret using LIME. We can use the same code as before, but we need to remember to pick the right feature values from the test set using `malignant_idx`. As an exercise, I encourage you to do that yourself. The resulting LIME interpretation is shown in figure 4.17. The two most important features are the same as the benign case, but the range of values is different. Moreover, the weight for the most important features (worst cell area) is also negative. This makes sense because we expect the feature to have a negative effect on the model's output. The DNN is trained to predict the probability of the positive class, which is, in this case, benign. Therefore, if the case is malignant, we expect the output of the model to be as low as possible; that is, the probability that the case is benign must be as low as possible.

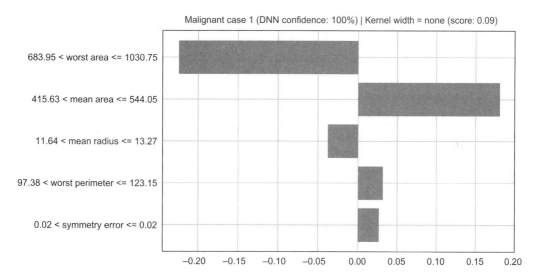

Figure 4.17 LIME interpretation of malignant case 1 where the DNN model predicted malignant with confidence of 100%

For this malignant case, the DNN predicts that the case is benign with a probability of 0. This means that the model is 100% confident that the case is malignant. Now let's inspect the feature value ranges. We can see that the model predicted malignant because the worst, or largest, cell area is greater than 683.95 but less than 1030.75. This makes sense because from the exploratory analysis, we observed more malignant cases than benign cases in that range (see figure 4.3). We can make similar observations for the other features.

IMPACT OF THE KERNEL WIDTH   It is important to point out that the kernel width is an important hyperparameter for LIME. Picking the right kernel width is important and has an impact on the quality of the interpretation. We can't pick the same kernel width for all instances that we wish to interpret. The choice of width has an impact on the weighted perturbed samples that LIME considers for the linear surrogate model. If we choose a large kernel width, samples further away from the picked instance will influence the linear surrogate model. This may not be desirable because we want the surrogate model to be as locally faithful to the original black-box model as possible. By default, the LIME library uses a kernel width that is the square root of the number of features multiplied by a factor of 0.75. So, if kernel_width = None, the default value is used. It may be the case that the same kernel width may not be applicable for all instances that need to be interpreted using LIME. To evaluate the quality of the interpretation, LIME provides an explanation, or fidelity score. The parameter is called score for the resulting LIME explanation. A higher score means that the linear model used by LIME is a good approximation of the black-box model. The kernel width and the LIME fidelity score are shown in the title for figures 4.16 and 4.17.

Let's now look at the impact of the kernel width by looking at another benign case. We have picked the second case here from the test set, as shown next:

```
benign_idx2 = np.where(y_test.numpy() == 1)[0][1]
```

The LIME explainer we created earlier used the default value, which is 0.75 × *sqrt(number of features)*. This evaluates to a kernel width of 4 because the number of features in the dataset is 30. We will also create another LIME explainer that is initialized with a smaller kernel width of 1 to see the impact on the interpretation. The following code shows how to create a LIME explainer with kernel width = 1:

```
explainer_kw1 = lime.lime_tabular.LimeTabularExplainer(X_train.numpy(),
feature_names=data.feature_names,
            class_names=data.target_names,
        kernel_width=1,              ◁——————   The kernel_width
            discretize_continuous=True)           parameter is set to 1.
```

The resulting LIME interpretations using the default kernel width and kernel width of 1 for the second benign case are shown in figure 4.18 (a) and figure 4.18 (b), respectively.

Let's first compare the default LIME interpretation of the second benign case with the first case shown earlier. The first most important feature is the same. We can see, however, that the range of values for the features is different. For the second benign

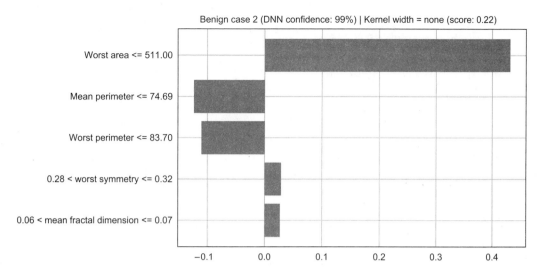

Figure 4.18a   LIME interpretation of benign case 2 with a default kernel width

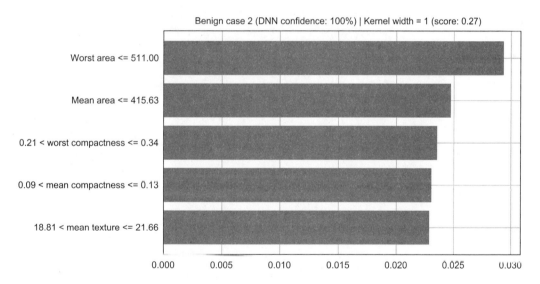

Figure 4.18b   LIME interpretation of benign case 2 with a kernel width of 1

case, we see that the model predicted benign because the worst cell area was less than 511, as opposed to being between 511 and 683.95, as seen for the first case. This is still a valid prediction because a lot more cases are benign when the worst area is less than 511. The fidelity score is also higher for default LIME interpretation of the second benign case. This means that the linear model in LIME reflects the DNN model more closely for this case than the first one.

If we now switch to figure 4.18 (b), we can see how different the interpretation is if we use a smaller kernel width. The top-most feature is still the same, but we see different features and a much smaller range of values for them because a small kernel width focuses the linear surrogate model on perturbed cases that are very close to the picked instance. Which kernel width is better for the second benign case? We can see that a kernel width of 1 achieves a fidelity score of only 0.27, as opposed to 0.22 for the default. Therefore, a kernel width of 1 is better in this case. As an exercise, I highly encourage you to increase the kernel width for the second case to see if you can achieve a higher fidelity score and to analyze the resulting LIME plot. I also suggest you tune the kernel width hyperparameter for the first case to see if you can get a better interpretation that is much more faithful to the DNN.

Figure 4.19 (a) and figure 4.19 (b) show the LIME interpretations for the second malignant case for two kernel widths—one default and the other with width 1. As an exercise, compare these interpretations with the first malignant case and see which kernel width gives you a higher quality interpretation.

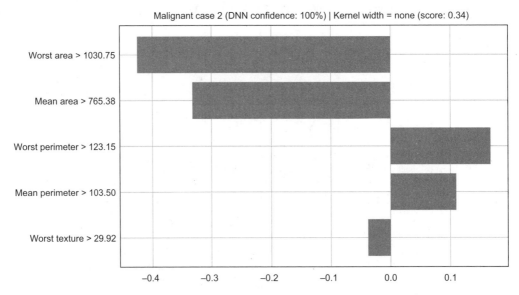

Figure 4.19a   LIME interpretation of malignant case 2 with a default kernel width

LIME is a great tool for interpreting black-box models. It is model-agnostic and can work with different types of models. LIME can also work with different types of data—tabular data, images, and text. We have seen it in action using tabular data in this section. We will explore images and text data in later chapters, and you can find examples in the library documentation (https://github.com/marcotcr/lime). It is a widely used library with lots of active contributors.

The quality of the LIME interpretation, however, depends greatly on the choice of the kernel width, which is an input to the kernel function that is used to weight the

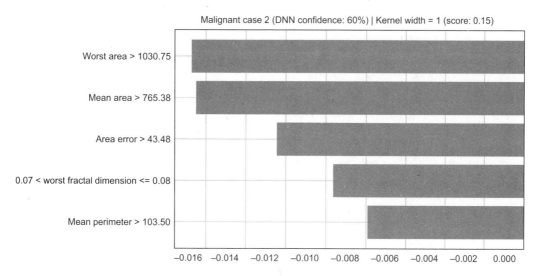

Figure 4.19b **LIME interpretation of malignant case 2 with a kernel width of 1**

perturbed samples. It is an important hyperparameter, and we have seen that the width could be different for different examples that we pick to interpret. We can use the fidelity score provided by the library to determine the right width, but the selection of the right kernel width is still ambiguous. Another limitation of LIME is that the perturbed dataset is created by sampling from a Gaussian distribution, and it ignores correlations between features. The perturbed dataset may, therefore, not have the same characteristics as the original training data.

4.6 *SHAP*

SHAP, an acronym for SHapley Additive exPlanations, was proposed in 2017 by Scott M. Lundberg and Su-In Lee. It unifies the idea behind LIME (and linear surrogate models) and game theory and provides more mathematical guarantees on the accuracy of the explanations than LIME. A *Shapley value* is a concept from game theory that quantifies the impact of a coalition of players in a cooperative game. Let's now see what we mean by a cooperative game, the players of the game, and coalitions of players. In the context of model interpretability, the cooperative game is the model and the predictions it comes up with. The input features to the model are equivalent to players, and coalitions of players are sets of features that interact with each other to come up with the final prediction. Shapley values could, therefore, be used to quantify the impact of features (i.e., players) and their interactions (i.e., player coalitions) on a model prediction (i.e., cooperative game). Let's break down the SHAP interpretability technique by looking at the concrete example shown in figure 4.20.

The idea behind SHAP is quite similar to that behind LIME. The first step is to pick an instance to explain. In figure 4.20, the picked instance is shown as the first row in index 0. Because SHAP uses game-theoretic concepts, the picked instance consists

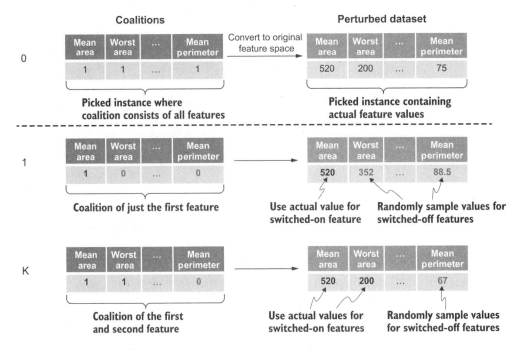

Figure 4.20   An illustration of creating the perturbed dataset for SHAP

of a coalition of all the features. When all the features are selected, or "switched on," it is represented by a vector containing all 1s for all the features in the dataset. The first column in figure 4.20 shows the *coalition vector* as a table. For the picked instance, the coalition vector consists of all 1s, so we pick all the actual feature values for that instance when we convert that vector into the feature space. This *feature vector* is shown as a table in the second column in figure 4.20.

Once we've picked the instance to interpret, the next step is to create the perturbed dataset. This process is the same as in LIME, but unlike with LIME, the idea in SHAP is to generate a bunch of coalition vectors where features are randomly "switched on" or "switched off." If a feature is switched on, its value in the coalition vector is 1. If the feature is switched off, its value in the coalition vector is 0. We know how to represent the feature in the feature space when it is switched on—we just pick the actual value from the instance that we've picked to interpret. If, however, the feature is switched off, we pick a value randomly from the training set for that feature.

After creating the perturbed dataset, the next step is to weight the dataset based on its proximity to the picked instance. This is again similar to LIME, but unlike with LIME, SHAP uses the *SHAP kernel* to determine the weights for the samples in the perturbed dataset as opposed to the exponential kernel function. The SHAP kernel function gives higher weight to coalitions that consist of very low or very high numbers of features. The next steps are then the same as with LIME, which is to fit a linear model on the weighted dataset and return the coefficients or weights of the linear model as the interpretation for that picked instance. These coefficients or weights are called *Shapley values.*

Let's now see SHAP in action on the breast cancer diagnostics model trained earlier. The authors of SHAP have created a Python library in GitHub. We can install this library using `pip` as follows:

```
pip install shap
```

We will use the same helper function called `prob` (introduced in the previous section on LIME) to provide the DNN model predictions for the perturbed dataset. You can now create the perturbed dataset and initialize the SHAP explainer as follows:

```
import shap                         Initializes JavaScript for      Uses the prob helper function
shap.initjs()    ←                  interactive visualizations      to obtain the DNN predictions

shap_explainer = shap.KernelExplainer(prob, ←                       Uses the logit link
                      X_train.numpy(),                              function because the
                      link="logit")  ←                              DNN is a classifier
```

Note that the `logit link` function is used for the linear surrogate model because we are dealing with a binary classifier that outputs a probability estimate for the positive class. For regression problems, you can switch the `link` parameter to `identity`. Next, obtain the SHAP values for all the data in the test set as follows:

```
shap_values = shap_explainer.shap_values(X_test.numpy())
```

You can now obtain the SHAP interpretation for the first benign case as a Matplotlib plot as shown here:

```
plot = shap.force_plot(shap_explainer.expected_value[0],
                      shap_values[0][benign_idx,:],
                      X_test.numpy()[benign_idx,:],
                      feature_names=data['feature_names'],
                      link="logit")
```

The resulting plot is shown in figure 4.21. Recall that for the first benign case, the DNN model predicted it was benign with a probability of 0.99 or confidence of 99%.

The SHAP library provides much nicer visualizations where you can see how each feature value pushes the base prediction up or down. In figure 4.21, you can see the base value at around 0.63. This is the positive class rate representing the proportion of

Figure 4.21   SHAP interpretation of benign case 1 where the DNN model predicts benign with a probability of 0.99 (or a confidence of 99%)

benign cases. When we explored the data in section 4.2, we observed that in the dataset, roughly 63% of the cases were benign. The idea behind the SHAP visualization is to see how the feature value pushes the baseline prediction probability from 0.63 up to 0.99. The impact of the feature is shown by the length of the bar. We can see from the figure that the worst cell area and mean cell area features have the largest Shapley values, which pushes the base prediction the most. The next most important feature is worst cell perimeter.

Figure 4.22 shows the SHAP interpretation for the second benign case where the DNN model predicted benign with a probability of 0.99.

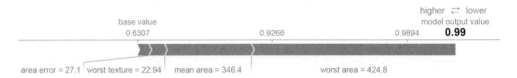

Figure 4.22   SHAP interpretation of benign case 2 where the DNN model predicts benign with a probability of 0.99 (or a confidence of 99%)

We can see that the two most important features here are the worst cell area and the mean cell area. Because the worst area and mean area are quite low, with values of 424.8 and 346.4, respectively, it was enough to push the baseline prediction all the way to 0.99. As an exercise, modify the code shown earlier to interpret the two malignant cases. The resulting plots are shown in figures 4.23 and 4.24.

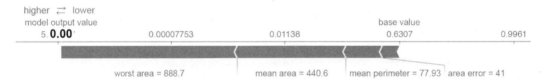

Figure 4.23   SHAP interpretation of malignant case 1 where the DNN model predicts benign with a probability of 0 (or malignant with a confidence of 100%)

For the first malignant case, the model predicted that it was benign with a probability of 0. In figure 4.23, we can see how the feature values push the baseline prediction probability down to 0. It looks like the features that have the most influence on the final prediction are the worst cell area, mean cell area, and perimeter.

For the second malignant case, the model also predicted that it was benign with a probability of 0. We can see that the most influential feature is again the worst cell area. Because the value was quite large—greater than 1417—it was enough to push the baseline prediction probability down to 0, as shown in figure 4.24.

SHAP is another great tool for interpreting black-box models. Like LIME, it is model-agnostic, and it uses concepts from game theory to quantify the impact of features on the model prediction of a single instance. It provides more mathematical

Figure 4.24 **SHAP interpretation of malignant case 2 where the DNN model predicts benign with a probability of 0 (or malignant with a confidence of 100%)**

guarantees on the accuracy of the explanations than LIME. The library also provides great visualizations of the impact of features, showing how the feature values push the baseline prediction up or down to the final prediction. Computing the Shapley values based on the SHAP kernel, however, is computationally intensive. The computational complexity increases exponentially with the number of input features.

4.7   *Anchors*

Anchors is another model-agnostic interpretability technique that is local in scope. It was proposed in 2018 by the same creators of LIME. It improves on LIME by providing high-precision rules, or predicates, for how the model arrives at the prediction and also by quantifying the coverage of these rules in terms of global scope. Let's break this down.

In this technique, model interpretations are generated in the form of anchors. An *anchor* is essentially a set of *if conditions*, or *predicates*, that contains the picked instance that we would like to interpret. This is shown by the box in figure 4.25. The anchor illustrated in the figure can be interpreted as two if conditions where the two features in the 2-D feature space are bounded by a lower bound and upper bound, thereby forming a bounding box around the picked instance. The first objective of the algorithm is to form high-precision anchors that contain the picked instance in terms of the target prediction. The *precision* is a measure of the quality of the anchor and is defined as the ratio of the number of perturbed samples with the same target prediction as that of the picked instance to the total number of samples within the anchor. An important hyperparameter for the algorithm is the *precision threshold*.

Once the algorithm has come up with a set of high-precision anchors, the next step is to quantify the scope of each anchor. The scope of an anchor is quantified by a metric called *coverage*. The coverage metric measures the probability that the anchor (or the set of predicates) will be present in other samples or other parts of the feature space. With this metric, we can tell how applicable the anchor's interpretation is at a global scale. The objective of the algorithm is to pick the anchor with the highest coverage.

Determining all possible predicates that meet the precision threshold and the coverage requirement is a computationally intensive task. The authors of the algorithm used a bottom-up approach in constructing the predicates or rules. The algorithm starts off with an empty set of rules, and in each iteration, the algorithm incrementally constructs an anchor that meets the precision threshold and the coverage requirement and adds it to the set. To estimate the precision of an anchor, the authors have

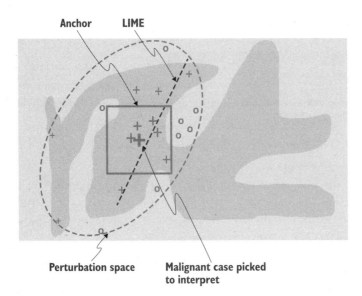

Figure 4.25   An illustration of an anchor

formulated this problem as a multiarmed bandit problem and specifically used the KL-LUCB algorithm to identify the rules with the highest precision.

Let's now interpret the breast cancer DNN model using anchors. The authors of the paper have created a library in Python that can be found in GitHub. You can install the library using `pip` as follows:

```
pip install anchors_exp
```

As we did with LIME and SHAP, let's now create the anchors tabular explainer for the breast cancer dataset as follows:

```
from anchor import anchor_tabular

anchor_explainer = anchor_tabular.AnchorTabularExplainer(
    data.target_names,
    data.feature_names,
    X_train.numpy(),
    categorical_names={})
anchor_explainer.fit(X_train.numpy(),
                     y_train.numpy(),
                     X_val.numpy(),
                     y_val.numpy())
```

- Imports the anchor_tabular module from the library
- Sets the target label names
- Sets the feature names for the dataset
- Provides categorical feature names, if any
- Fits the anchors explainer on the train and validation sets

We need to create a different helper function for anchors that provides the DNN predictions as discrete labels rather than probabilities. This helper function is shown next:

```
def pred(data):
    pred = model.forward(
        Variable(torch.from_numpy(data)).float()).\
    detach().numpy().reshape(-1) > 0.5
    return np.array([1 if p == True else 0 for p in pred])
```

Predicts 1 if the output probability is greater than 0.5, else 0

Let's now interpret the first benign case using anchors. The following code shows how to interpret the instance, extract the predicates or rules, and obtain the precision and coverage of the interpretation:

Provides the helper function that provides the model label predictions

Passes the picked instance as the first parameter

```
exp = anchor_explainer.explain_instance(X_test.numpy()[benign_idx],
                                        pred,
                                        threshold=0.95)
print('Prediction: ',
    anchor_explainer.class_names[pred(X_test.numpy()[benign_idx])][0])
print('Anchor: %s' % (' AND '.join(exp.names())))
print('Precision: %.3f' % exp.precision())
print('Coverage: %.3f' % exp.coverage())
```

Sets the precision threshold

Prints the label prediction made by the model

Prints the rules or predicates

Prints the precision of the anchor

Prints the coverage of the anchor

Note that the precision threshold is set to 0.95. The rules or predicates are obtained as a list of strings and are strung together using the AND clause. The resulting output from the code is shown here:

```
Prediction:  benign
Anchor: worst area <= 683.95 AND mean radius <= 13.27
Precision: 1.000
Coverage: 0.443
```

You can see that the model predicted benign correctly, and the interpretation, or anchor, with the highest precision consists of two rules, or predicates. If the worst area is less than or equal to 683.95 and the mean radius is less than or equal to 13.27, the model predicts benign 100% of the time in the region around the picked instance. In terms of coverage, this anchor does pretty well with a coverage of 44.3%. This means that the rule is applicable to quite a lot of benign cases globally. You can also obtain an HTML visualization of this interpretation, shown in figure 4.26, using the following line of code:

```
exp.save_to_file('anchors_benign_case1_interpretation.html')
```

The anchors library as it stands now does not provide Matplotlib visualizations.

Figure 4.26   Anchor interpretation of benign case 1 where precision is 100% and coverage is 44.3%

As an exercise, extend this code to the other benign and malignant cases. The resulting visualization for the second benign case is shown in figure 4.27. You can see that the model predicted benign correctly and the anchors algorithm came up with two rules with precision 1: if the worst cell area is less than or equal to 683.95 and the worst cell radius is less than or equal to 12.98, the model predicts benign 100% of the time. The coverage of this anchor is, however, 20.9% lower than the first benign case. This means that the interpretation for the second benign case is a lot more local than the first one.

Figure 4.27   Anchor interpretation of benign case 2 where precision is 100% and coverage is 20.9%

The anchor's interpretation for the first malignant case is shown in figure 4.28. The model correctly predicted it was malignant, and the interpretation consists of two rules, or predicates, with a precision of 1. The rules follow: if the worst cell area is greater than 683.95 and the mean cell radius is less than or equal to 544.05, the model predicts malignant 100% of the time. The anchor has a very low coverage of just 1.2%, however. The interpretation is, therefore, extremely local and is not really applicable to a lot of the other malignant cases.

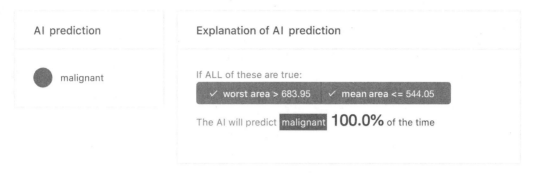

Figure 4.28   Anchor interpretation of malignant case 1 where precision is 100% and coverage is 1.1%

Finally, the anchor's interpretation of the second malignant case is shown in figure 4.29. The model again predicted malignant correctly, and the interpretation consists of one rule with a precision of 1. The rule follows: if the worst cell area is greater than 1030.75, the model predicts malignant 100% of the time. The coverage of this anchor is a lot better than the first case at 27.1%. This makes sense because if we go back to the exploratory analysis we did in section 4.2 and look closely at figure 4.3, we see many more malignant cases with worst cell areas greater than 1030.

Figure 4.29   Anchor interpretation of malignant case 2 where precision is 100% and coverage is 27.1%

Anchors are a powerful model-agnostic interpretability technique because they provide interpretations as a set of high-precision rules, predicates, or human-readable if conditions. The technique also gives us a sense of the coverage or scope of the rules, that is, how applicable the rules are at a global scale. The Python library, however, is still a work in progress and is not as actively developed as LIME or SHAP.

In the next and subsequent chapters, we will go deeper into the world of neural networks and learn about more complex structures like CNNs and RNNs. We will also learn how to perform feature attributions on neural networks and how to dissect them to get a much better understanding of what the network has learned.

Summary

- An artificial neural network (ANN) is a system that is designed to loosely model a biological brain. It belongs to a broad class of machine learning methods called deep learning. The central idea of deep learning based on ANNs is to build complex concepts or representations from simpler concepts or features.

- An ANN with two or more hidden layers is called a deep neural network (DNN).

- An efficient algorithm to determine the weights in a DNN is backpropagation.

- The activation function is an important feature within a neural network. It decides whether a neuron should be activated and by how much. The properties of an activation function are that it is differentiable and monotonic.

- ReLUs are the most widely used activation functions in neural networks because they handle the vanishing gradient problem well. They are also more computationally efficient.

- We can interpret neural networks in multiple ways. We can use model-agnostic methods that are global in scope, such as PDPs. In this chapter, we learned about more advanced perturbation-based model-agnostic techniques such as LIME, SHAP, and anchors. These interpretability techniques are local in scope, meaning they focus on a specific instance or example to interpret.

- LIME stands for local interpretable model-agnostic explanations. It is based on picking an example, randomly perturbing it, weighting the perturbed samples based on its proximity to the picked instance, and fitting a simpler white-box model on the weighted samples.

- The quality of the LIME interpretation depends greatly on the choice of the kernel width, which is an input to the kernel function used to weight the perturbed samples. It is an important hyperparameter, and we have seen that the width could be different for different examples that we pick to interpret. We can use the fidelity score provided by the library to determine the right width, but the selection of the right kernel width is still ambiguous.

- Another drawback of LIME is that the perturbed dataset is created by sampling from a Gaussian distribution, and it ignores correlations between features. The perturbed dataset may, therefore, not have the same characteristics as the original training data.

- SHAP stands for SHapley Additive exPlanations. Like LIME, it is model-agnostic, and it uses concepts from game theory to quantify the impact of features on the model prediction of a single instance. In theory, SHAP provides more mathematical guarantees on the accuracy of the explanations than LIME.

- The SHAP library provides great visualizations of the impact of features, showing how the feature values push the baseline prediction up or down to the final prediction.

- Computing the Shapley values based on the SHAP kernel is, however, computationally intensive. The computational complexity increases exponentially with the number of input features.
- Anchors is another technique that improves on LIME by providing interpretations as a set of high-precision rules, predicates, or human-readable if conditions. The technique also gives us a sense of the coverage or scope of the rules, that is, how applicable the rules are at a global scale. The Python library, however, is still a work in progress and is not as actively developed as LIME or SHAP.

Saliency mapping

This chapter covers

- Characteristics that make convolutional neural networks inherently black-box
- How to implement convolutional neural networks for image classification tasks
- How to interpret convolutional neural networks using saliency mapping techniques, such as vanilla backpropagation, guided backpropagation, guided Grad-CAM, and SmoothGrad
- Strengths and weaknesses of these saliency mapping techniques and how to perform sanity checks on them

In the previous chapter, we looked at deep neural networks and learned how to interpret them using model-agnostic methods that are local in scope. We specifically learned three techniques: LIME, SHAP, and anchors. In this chapter, we will focus on convolutional neural networks (CNNs), a more complex neural network architecture used mostly for visual tasks such as image classification, image segmentation, object detection, and facial recognition. We will learn how to apply techniques learned in the previous chapter to CNNs. In addition, we will also focus on saliency mapping, which is a local, model-dependent, and post hoc interpretability technique. Saliency mapping is a great tool for interpreting CNNs because it helps us visualize the salient or important features for the model. We will specifically cover techniques such as vanilla backpropagation, guided backpropagation, integrated gradients, SmoothGrad, Grad-CAM, and guided Grad-CAM.

This chapter follows a similar structure to the previous chapters'. We will start off with a concrete example where we will extend the breast cancer diagnosis example from chapter 4. We will explore this new dataset containing images and learn how to train and evaluate CNNs in PyTorch and how to interpret them. It is worth reiterating that although the main focus of this chapter is interpreting CNNs using saliency mapping, we will also cover model training and testing. We will also glean some key insights in the earlier sections that will be useful during model interpretation. Readers who are already familiar with training and testing CNNs are free to skip the earlier sections and jump straight to section 5.4, which covers model interpretability.

5.1 Diagnostics+ AI: Invasive ductal carcinoma detection

Invasive ductal carcinoma (IDC) is the most common form of breast cancer. In this chapter, we will extend the breast cancer diagnosis example from the previous chapter to detecting IDC. Pathologists at Diagnostics+ currently perform biopsies on patients where they remove small tissue samples and analyze them under the microscope to determine whether the patient has IDC. The pathologist splits the whole mount sample of the tissue into patches and determines whether each patch is IDC positive or negative. By delineating the exact regions of IDC in the tissue, the pathologist determines how aggressive or advanced the cancer is and which grade to assign to the patient.

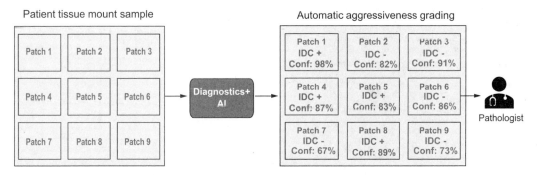

Figure 5.1 Diagnostics+ AI for invasive ductal carcinoma (IDC) detection

Diagnostics+ would like to expand the capabilities of the their AI system that we built in chapter 4 to automatically assess images of tissue samples. The goal is for the AI system to determine whether each patch in the tissue mount sample is IDC positive or negative and to assign a confidence measure to it. This is shown in figure 5.1. By using this AI system, Diagnostics+ can automate the preprocessing step of delineating the regions of IDC in the tissue so that the pathologist can easily assign a grade to it to determine how aggressive the cancer is. Given this information, how would you formulate this as a machine learning problem? Because the target of the model is to predict whether a given image or patch is IDC positive or negative, we can formulate this problem as a *binary classification* problem. The formulation is similar to chapter 4, but the inputs to the classifier are images, not structured tabular data.

5.2 *Exploratory data analysis*

Let's now try to understand this new image dataset better. A lot of the insights gleaned in this section will help us with model training, evaluation, and interpretation. In this dataset, we have tissue samples from 279 patients and 277,524 images of tissue patches. The raw dataset is obtained from Kaggle (http://mng.bz/0wBl) and is preprocessed to extract the metadata associated with these images. The preprocessing notebook and the preprocessed dataset can be found in the GitHub repository (http://mng.bz/KBdZ) associated with this book.

In figure 5.2, we can see the distribution of IDC-positive and -negative patches. Out of the 277,524 patches, roughly 70% are IDC negative and 30% are IDC positive. The dataset is, therefore, highly imbalanced. To recapitulate, we need to note the following two things when dealing with imbalanced datasets:

- Use the right performance metrics (like precision, recall, and F1) when testing and evaluating the models.
- Resample the training data such that the majority class is either undersampled or the minority class is oversampled.

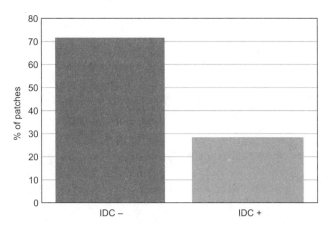

Figure 5.2   Distribution of IDC-positive and -negative patches

Let's look at a few random samples of patches. By visualizing these images, we can see if there are some distinct characteristics for IDC-positive and -negative patches. This will help us later when we have to interpret the model. Figure 5.3 shows a random sample of four IDC-positive patches, and figure 5.4 shows a random sample of four IDC-negative patches. The dimension of each patch image is 50×50 pixels. We can observe that the IDC-positive patches have more dark-stained cells. The density of the dark stains is also higher. The darker color is typically used to stain nuclei. For IDC-negative samples, on the other hand, the density of lighter stains is higher. The lighter color is typically used to highlight the cytoplasm and extracellular connective tissue. We can, therefore, visually say that a given patch is more likely to be IDC positive if it has a high density of dark stains or cell nuclei. On other hand, a given patch is more likely to be IDC negative if it has a high density of lighter stains and a very low density of cell nuclei.

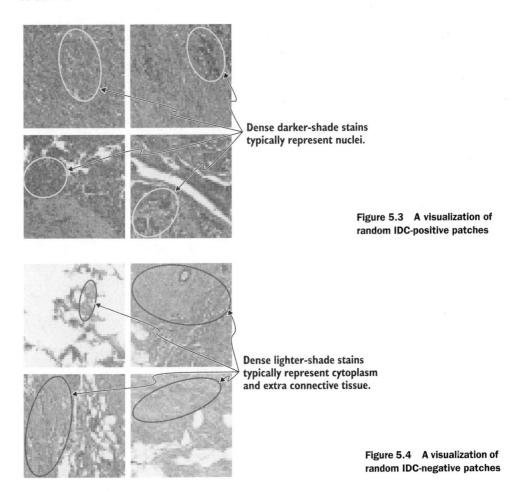

Dense darker-shade stains typically represent nuclei.

Figure 5.3   A visualization of random IDC-positive patches

Dense lighter-shade stains typically represent cytoplasm and extra connective tissue.

Figure 5.4   A visualization of random IDC-negative patches

Now let's visualize all the patches for one patient or tissue sample and the regions that are IDC positive. Figure 5.5 visualizes this for one patient. The plot on the left shows all the patches stitched together for the tissue sample. The plot on the right shows the same image but highlights the IDC-positive patches in a darker shade. This confirms our observation earlier that patches are much more likely to be IDC positive if they

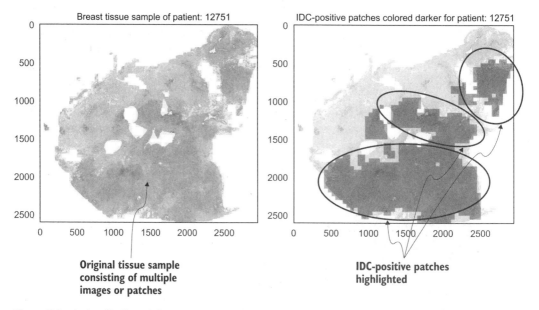

Figure 5.5   A visualization of tissue sample and IDC-positive patches

have a very high density of darker stains. We will come back to this visualization when we have to interpret the CNN that we will be training for IDC detection.

In the next section, we will prepare the data and train a CNN. The CNN will be used to classify each image or patch as either IDC positive or negative. Because the dataset is quite imbalanced, we need to evaluate the CNN using metrics such as precision, recall, and F1.

5.3   *Convolutional neural networks*

A convolutional neural network (CNN) is a neural network architecture commonly used for visual tasks such as image classification, object detection, and image segmentation. Why are CNNs used for visual tasks and not fully connected deep neural networks (DNNs)? Fully connected DNNs do not capture pixel dependencies in an image well because images need to be flattened into a 1-D structure before being fed into the neural network. CNNs, on the other hand, take advantage of the multidimensional structure of images and capture pixel dependencies or spatial dependencies in an image well. CNNs are also translation invariant, meaning they are great at detecting shapes in an image, irrespective of where the shapes occur in the image. In addition, the CNN architecture can also be trained more efficiently to fit the input dataset because weights in the network are reused. Figure 5.6 shows an illustration of a CNN architecture used for binary image classification.

The architecture in figure 5.6 consists of a sequence of layers called *convolution and pooling layers*. The combination of these two types of layers is called the *feature learning layers*. The objective of the feature learning layers is to extract hierarchical features

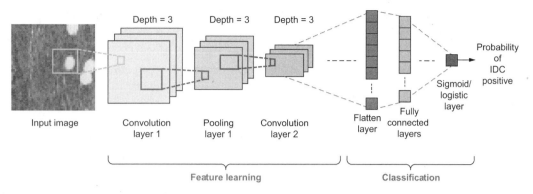

Figure 5.6 An illustration of CNN for image classification

from the input image. The first few layers will be extracting low-level features such as edges, colors, and gradients. By adding more convolution and pooling layers, the architecture learns high-level features, giving us a much better understanding of the characteristics of images in the dataset. We will cover convolutional and pooling layers in more depth later in this section.

Following the feature learning layers are layers of neurons or units that are fully connected, just like the DNN architecture we saw in chapter 4. The purpose of these fully connected layers is to perform classification. The inputs to the fully connected layer are the high-level features learned by the convolution and pooling layers, and the output is a probability measure for the classification task. Because we covered how DNNs work in chapter 4, we will focus most of our attention now on the convolution and pooling layers.

In chapter 1, we saw how to represent an image so that a CNN can easily process it, as summarized in figure 5.7. In this example, the image of a tissue patch is a colored

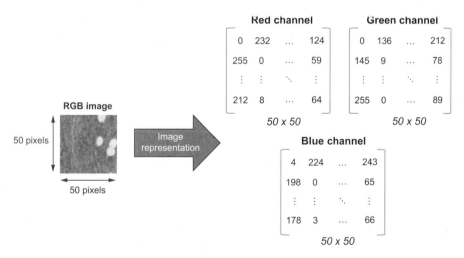

Figure 5.7 An illustration of how to represent a 50 × 50 image of a tissue patch

image of size 50×50 pixels consisting of three primary channels: red (R), green (G) and blue (B). This RGB image can be represented in mathematical form as three matrices of pixel values, one for each channel and each of size 50×50.

Let's now see how the convolution layer processes an image represented as a matrix of pixel values. This layer consists of a kernel or filter and is convolved with the input image to obtain a representation of the image called the *feature image*. Let's break this down and look at it step by step. Figure 5.8 shows a simplified illustration of the operation performed in the convolution layer. In the figure, the image is represented as a matrix of dimension 3×3, and the kernel or filter is represented as a matrix of dimension 2×2. The kernel starts off at the top-left corner of the image and moves from left to right until it processes the complete width of the image. The kernel then moves down and starts again from the left of the image, repeating this movement until the whole image is processed. Each movement of the kernel is called a *stride*. An important hyperparameter for the kernel is the stride length. If the stride length is 1, the kernel moves one step during each stride. Figure 5.8 illustrates a kernel with a stride length of 1. As you can see, the kernel starts at the top-left corner of the image and needs to perform three strides to process the whole image.

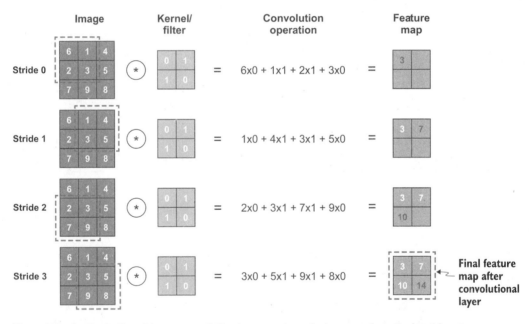

Figure 5.8   An illustration of how a convolution layer creates a feature map from the input image

During each stride, the part of the image that is processed is convolved with the kernel. As we saw in chapter 2 in the context of GAMs, the convolution operation is essentially a dot product. An element-wise product is taken of the part of the image that is processed with the kernel, followed by a sum. In figure 5.8, we can see this illustrated for all the strides. For stride 0, for instance, the part of the image that is processed by the kernel is highlighted by the dashed box. The value obtained by taking the dot product of this image with the kernel is 3, and this value is placed on the top-left corner of the feature map matrix. In stride 1, we move one step to the right and perform the convolution operation again. The value that is obtained after convolution is 7, and this is placed on the top-right corner of the feature map matrix. This process is repeated until the whole image is processed. At the end of the convolution operation, we obtain a feature map matrix of size 2 × 2 that is meant to capture a high-level feature representation of the input image. The numbers within the kernel or filter are called *weights*. Note that in figure 5.8, the same weights are used for the convolution layer. This weight sharing allows the CNN to be trained a lot more efficiently than DNNs.

The objective of the learning algorithm is to determine the weights within the kernel or filter in the convolution layer. This is done during backpropagation. The size of the feature map matrix is determined by a few hyperparameters—the size of the input image, the size of the kernel, the stride length, and another hyperparameter called the padding. *Padding* refers to the number of pixels added to the image before performing the convolution operation. In figure 5.8, a padding of 0 is used where no additional pixels are added to the image. If the padding is set to 1, a border of pixels is added around the image where all the pixel values in the border are set to 0, as illustrated in figure 5.9. Adding padding increases the size of the feature map and allows for a more accurate representation of the image. In practice, the convolution layer consists of multiple filters or kernels. The number of filters is another hyperparameter that we must specify before training.

Padding = 1

Padding = 0

Input image

Figure 5.9   An illustration of padding

The convolution layer in a CNN is usually followed by a pooling layer. The purpose of the pooling layer is to reduce the dimensionality of the feature map further to reduce the computational power required during model training. A common pooling layer is max pooling. Like in the convolution layer, the pooling layer also consists of a filter. A max pooling filter returns the maximum of all the values covered by that filter, as illustrated in figure 5.10.

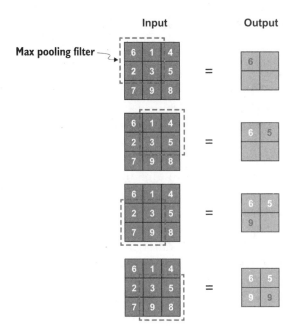

Figure 5.10   An illustration of max pooling

Rapid advances in CNNs have occurred in the last decade in various tasks, such as image recognition, object detection, and image segmentation. This is thanks to massive amounts of annotated data (ImageNet [http://www.image-net.org/] and CIFAR-10 and CIFAR-100 [https://www.cs.toronto.edu/~kriz/cifar.html] being some of them) and advances in computation where deep learning models are leveraging the strengths of graphics processing units (GPUs). Figure 5.11 shows advances in CNN research over the last decade, especially in the image classification task using the ImageNet dataset. The ImageNet dataset is a large database of annotated images typically used for image classification and object detection tasks. It consists of more than a million images organized in a hierarchical structure consisting of more than 20,000 labeled categories. Figure 5.11 was obtained from Papers with Code (http://mng.bz/9K8o), a useful repository of state-of-the-art (SoTA) machine learning techniques. One of the major breakthroughs in terms of performance occurred in 2013 using the AlexNet architecture. The current best CNNs are based on an architecture called residual network (ResNet). Some of these SoTA architectures have been implemented in deep learning frameworks like PyTorch and Keras. We will see how to use them in the next section where we will train a CNN for the IDC detection task. We will specifically focus on the ResNet architecture because it is one of the most widely used architectures.

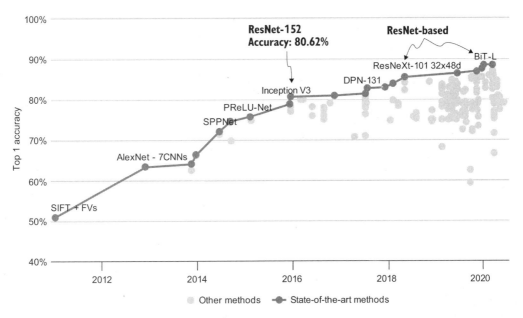

Figure 5.11 State-of-the-art CNN architectures for image classification on the ImageNet dataset (Source: http://mng.bz/9K8o)

5.3.1 Data preparation

In this section, we will prepare the data for model training. Data preparation is slightly different than in the previous chapters because we are dealing with images and not structured tabular data. Please note that the preprocessed dataset is used here. The code used for preprocessing and the preprocessed dataset can be found in the GitHub repository (http://mng.bz/KBdZ) associated with this book. First, let's prepare the training, validation, and test sets. It is important that we do not split the data by patches but rather using the patient ID. This prevents data leakage across the training, validation, and test sets. If we randomly split the dataset by patches, patches for one patient may be in all three sets and, therefore, leak some information about the patient. The following code snippet shows how to split the dataset by patient ID:

Loads the data into a Pandas DataFrame

```
df_data = pd.read_csv('data/chapter_05_idc.csv')
patient_ids = df_data.patient_id.unique()
train_ids, val_test_ids = train_test_split(patient_ids,
                              test_size=0.4,
                              random_state=24)

val_ids, test_ids = train_test_split(val_test_ids,
                              test_size=0.5,
                              random_state=24)
```

Extracts all unique patient IDs from the data

Splits the data into train and validation/test sets

Splits the validation/test set into separate validation and test sets

**Extracts all patches for patient
IDs in the validation set**

```
                                        Extracts all patches for patient IDs in the train set
   df_train =
⇒ df_data[df_data['patient_id'].isin(train_ids)].reset_index(drop=True)  ◄──
└▷ df_val = df_data[df_data['patient_id'].isin(val_ids)].reset_index(drop=True)
   df_test =
▷ ⇒ df_data[df_data['patient_id'].isin(test_ids)].reset_index(drop=True)
```

Extracts all patches for patient IDs in the test set

Note that 60% of the patients are in the training set, 20% in the validation set, and the remaining 20% in the test set. Let's now check to see whether the distribution of the target variable is similar across the three sets, as shown in figure 5.12. We can see that roughly 25–30% of the patches are IDC positive and 70–75% are IDC negative in all three sets.

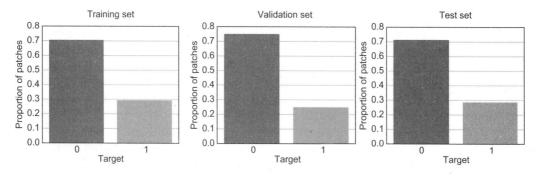

Figure 5.12   Target variable distribution across the training, validation, and test sets

Let's now create a custom class to easily load the images of patches and their corresponding labels. PyTorch provides a class called `Dataset` for this purpose. We will extend this class for the IDC dataset in this chapter. For more details on the `Dataset` class and also on PyTorch, please see appendix A. See the following code sample:

Loads the dataset class provided by PyTorch

```
                                        Creates a new dataset class
└▷ from torch.utils.data import Dataset     for the image patches that
                                            extends the PyTorch class
   class PatchDataset(Dataset):   ◄──
       def __init__(self, df_data, images_dir, transform=None):
           super().__init__()
           self.data = list(df_data.itertuples(name='Patch', index=False))
           self.images_dir = images_dir
           self.transform = transform

       def __len__(self):
           return len(self.data)

       def __getitem__(self, index):
```

**Overrides the
__getitem__ method
to return the image
and label from the
dataset at the
position index**

**Overrides the __len__ method
to return the number of image
patches in the dataset**

**A constructor that initializes the list of
patches, and a directory that contains
the images and any image transformer**

Extracts the image ID and label from the dataset

```
image_id, label = self.data[index].image_id, self.data[index].target
image = Image.open(os.path.join(self.images_dir, image_id))
image = image.convert('RGB')
if self.transform is not None:
    image = self.transform(image)
return image, label
```

Opens the image and converts it to RGB

Applies the transformation on the image if defined

Returns the image and label

Let's now define a function to transform the image of the patch. Common image transformations such as crops, flips, rotations, and resizing are implemented in the torchvision package. The full list of transformations can be found at http://mng.bz/jy6p. The following code snippet shows five transformations being performed on an image in the training set. As a data augmentation step, the second and third transforms flip the image randomly about the horizontal and vertical axes. As an exercise, create transforms for both the validation and test sets. Note that on the validation and test sets, you do not need to augment the data by flipping the image horizontally or vertically. You can name the transforms trans_val and trans_test:

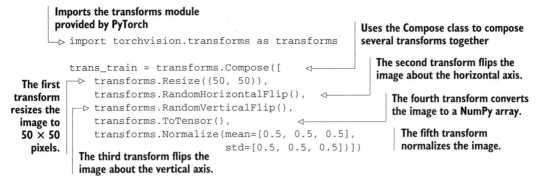

Imports the transforms module provided by PyTorch

```
import torchvision.transforms as transforms
```

Uses the Compose class to compose several transforms together

```
trans_train = transforms.Compose([
    transforms.Resize((50, 50)),
    transforms.RandomHorizontalFlip(),
    transforms.RandomVerticalFlip(),
    transforms.ToTensor(),
    transforms.Normalize(mean=[0.5, 0.5, 0.5],
                         std=[0.5, 0.5, 0.5])])
```

The first transform resizes the image to 50 × 50 pixels.

The second transform flips the image about the horizontal axis.

The fourth transform converts the image to a NumPy array.

The fifth transform normalizes the image.

The third transform flips the image about the vertical axis.

With the dataset class and transforms in place, we can now initialize the datasets and loaders. The following code snippet shows you how to initialize it for the training set. The DataLoader class provided by PyTorch allows you to batch data, shuffle it, and load it in parallel using multiprocessing workers:

Uses the DataLoader class in PyTorch to iterate through the data in batches

```
from torch.utils.data import DataLoader

dataset_train = PatchDataset(df_data=df_train,
                             images_dir=all_images_dir,
                             transform=trans_train)
batch_size = 64
loader_train = DataLoader(dataset=dataset_train,
                          batch_size=batch_size,
                          shuffle=True,
                          num_workers=0)
```

Loads images and labels of the patches in batches of 64

Creates the dataset for the patches in the training set

Creates the data loader for the training set

As an exercise, I encourage you to create similar datasets and loaders for the validation and test sets and name the objects dataset_val and dataset_test, respectively.

The solutions to these exercises can be found in the GitHub repository associated with this book (http://mng.bz/KBdZ).

5.3.2   *Training and evaluating CNNs*

With the datasets and loaders in place, we are now ready to create the CNN model. We will use the ResNet architecture that is implemented in the `torchvision` package in PyTorch. Using `torchvision` (http://mng.bz/jy6p), you can initialize other state-of-the-art architectures as well, such as AlexNet, VGG, Inception, and ResNeXt. You can also load these model architectures with pretrained weights by setting the pretrained flag to true. If set to true, the package returns a model pretrained on the ImageNet dataset. For the IDC detection example in this chapter, we will not use the pretrained model because it initializes the model weights randomly, and the model would be trained from scratch using the new dataset containing images of tissue patches. As an exercise, I encourage you to set the `pretrained` parameter to `True` to initialize the weights obtained by training on the ImageNet dataset.

We also need to concatenate fully connected layers to the CNN to perform the binary classification task. We can use the next code snippet to initialize the CNN:

```
# Hyper parameters        Sets the number of classes in the      Uses the GPU device
num_classes = 2           dataset, which is binary in this case   if CUDA is available;
                                                                  otherwise, sets the
                                                                  device as the CPU
# Device configuration
device = torch.device('cuda:0' if torch.cuda.is_available() else 'cpu')

# Use the ResNet architecture for the CNN
model = torchvision.models.resnet18(pretrained=False)
num_features = model.fc.in_features              Initializes the ResNet
                                                 model and extracts the
# Create the fully connected layers for classification   number of features
model.fc = nn.Sequential(                        from the model
    nn.Linear(num_features, 512),
    nn.ReLU(),                       Concatenates the fully connected
    nn.BatchNorm1d(512),             layers to the ResNet model for
    nn.Dropout(0.5),                 classification
    nn.Linear(512, 256),
    nn.ReLU(),
    nn.BatchNorm1d(256),
    nn.Dropout(0.5),
    nn.Linear(256, num_classes))

model = model.to(device)        Transfers the model to the device
```

Note that the model is loaded on the CPU by default. For faster processing, you can load the model on a GPU. All the popular deep learning frameworks, including PyTorch, use CUDA, which stands for compute unified device architecture, to perform general-purpose computing on GPUs. CUDA is a platform built by NVIDIA that provides APIs to directly access the GPU.

We can train the model using the following code snippet. Note that in this example, the model is trained for five epochs. The training time of this complex model using the IDC dataset is about 17 hours on a CPU. The training time would be a lot shorter if it were done on a GPU instance. You could also achieve better performance by increasing the number of epochs and training the model for longer:

```
# Hyper parameters
num_epochs = 5
learning_rate = 0.002

# Criterion or loss function
criterion = nn.CrossEntropyLoss()

# Optimizer for CNN
optimizer = torch.optim.Adamax(model.parameters(), lr=learning_rate)

for epoch in range(num_epochs):
    model.train()

    for idx, (inputs, labels) in enumerate(loader_train):
            inputs = inputs.to(device, dtype=torch.float)
            labels = labels.to(device, dtype=torch.long)

            # zero the parameter gradients
            optimizer.zero_grad()

            with torch.set_grad_enabled(True):
                outputs = model(inputs)
                _, preds = torch.max(outputs, 1)
                loss = criterion(outputs, labels)

                # backpropagation
                loss.backward()
                optimizer.step()
```

Let's now see how well this model performs on the test set. As we did in the previous chapters, we compare the model performance with a reasonable baseline. We saw in section 5.2 that the target class is highly imbalanced (see figure 5.2), where IDC-negative is the majority class. One option for the baseline model is to predict the majority class always, that is, always predict that a tissue patch is IDC negative. This baseline is not reasonable, however, because the cost of a false negative is a lot larger than a false positive when it comes to healthcare, especially a cancer diagnosis. A much more reasonable strategy would be to err on the side of false positives—always predict that a given tissue patch is IDC positive. Although this strategy is not ideal, it at least gets all the positive cases right. In a real-life situation, the baseline model is typically predictions made by a human or expert (in this case, the assessments made by an expert pathologist) or an existing model that the business is using. For this example, unfortunately, we do not have access to that information and so use a baseline model that always predicts IDC positive.

Table 5.1 shows the three key performance metrics used to benchmark the models: precision, recall, and F1. Precision measures the proportion of predicted classes that are accurate. Recall measures the proportion of actual classes that the model predicted accurately. The F1 score is the harmonic mean of precision and recall. Please see chapter 3 for a more detailed explanation of these metrics.

If we look at the recall metric in table 5.1, the baseline model does better than the CNN. This is expected because the baseline model is predicting IDC positive all the time. Overall, though, the CNN model does much better than the baseline, achieving a precision of 74.4% (+45.8% better than the baseline) and an F1 score of 74.2% (+29.7% better than the baseline). As an exercise, I encourage you to tune the model and achieve higher performance either by training for longer by increasing the number of epochs or by changing the CNN architecture.

Table 5.1 Performance comparison of baseline model with the CNN model

	Precision (%)	Recall (%)	F1 score (%)
Baseline model	28.6	100	44.5
CNN model (ResNet)	74.4 (+45.8)	74.1 (−25.9)	74.2 (+29.7)

With the CNN model performing better than the baseline, let's now interpret it and understand how the black-box model arrived at the final prediction.

5.4 Interpreting CNNs

As we saw in the previous section, to make a prediction using a CNN, an image goes through multiple convolutional and pooling layers for feature learning, followed by multiple layers of a fully connected deep neural network for classification. For the ResNet model used for IDC detection, the total number of parameters learned during training was 11,572,546. Millions of complex operations are being performed in the network, and it becomes incredibly difficult to understand how the model arrived at the final prediction. This is what makes CNNs black boxes.

5.4.1 Probability landscape

In the previous chapter, we saw that one way of interpreting DNNs is by visualizing the strengths of the edge weights. Through this technique, we could see at a high level what influence input features had on the final model prediction. This technique cannot be applied to CNNs because it is not trivial to visualize the kernels (or filters) in the convolution layers and the influence they have on the intermediate features that are learned and the final model output. We could, however, visualize the probability landscape of the CNN. What is the probability landscape? Using the CNN in the context of a binary classifier, we are essentially getting a probability measure for the target class. In the case of IDC detection, we are getting from the CNN the probability that a given input patch is IDC positive. For all the patches in the tissue, we can then plot the output probability of the classifier and visualize it as a heat map. Overlaying this heat map over the image can give us an indication of hot spots where the CNN detects highly likely IDC-positive regions. This is the probability landscape.

Figure 5.13 shows three plots. The left-most plot is a visualization of all the patches for patient 12930. The middle plot highlights the patches that are IDC positive based on the ground truth labels collected from the expert pathologists. These first two plots are similar to the one we saw in section 5.2 (see figure 5.5). The right-most plot shows the probability landscape of the ResNet model trained to detect IDC. The brighter the color, the greater the probability that a given patch is IDC positive. By comparing with the ground truth, we can see a good overlap between the model predictions and the ground truth. There are, however, some false positives where the model highlights regions that are not necessarily IDC positive. The implementation of figure 5.13 can be found in the GitHub repository (http://mng.bz/KBdZ) associated with this book. You can load the model trained in section 5.3.2 to jump straight into model interpretability.

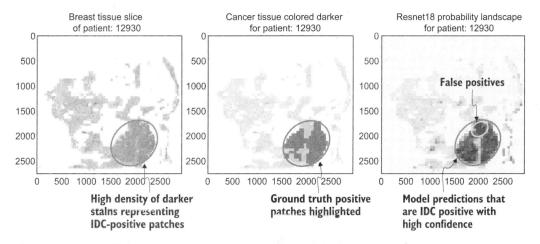

Figure 5.13 Probabilistic landscape of a ResNet model for a whole-tissue sample

Visualizing the probability landscape is a great way of validating the output of the model. By comparing with the ground truth labels, we can see which cases the model gets wrong and tune the model accordingly. It is also a great way to visualize and monitor the output of the model after deploying it in production. The probability landscape, however, does not give us any information on how the model arrived at the prediction.

5.4.2   LIME

One way of interpreting a CNN is by using any one of the model-agnostic interpretability techniques that we learned in the previous chapter. Let's specifically look at how to apply the LIME interpretability technique to images and CNNs. To recapitulate, the

LIME technique is a model-agnostic technique that is local in scope. On a tabular dataset, the technique works as follows:

1 Pick one example to interpret.
2 Create a perturbed dataset by sampling from a Gaussian distribution given the mean and standard deviation of the features in the tabular dataset.
3 Run the perturbed dataset through the black-box model, and obtain the predictions.
4 Weight the samples based on their proximity with the picked example, where samples that are closer to the picked example are given a higher weight. As we saw in chapter 4, a hyperparameter called the kernel width is used for weighting the samples. If the kernel width is small, only samples that are close to the picked instance will influence the interpretation.
5 Finally, fit a white-box model that is easily interpretable on the weighted samples. For LIME, linear regression is used.

The weights of the linear regression model can be used to determine the importance of features for that picked example. The interpretation is obtained using a surrogate model that is locally faithful to the example that we wish to interpret. Now, how do we apply LIME to images? As with tabular data, we first need to pick an image that we wish to interpret. Next, we have to create a perturbed dataset. We cannot perturb the dataset the same way as we do for tabular data, by sampling from a Gaussian distribution. Instead, we randomly turn pixels off and on in the image. This is computationally intensive because to come up with an interpretation that is locally faithful, we have to generate a lot of samples to run through the model. Moreover, pixels could be spatially correlated, and multiple pixels could contribute to one target class. We, therefore, segment the image into multiple segments, also called *superpixels*, and turn random superpixels on and off, as illustrated in figure 5.14.

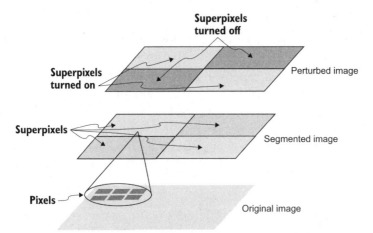

Figure 5.14   An illustration of how to create a perturbed image for LIME

We can read figure 5.14 from bottom to top. The idea is to segment the original image by grouping multiple pixels into a superpixel. In this illustration, we are using a simple segmentation algorithm where the original image is segmented into four nonoverlapping rectangular segments. Once you have formed the segmented image with superpixels, you can create the perturbed image by turning random superpixels on and off. By default, the LIME implementation uses the quickshift (http://mng.bz/ W7mw) segmentation algorithm. Once you have created the perturbed dataset, the rest of the technique is the same as with tabular data. The weights of the linear surrogate model will give us an idea of the influence of features or superpixels in the final model prediction for the picked input image. We segment the image into superpixels because we are attempting to group correlated pixels together and to look at the effects on the final prediction.

Let's now see how to implement LIME for the ResNet model trained earlier. We will first need to split the one PyTorch transform that we used earlier into two. The first one will transform the input Python Imaging Library (PIL) image into a 50 × 50 tensor, and the second one will normalize it. The first transformation, shown next, is required for the image segmentation algorithm in LIME:

The first transformation to resize the input image to 50 × 50 pixels required for the image segmentation algorithm

The second transformation to normalize the transformed 50 × 50 input image

```
trans_pil = transforms.Compose([transforms.Resize((50, 50)),])
trans_pre = transforms.Compose([transforms.ToTensor(),
                    transforms.Normalize(mean=[0.5, 0.5, 0.5],
                                         std=[0.5, 0.5, 0.5])])
```

Next, we will need two helper functions—one to load the image file as a PIL image and the other to perform predictions on the perturbed dataset using the model. The next code snippet shows these functions, where `get_image` is the function to load the PIL image and `batch_predict` is the function that runs the perturbed `images` through the `model`. We also create a partial function that presets the model parameter with the ResNet model that we trained in the previous section:

A helper function to read the input RGB image into memory

Returns the image

Opens the image and converts it to RGB

A helper function to perform predictions on images in the perturbed dataset

A function to compute the sigmoid of the input parameter

Stacks all the transformed tensors for the input images

Detaches the output tensor and converts it to a NumPy array

Runs through the model to obtain the output for all images

```
def get_image(images_dir, image_id):
    image = Image.open(os.path.join(images_dir, image_id))
    image = image.convert('RGB')
    return image

def batch_predict(images, model):
    def sigmoid(x):
        return 1. / (1 + np.exp(-x))
    batch = torch.stack(tuple(trans_pre(i) for i in images), dim=0)
    outputs = model(batch)
    proba = outputs.detach().cpu().numpy().astype(np.float)
```

```
        return sigmoid(proba)      ◁──┐  Returns the predictions as probabilities by
                                       │  passing them through the sigmoid function
      from functools import partial
    ┌ batch_predict_with_model = partial(batch_predict, model=model)
```
**A partial function to perform batch prediction
using a pretrained ResNet model**

Note that in this code, we define a partial function called batch_predict_with_model. Partial functions in Python allow us to set a certain number of arguments in a function and generate a new function. We are using the batch_predict function and setting the model parameter with the ResNet model trained earlier. You can replace this with any other model that you wish to interpret using LIME.

Because LIME is a local interpretability technique, we need to pick an example to interpret. For the ResNet model, we will pick two patches to interpret—one that is IDC negative and the other that is IDC positive—from the test set, as shown here:

An IDC-negative example with ID 142   **Loads the PIL image
                                                                        for the IDC-negative
                                       An IDC-positive   example
```
 ──▷ non_idc_idx = 142              example with ID 41291**
     idc_idx = 41291      ◁─────┘
     non_idc_image = get_image(all_images_dir,
                          df_test.iloc[non_idc_idx, :]['image_id'])
     idc_image = get_image(all_images_dir,
                       df_test.iloc[idc_idx, :]['image_id'])
```
**Loads the PIL image
for the IDC-positive
example**

Now we will initialize the LIME explainer and use that to interpret the two examples that we picked. The following code snippet shows how to obtain the LIME explanation for the IDC-negative example. As an exercise, obtain the LIME explanation for the IDC-positive example and set it to a variable named idc_exp:

**Imports the lime_image module
from the LIME library**   **Initializes the LIME
                                          image explainer**   **First transforms the IDC-
                                                                     negative image for
```
──▷ from lime import lime_image                                     segmentation**
    explainer = lime_image.LimeImageExplainer()   ◁──┘

    non_idc_exp = explainer.explain_instance(np.array(trans_pil(non_idc_image)),◁─┘
                          batch_predict_with_model,  ◁─┐
**Perturbs the segmented image    ┌──▷ num_samples=1000)      **Passes the partial function
  to create 1,000 samples**       │                           to predict on the perturbed
                                                               dataset using the ResNet model**
```

Using the LIME explanation variable shown in the previous code, obtain the RGB image and the 2-D mask that contains the explanation. As an exercise, obtain the masked LIME image for the IDC-positive example, and name the masked image i_img_boundary. To do this, you need to complete the previous exercise and obtain the LIME explanation for the IDC-positive example first. The solutions to these exercises can be found in the GitHub repository (http://mng.bz/KBdZ) associated with this book:

Imports the mark_boundaries function from the skimage library to plot the segmented image

Obtains the masked LIME image for the IDC-negative example

```
from skimage.segmentation import mark_boundaries
ni_tmp, ni_mask = non_idc_exp.get_image_and_mask(non_idc_exp.top_labels[0],
                                                 positive_only=False,
                                                 num_features=20,
                                                 hide_rest=True)
```

Plots the masked image using the mark_boundaries function

```
ni_img_boundary = mark_boundaries(ni_tmp/255.0, ni_mask)
```

We can now visualize the LIME explanations for both the IDC-positive and -negative patches using the following code:

Obtains the image of the IDC-positive patch

Obtains the image of the IDC-negative patch

Obtains the model confidence for the IDC-negative patch

Obtains the model confidence for the IDC-positive patch

```
non_idc_conf = 100 - df_test_with_preds.iloc[non_idc_idx]['proba'] * 100
idc_conf = df_test_with_preds.iloc[idc_idx]['proba'] * 100
non_idc_image = df_test.iloc[non_idc_idx]['image_id']
idc_image = df_test.iloc[idc_idx]['image_id']
non_idc_patient = df_test.iloc[non_idc_idx]['patient_id']
idc_patient = df_test.iloc[idc_idx]['patient_id']
```

Obtains the patient ID for the IDC-negative patch

Obtains the patient ID for the IDC-positive patch

Creates a 2 × 2 figure to plot the original images and LIME explanations

```
f, ax = plt.subplots(2, 2, figsize=(10, 10))
```

```
# Plot the original image of the IDC negative patch
ax[0][0].imshow(Image.fromarray(imread(os.path.join(all_images_dir,
➡ non_idc_image))))
ax[0][0].axis('off')
ax[0][0].set_title('Patch Image (IDC Negative)\nPatient Id: %d' %
➡ non_idc_patient)
```

Plots the original image of the IDC-negative patch on the top-left cell

```
# Plot the LIME explanation for the IDC negative patch
ax[0][1].imshow(ni_img_boundary)
ax[0][1].axis('off')
ax[0][1].set_title('LIME Explanation (IDC Negative)\nModel Confidence:
➡ %.1f%%' % non_idc_conf)
```

Plots the LIME explanation for the IDC-negative patch on the top-right cell

```
# Plot the original image of the IDC positive patch
ax[1][0].imshow(Image.fromarray(imread(os.path.join(all_images_dir,
➡ idc_image))))
ax[1][0].axis('off')
ax[1][0].set_title('Patch Image (IDC Positive)\nPatient Id: %d' %
➡ idc_patient)
```

Plots the original image of the IDC-positive patch on the bottom-left cell

```
# Plot the LIME explanation for the IDC positive patch
ax[1][1].imshow(i_img_boundary)
ax[1][1].axis('off')
ax[1][1].set_title('LIME Explanation (IDC Positive)\nModel Confidence:
➡ %.1f%%' % idc_conf);
```

Plots the LIME explanation for the IDC-positive patch on the bottom-right cell

Figure 5.15 shows the resulting visualization. The figure has been annotated where the top-left image is the original image of the IDC-negative patch. The top-right image is the LIME explanation of the IDC-negative patch. We can see that the model predicts that the patch is IDC negative with 82% confidence. From the original image, we can see that the density of the lighter stain is higher, which matches the pattern that we saw in section 5.2 (figure 5.4). The lighter stain is typically used to highlight the cytoplasm and extracellular connective tissue. If we look at the LIME explanation, we can see that the segmentation algorithm has highlighted two superpixels where the segmentation boundary separates the highly dense lighter stains from the rest of the image. The segment or superpixel that positively influences the prediction is shown in red (darker shade). This is annotated as the left half of the segmented image. The segment or superpixel that negatively influences the prediction is shown in green (lighter shade). This is annotated as the right half of the segmented image. The LIME explanation, therefore, seems to have correctly highlighted the dense lighter stains as contributing positively to predicting IDC negative with high confidence.

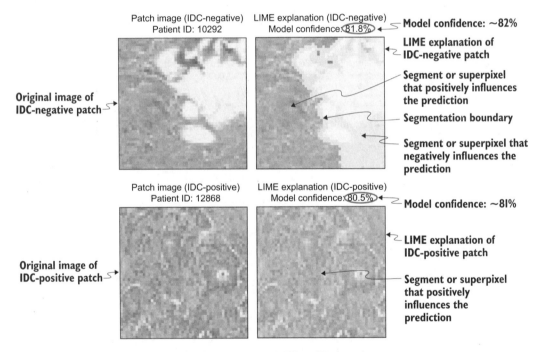

Figure 5.15   The LIME explanation for IDC-negative and IDC-positive patches

The bottom-left image in figure 5.15 is the original image of the IDC-positive patch. The LIME explanation for this patch is shown on the bottom right of the figure. We can see from the original image that the density of darker stains is a lot higher, which matches the pattern that we saw in section 5.2 (figure 5.3). If we look at the LIME explanation now, we can see that the segmentation algorithm treats the entire image as the superpixel, and the whole superpixel contributes positively to predict IDC positive with high confidence. Although this explanation makes sense at a high level because the whole image consists of a high density of darker stains, it does not give us any additional information about what specific pixels are influencing the model prediction.

This brings us to some of the drawbacks of LIME. As we saw in chapter 4 and in this section, LIME is a great interpretability technique as it is model-agnostic and can be applied to any complex model. It has a few disadvantages, however. The quality of the LIME explanation depends heavily on the choice of the kernel width. As we saw in chapter 4, this is an important hyperparameter, and the same kernel width may not be applicable for all examples that we wish to interpret. LIME explanations can also be unstable because they depend on how the perturbed dataset is sampled. The interpretation is also dependent on the specific segmentation algorithm we use. As we saw in figure 5.15, the segmentation algorithm treats the entire image as a superpixel. The computation complexity of LIME is also high, depending on the number of pixels or superpixels that need to be turned on or off.

5.4.3 *Visual attribution methods*

Now let's take a step back and look at LIME from the context of a broader class of interpretability methods called *visual attribution methods*. Visual attribution methods are used to attribute importance to parts of an image that influence the prediction made by the CNN. Three broad categories of visual attribution methods follow and are shown in figure 5.16:

- Perturbations
- Gradients
- Activations

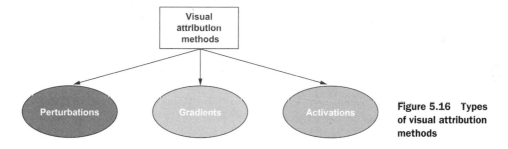

Figure 5.16 Types of visual attribution methods

Interpretability techniques like LIME and SHAP are *perturbation-based methods.* As we saw in chapter 4 and in the previous section, the idea is to perturb the input and probe its effects on the predictions made by the CNN. These techniques are *model-agnostic, post hoc,* and *local* interpretability techniques. Perturbation-based methods are, however, computationally inefficient because each perturbation requires us to perform a forward pass on the complex CNN model. These techniques can also underestimate the importance of features, where the features are parts of the image that are based on the segmentation done on the original image.

Gradient-based methods are used to visualize the gradient of the target class with respect to the input image. The idea is to pick an example or image to interpret. We then run this image through the CNN in the forward direction to obtain the output prediction. We apply the backpropagation algorithm to compute the gradient of the output class with respect to the input image. The gradient is a good importance measure because it tells us which pixels need to be changed to affect the model output. If the magnitude of the gradient is large, then a small change to the pixel value will result in a large change in the input. Therefore, pixels with large gradient measures are considered most important, or salient, for the model. Gradient-based methods are sometimes also called *backpropagation methods* because the backpropagation algorithm is used to determine feature importance. They are also called *saliency maps* because a map of salient, or important, features is obtained. Popular gradient-based methods are *vanilla backpropagation, guided backpropagation, integrated gradients,* and *SmoothGrad,* which will be covered in the sections 5.5–5.7. These techniques are local in scope and also post hoc. They are not entirely model-agnostic, however, and are weakly model-dependent. They are much more computationally efficient when compared to perturbation-based methods because only one forward and backward pass is required for one image.

Activation-based methods look at the feature maps or activations in the final convolutional layer and weight them based on the gradient of the target class with respect to those feature maps. The weights of the feature maps act as a proxy for the importance of the input features. This technique is called *gradient-weighted class activation mapping* (*Grad-CAM*). Because we are looking at the importance of the feature map in the final convolutional layer, Grad-CAM provides a coarse-grained activation map. To obtain more fine-grained activation maps, we can combine Grad-CAM and guided backpropagation—this technique is called *guided Grad-CAM.* We will see how Grad-CAM and guided Grad-CAM work in more detail in section 5.8. Activation-based methods are also weakly model-dependent, post hoc, and local interpretability techniques.

5.5   *Vanilla backpropagation*

In this section, we will learn about a gradient-based attribution method called *vanilla backpropagation.* Vanilla backpropagation was proposed in 2014 by Karen Simonyan et al, and this technique is illustrated in figure 5.17.

The first step is to pick an image or example to interpret. Because we are looking at interpreting a single instance, the scope of this interpretability technique is local. The second step is to perform a forward pass on the CNN to obtain the output class prediction. Once you have obtained the output class, the next step is to obtain the gradient of the output with respect to the penultimate layer and perform a backward pass—which we learned about in chapter 4—to ultimately obtain the gradient of the output class with respect to the pixels in the input image. The gradients for the input pixels or

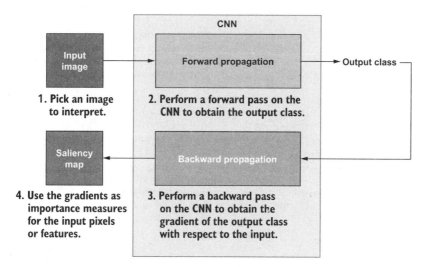

Figure 5.17 An illustration of vanilla backpropagation

features are used as important measures. The larger the gradient for the pixel, the more important that pixel is for the model to predict the output class. The intuition behind it is that if the magnitude of the gradient is large for a given pixel, then a small change in the pixel value will have a larger impact on the model prediction.

Vanilla backpropagation and other gradient-based methods have been implemented in PyTorch by Utku Ozbulak and open sourced in this GitHub repository: http://mng.bz/8l8B. These implementations cannot be directly applied to the Res-Net architecture or ResNet-based architectures, however, and I have adapted them in this book so that they can be applied to these more advanced architectures. The next code snippet implements the vanilla backpropagation technique as a Python class:

**A constructor for vanilla backpropagation that takes
in the model and the start of the feature layers**

```
# Code below adapted from: http://mng.bz/8l8B

class VanillaBackprop():
    """
        Produces gradients generated with vanilla back propagation from the
    ⇒  image
    """
    def __init__(self, model, features):          Initializes the model object
        self.model = model                        Initializes the gradients object as None
        self.gradients = None
        # Put model in evaluation mode            Sets the model in evaluation mode
        self.model.eval()
        # Set feature layers                      Sets the features object that points to
        self.features = features                  the start of the feature layers in the
        # Hook the first layer to get the gradient  model
        self.hook_layers()
                                         Hooks the layers so that you can compute the gradient
    def hook_layers(self):               of the output with respect to the input pixels
```

A function to hook the first layer to get the gradient

Sets the grad_out object to the gradient obtained from the current layer

Obtains the gradients with respect to the pixels in the feature map for the current layer

Resets the gradient to 0 before backpropagating

A helper function used to process the input and output gradients during backpropagation

Sets the grad_in object to the gradient obtained from the previous layer

Obtains the first feature layer

Registers the backward hook function to obtain the gradient of the output class with respect to the input pixels

Obtains the model output by propagating the image through the model in the forward direction

A function to perform backpropagation to obtain the gradients

Creates a one-hot-encoded tensor where the target class is set to I

Performs backward propagation

Returns the gradients object obtained through the hook function

```python
def hook_function(module, grad_in, grad_out):
    self.grad_in = grad_in
    self.grad_out = grad_out
    self.gradients = grad_in[0]
    # Register hook to the first layer
    first_layer = list(self.features._modules.items())[0][1]
    first_layer.register_backward_hook(hook_function)

def generate_gradients(self, input_image, target_class):
    # Forward
    model_output = self.model(input_image)
    # Zero grads
    self.model.zero_grad()
    # Target for backprop
    one_hot_output = torch.FloatTensor(1, model_output.size()[-1]).zero_()
    one_hot_output[0][target_class] = 1
    # Backward pass
    model_output.backward(gradient=one_hot_output)
    gradients_as_arr = self.gradients.data.numpy()[0]
    return gradients_as_arr
```

Note that the features layers for the ResNet model and other architectures like Inception v3 and ResNeXt can be found in the parent model and are not stored in a hierarchical structure as in VGG16 and AlexNet architectures, where the features layers are stored within the `features` key in the model. You can test this by initializing the VGG16 model, as follows, and printing it to see its structure:

```python
vgg16 = torchvision.models.vgg16()
print(vgg16)
```

The output of this print statement is shown next. The output is clipped and is meant to show how the feature layers are stored within the features key. You will get similar output if you replace `vgg16` with `alexnet` in the previous code:

```
VGG(
  (features): Sequential(
    (0): Conv2d(3, 64, kernel_size=(3, 3), stride=(1, 1), padding=(1, 1))
    (1): ReLU(inplace=True)
    (2): Conv2d(64, 64, kernel_size=(3, 3), stride=(1, 1), padding=(1, 1))
    (3): ReLU(inplace=True)
    (4): MaxPool2d(kernel_size=2, stride=2, padding=0, dilation=1,
     ceil_mode=False)
    (5): Conv2d(64, 128, kernel_size=(3, 3), stride=(1, 1), padding=(1, 1))
    (6): ReLU(inplace=True)
...
(output clipped)
```

The implementation by Utku Ozbulak expects the architecture to have the same hierarchical structure as VGG16 and AlexNet. In the vanilla backpropagation implementation earlier, on the other hand, the feature layers are explicitly passed to the constructor so that it can be used for more complex architectures. You can now instantiate this class for the ResNet model as follows:

```
vbp = VanillaBackprop(model=model, features=model)
```

We will now create a helper function to obtain the gradients of the output with respect to the input, as shown next:

The get_grads function takes in the gradient-based method, the dataset, and the index of the example to be interpreted.

```
def get_grads(gradient_method, dataset, idx):
    image, label = dataset[idx]

    X = image.reshape(1,
                      image.shape[0],
                      image.shape[1],
                      image.shape[2])
    X_var = Variable(X, requires_grad=True)
    grads = gradient_method.generate_gradients(X_var, label)
    return grads
```

Obtains the image and label at index idx

Reshapes the image to be able to run through the model

Creates the PyTorch variable where requires_grad is True to obtain the gradients through backpropagation

Returns the gradients with respect to the input pixels

Obtains the gradients using the generate_gradients function

We will use the same two examples that we used for the LIME technique in section 5.4.2—one IDC-negative patch and one IDC-positive patch. We can now obtain the gradients using the vanilla backpropagation technique as follows:

```
non_idc_vanilla_grads = get_grads(vbp, dataset_test, non_idc_idx)
idc_vanilla_grads = get_ grads(vbp, dataset_test, idc_idx)
```

Note that the test dataset is the `PatchDataset` for the test set that we initialized in section 5.3.1. The resulting gradients array shown here will have the same dimension as the input image. The input image has dimension $3 \times 50 \times 50$ where there are three channels (red, green, blue) and the height and width of the image are 50 pixels each. The resulting gradients will also have the same dimension and can be visualized as a color image. For ease of visualization, though, we will convert the gradients image to grayscale. We can use the following helper function to convert from color to grayscale:

```
# Code below from: http://mng.bz/818B

def convert_to_grayscale(im_as_arr):
    """
        Converts 3d image to grayscale
    Args:
        im_as_arr (numpy arr): RGB image with shape (D,W,H)
    returns:
        grayscale_im (numpy_arr): Grayscale image with shape (1,W,D)
```

```
"""
grayscale_im = np.sum(np.abs(im_as_arr), axis=0)
im_max = np.percentile(grayscale_im, 99)
im_min = np.min(grayscale_im)
grayscale_im = (np.clip((grayscale_im - im_min) / (im_max - im_min), 0, 1))
grayscale_im = np.expand_dims(grayscale_im, axis=0)
return grayscale_im
```

Now that we have the gradients obtained through vanilla backpropagation, we can visualize them the same way as we visualized the LIME explanation. As an exercise, I encourage you to extend the visualization code in section 5.4.2 to replace the LIME explanation with the grayscale representation of the gradients. The resulting figure is shown in figure 5.18.

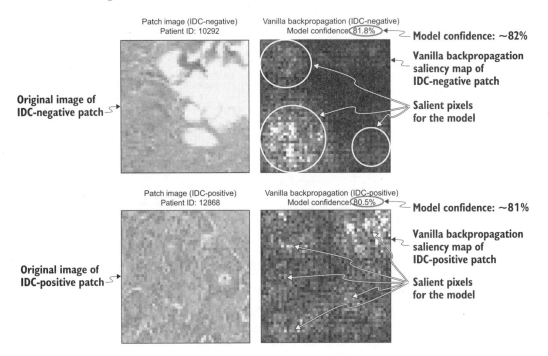

Figure 5.18   A saliency map using vanilla backpropagation

Let's focus on the IDC-negative patch first. The original image of the patch is shown on the top left. The grayscale representation of the gradients obtained through vanilla backpropagation is shown on the top right. We can see pixels with various shades of gray in the image. Larger gradients have a higher intensity of gray or appear white. This is a great way to visualize what pixels the CNN is focusing on to predict that the image is IDC negative with a confidence of 82%. The salient, or important, pixels correspond to the dense lighter stains in the original image. Because gradients are shown at the pixel level, this is a much more fine-grained interpretation than LIME, where

LIME focuses only on superpixels. Saliency maps are a great way to debug the CNN as a data scientist or engineer and also help the expert pathologist understand what parts of the image the CNN is paying attention to.

Let's now look at the IDC-positive patch. The original image is shown on the bottom left, and the interpretation obtained through vanilla backpropagation is shown on the bottom right. We can see that a lot more pixels are lit up, which corresponds to the darker stains or the nuclei in the input image. This interpretation is a lot better than the LIME interpretation, where in LIME, the whole image was treated as a superpixel.

5.6 *Guided backpropagation*

Guided backpropagation is another gradient-based attribution method proposed in 2015 by J. T. Springenberg et al. It is similar to vanilla backpropagation, with the only difference being in the way it handles the gradient when it passes through a rectified linear unit (ReLU). As we saw in chapter 4, ReLU is a nonlinear activation function that clips negative input values to zero. The guided backpropagation technique zeroes out the gradient into a ReLU if the gradient is negative or if input to the ReLU during the forward pass is negative. The idea behind guided backpropagation is to focus only on input features that positively influence the model prediction.

The guided backpropagation technique has also been implemented in PyTorch in the repository at http://mng.bz/8l8B, but it has been adapted in this book so that it can be applied to more complex architectures like ResNet, where there are nested layers with ReLUs. The following code snippet shows the improved implementation:

```
# Code below adapted from: http://mng.bz/8l8B
from torch.nn import ReLU, Sequential
```
Imports the ReLU activation function and the Sequential container

```
class GuidedBackprop():
    """
        Produces gradients generated with guided back propagation from the
        given image
    """
    def __init__(self, model, features):
        self.model = model
        self.gradients = None
        self.features = features
        self.forward_relu_outputs = []
        # Put model in evaluation mode
        self.model.eval()
        self.update_relus()
        self.hook_layers()
```
A function to hook the first layer to get the gradient, similar to vanilla backpropagation

The contructor for guided backpropagation is similar to vanilla backpropagation with one additional function call to update the ReLUs during backpropagation.

```
    def hook_layers(self):
        def hook_function(module, grad_in, grad_out):
            self.gradients = grad_in[0]
        # Register hook to the first layer
        first_layer = list(self.features._modules.items())[0][1]
        first_layer.register_backward_hook(hook_function)
    def update_relus(self):
```
A function to update the ReLUs

A function to impute zero for gradient values that are less than 0

```
"""
        Updates relu activation functions so that
            1- stores output in forward pass
            2- imputes zero for gradient values that are less than zero
"""
def relu_backward_hook_function(module, grad_in, grad_out):
        """
        If there is a negative gradient, change it to zero
        """
        # Get last forward output
        corresponding_forward_output = self.forward_relu_outputs[-1]
        corresponding_forward_output[corresponding_forward_output > 0] = 1
        modified_grad_out = corresponding_forward_output *
            torch.clamp(grad_in[0], min=0.0)
        del self.forward_relu_outputs[-1]  #
        return (modified_grad_out,)

def relu_forward_hook_function(module, ten_in, ten_out):
        """
        Store results of forward pass
        """
        self.forward_relu_outputs.append(ten_out)

# Loop through layers, hook up ReLUs
for pos, module in self.features._modules.items():
    if isinstance(module, ReLU):
        module.register_backward_hook(relu_backward_hook_function)
        module.register_forward_hook(relu_forward_hook_function)
    elif isinstance(module, Sequential):
        for sub_pos, sub_module in module._modules.items():
            if isinstance(sub_module, ReLU):
sub_module.register_backward_hook(relu_backward_hook_function)

sub_module.register_forward_hook(relu_forward_hook_function)
            elif isinstance(sub_module, torchvision.models.resnet.BasicBlock):
                for subsub_pos, subsub_module in
                    sub_module._modules.items():
                    if isinstance(subsub_module, ReLU):
subsub_module.register_backward_hook(relu_backward_hook_function)

subsub_module.register_forward_hook(relu_forward_hook_function)

def generate_gradients(self, input_image, target_class):
    # Forward pass
    model_output = self.model(input_image)
    # Zero gradients
    self.model.zero_grad()
    # Target for backprop
    one_hot_output = torch.FloatTensor(1, model_output.size()[--1]).zero_()
    one_hot_output[0][target_class] = 1
    # Backward pass
    model_output.backward(gradient=one_hot_output)
    gradients_as_arr = self.gradients.data.numpy()[0]
    return gradients_as_arr
```

Annotations:
- **Obtains the output of the ReLU in the forward pass**
- **Sets the identifier variable where positive values are set to 1**
- **Removes the last forward output**
- **Imputes negative gradient values with 0**
- **Returns the modified gradients**
- **A helper function to store the outputs of the ReLUs during the forward pass**
- **Iterates through all the feature layers**
- **If the module is ReLU, registers the hook functions to obtain the values during forward pass and clip the gradients during backprop**
- **If the module is a Sequential container, iterates through its submodules**
- **If the submodule is a ReLU, registers the hook functions as before**
- **If the sub-submodule is a ReLU, registers the hook functions as before**
- **If the submodule is a BasicBlock, iterates through its submodules**
- **A function to perform backpropagation to obtain the gradients, similar to vanilla backpropagation**

We can use this adapted implementation for model architectures with up to three nested layers with ReLUs. Let's now instantiate the guided backpropagation class for the ResNet model as follows:

```
gbp = GuidedBackprop(model= model,
                     features=model)
```

We can now obtain the gradients using the same `get_gradients` helper function defined in section 5.5. As an exercise, obtain the gradients for the two examples, convert them to grayscale, and then visualize them. The resulting figure is shown in figure 5.19.

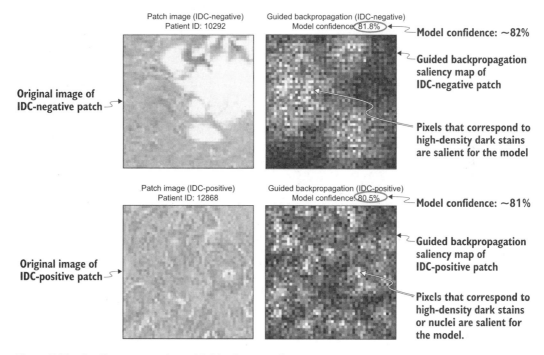

Figure 5.19 A saliency map using guided backpropagation

The interpretation using guided backpropagation seems to show the model focusing on a lot more pixels for both the IDC-negative and IDC-positive patches. The pixels seem to correspond to regions of high-density lighter stains for the IDC-negative patch and high-density darker stains for the IDC-positive patch. The interpretations using vanilla backpropagation and guided backpropagation both seem to be legitimate, but which one should we use? We will discuss this in section 5.9.

5.7   *Other gradient-based methods*

The vanilla and guided backpropagation methods both underestimate the importance of features in a model that exhibits saturation. What does this mean? Let's take a look at a simple example as highlighted in a 2017 paper by Avanti Shrikumar et al., available at https://arxiv.org/pdf/1704.02685;Learning. Figure 5.20 illustrates a simple network that exhibits saturation in the output signal. The network takes in two inputs, *x1* and *x2*. The numbers on the arrows or edges are the weights that are used to multiply with the input unit that it connects. The final output of the network (or output signal) *y* can be evaluated as follows:

```
y=1+max(0,1- (x₁+x₂))
```

If *x1* + *x2* is greater than 1, then the output signal y is saturated at 1. We can see that the gradient of the output with respect to the inputs is zero when the sum of the inputs is greater than 1. At this point, both vanilla backpropagation and guided backpropagating underestimate the importance of the two input features because the gradients are 0.

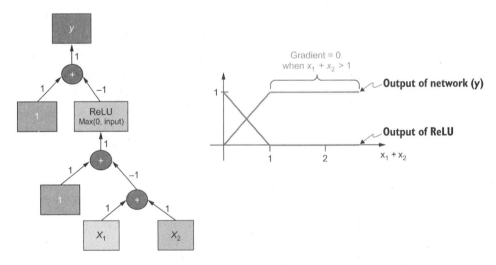

Figure 5.20   An illustration of a simple network that exhibits output signal saturation

To overcome the saturation problem, two gradient-based methods were proposed recently called integrated gradients (https://arxiv.org/pdf/1703.01365.pdf) and SmoothGrad (https://arxiv.org/pdf/1706.03825.pdf). Integrated gradients were proposed in 2017 by Mukund Sundararajan et al. For a given input image, integrated gradients integrate the gradients as the input pixels are scaled from a starting value (e.g., all zeros) to their actual values. SmoothGrad was also proposed in 2017 by Daniel Smilkov et al. SmoothGrad adds pixelwise Gaussian noise to copies of the input image and then averages the resulting gradients obtained through vanilla backpropagation.

Both of these techniques require integrating/averaging over multiple samples, similar to perturbation-based methods, thereby increasing the computational complexity. The resulting interpretations are also not guaranteed to be reliable, which is why we don't explicitly cover them in this book. We will discuss them further in section 5.9. For those interested, you can play around with these techniques using the implementation in PyTorch in the repository at http://mng.bz/8l8B.

5.8 *Grad-CAM and guided Grad-CAM*

We will now focus our attention on activation-based methods. Grad-CAM was proposed in 2017 by R. R. Selvaraju et al. and is an activation-based attribution method that exploits the features learned through the convolutional layers. Grad-CAM looks at the feature map learned by the final convolutional layer in the CNN, and we obtain the importance of that feature map by calculating the gradient of the output with respect to the pixels in the feature map. Because we are looking at the feature map from the final convolutional layer, the activation map produced by Grad-CAM is coarse. The Grad-CAM technique is also implemented in the repository at http://mng.bz/8l8B and is adapted as follows so that it can be applied to any CNN architecture. First, we will define a class called `CamExtractor` to obtain the output or feature map of the final convolutional layer and also the output of the classifier or fully connected layers:

The second argument sets the start of the features layers in the CNN.

The first argument sets the CNN model object.

A constructor for CamExtractor that takes in five input arguments

```
# Code below adapted from: http://mng.bz/8l8B

class CamExtractor():
    """
        Extracts cam features from the model
    """
    def __init__(self, model, features, fc, fc_layer, target_layer):
        self.model = model
        self.features = features
        self.fc = fc
        self.fc_layer = fc_layer
        self.target_layer = target_layer
        self.gradients = None

    def save_gradient(self, grad):
        self.gradients = grad

    def forward_pass_on_convolutions(self, x):
        """
            Does a forward pass on convolutions,
            hooks the function at given layer
        """
        conv_output = None
        for module_pos, module in self.features._modules.items():
            if module_pos == self.fc_layer:
                break
```

The third argument sets the start of the fully connected layers in the CNN.

The fourth argument is the name of the fully connected layer.

The fifth argument is the name of the target or the final convolutional layer.

Initializes the gradients object as None

A method to save the gradients

A method to do a forward pass and obtain the output of the final convolutional layer and to register a hook function to obtain the gradient of the output with respect to that layer

Initializes the output of the final convolutional layer as None

Iterates through all the modules in the features layers of the CNN

Breaks once the name of the module matches the name of the fully connected layer

Obtains the output of the module using the input from the previous layer

```
x = module(x)
    if module_pos == self.target_layer:
        x.register_hook(self.save_gradient)
        conv_output = x
return conv_output, x
```

Returns the feature map for the final convolutional layer and the input to the fully connected layers

If the module name matches the name of the final convolutional layer, registers a hook to obtain the gradient of the output with respect to this layer during backpropagation

A method to perform a forward pass on the model

```
def forward_pass(self, x):
    """
        Does a full forward pass on the model
    """
    # Forward pass on the convolutions
    conv_output, x = self.forward_pass_on_convolutions(x)
    x = x.view(x.size(0), -1)
    # Forward pass on the classifier
    x = self.fc(x)
    return conv_output, x
```

Flattens the input to the fully connected layer

Obtains the feature map for the final convolutional layer and the input to the fully connected layer

Passes through the fully connected layer to obtain the classifier output

Returns the feature map for the final convolutional layer and the output of the classifier

The CamExtractor class shown in this code snipper takes in the following five input arguments:

- model—The CNN model used for image classification
- features—The layer that indicates the start of the feature layers in the CNN
- fc—The layer that indicates the start of the fully connected layer in the CNN use for classification
- fc_layer—The name of the fully connected layer in the model object
- target_layer—The name of the final convolutional layer in the model object

As we saw for vanilla backpropagation and guided backpropagation, the model object is called model and the layer that indicates the start of the feature layers is the same object. The layer that indicates the start of the fully connected layer in the model object is model.fc. The name of the fully connected layer in the model object is fc, and the name of the final convolutional layer in the model is layer4. We now define the GradCam class to produce the class activation map, as shown here:

```
# Code below adapted from: http://mng.bz/818B

class GradCam():
    """
        Produces class activation map
    """
    def __init__(self, model, features, fc, fc_layer, target_layer):
        self.model = model
        self.features = features
        self.fc = fc
        self.fc_layer = fc_layer
        self.model.eval()
```

A constructor for GradCam takes the same five arguments as CamExtractor.

Sets the appropriate objects

Sets the model in evaluation mode

Uses the extractor to get the feature map from the final convolution layer and the output of the classifier

A function to generate the CAM given an input image and target class

Initializes the CamExtractor object

If the target class is not specified, obtains the output class based on the model prediction

Converts the target class into a one-hot-encoded tensor

Resets the gradients before backpropagation

Obtains the gradients of the output class with respect to the feature map

Performs backpropagation

Obtains the CAM by weighting the feature map by the gradients

Clips the CAM and removes negative values

Normalizes the CAM between 0 and 1

Scales the CAM to 0–255 to visualize as a grayscale image

Returns the CAM

Zooms the CAM and interpolates to the same dimension as the input image

```python
self.extractor = CamExtractor(self.model,
                              self.features,
                              self.fc,
                              self.fc_layer,
                              target_layer)

def generate_cam(self, input_image, target_class=None):
    conv_output, model_output = self.extractor.forward_pass(input_image)
    if target_class is None:
        target_class = np.argmax(model_output.data.numpy())
    one_hot_output = torch.FloatTensor(1, model_output.size()[-1]).zero_()
    one_hot_output[0][target_class] = 1

    self.features.zero_grad()
    self.fc.zero_grad()

    model_output.backward(gradient=one_hot_output, retain_graph=True)

    guided_gradients = self.extractor.gradients.data.numpy()[0]

    target = conv_output.data.numpy()[0]
    weights = np.mean(guided_gradients, axis=(1, 2))
    cam = np.ones(target.shape[1:], dtype=np.float32)
    for i, w in enumerate(weights):
        cam += w * target[i, :, :]
    cam = np.maximum(cam, 0)
    cam = (cam - np.min(cam)) / (np.max(cam) - np.min(cam))
    cam = np.uint8(cam * 255)
    cam = np.uint8(Image.fromarray(cam).resize((input_image.shape[2],
                   input_image.shape[3]), Image.ANTIALIAS))/255
    return cam
```

You can initialize the Grad-CAM object as follows. As an exercise, I encourage you to create activation maps for the two examples we used earlier. The solution to this exercise can be found in the GitHub repository associated with this book (http://mng.bz/KBdZ):

```python
grad_cam = GradCam(resnet18_model,
                   features=resnet18_model,
                   fc=resnet18_model.fc,
                   fc_layer='fc',
                   target_layer='layer4')
```

Figure 5.21 contains the resulting Grad-CAM activation maps. We can see from the figure that the activation map shows the importance of the feature map from the final convolutional layer and is quite coarse-grained. The regions in gray or white show highly important regions for the model prediction.

To get a more fine-grained activation map, we can use the guided Grad-CAM technique. The guided Grad-CAM technique, proposed in 2017 by the same authors as Grad-CAM, essentially combines the Grad-CAM and guided backpropagation

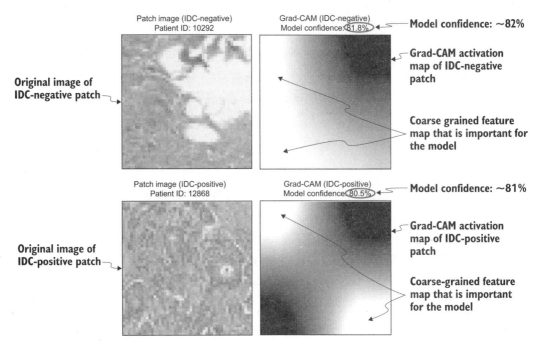

Figure 5.21   An activation map using Grad-CAM

techniques. The final activation map produced by guided Grad-CAM is an element-wise dot product of the activation map produced by Grad-CAM and the saliency map produced by guided backpropagation. This is implemented in the following function:

```
# Code below from: http://mng.bz/818B
def guided_grad_cam(grad_cam_mask, guided_backprop_mask):
    """
        Guided grad cam is just pointwise multiplication of cam mask and
        guided backprop mask
    Args:
        grad_cam_mask (np_arr): Class activation map mask
        guided_backprop_mask (np_arr):Guided backprop mask
    """
    cam_gb = np.multiply(grad_cam_mask, guided_backprop_mask)
    return cam_gb
```

This function takes the mask in grayscale obtained from Grad-CAM and guided backpropagation and returns an element-wise product of them. Figure 5.22 shows the activation maps produced by guided Grad-CAM for the two examples of interest. We can see that visualization is a lot cleaner than guided backpropagation and highlights areas that are consistent with IDC-negative and -positive patches.

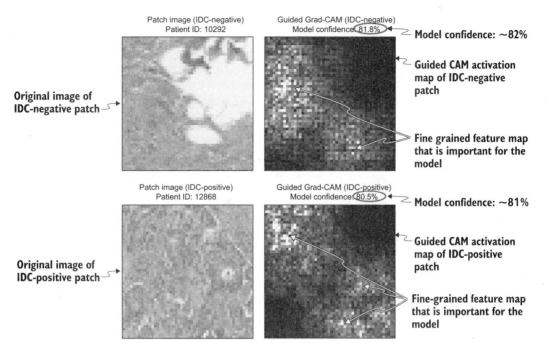

Figure 5.22   An activation map using guided Grad-CAM

5.9   *Which attribution method should I use?*

Now that we have all these techniques in our arsenal, which techniques should we apply? In other words, which techniques produce reliable interpretations? From visually inspecting the interpretations using a couple of examples, we found all the saliency techniques to provide a measure of importance for pixels. By visually assessing them, we found those importance measures to be reasonable. Relying solely on visual or qualitative assessment, however, can be misleading.

A paper that was published in 2018 by Julius Adebayo, et al., available at http:// mng.bz/Exjj, did a thorough quantitative assessment of the saliency methods discussed in this chapter. The following two broad classes of tests were done:

1 *Model parameter randomization test*—Checks whether any effect on the saliency map occurs by randomizing the weights of the model, from which we would expect the model to make random or garbage predictions. If the output of the saliency method is the same for the trained model and the random model, then we can say that the saliency map is insensitive to the model parameters. The saliency map would, therefore, not be reliable for debugging the model.

2 *Data randomization test*—Checks whether any effect on the saliency map occurs by randomizing the labels in the training data. When we train the same model architecture on a copy of the training dataset where the target labels are randomized, we would expect the output of the saliency method to also be sensitive

to it. If by randomizing the labels, there is no effect on the saliency map, then the method is not dependent on the input images and labels that exist in the original training set. The saliency map is, therefore, not reliable for understanding input-output relationships.

The paper provides a couple of sanity checks that can be used in practice to determine how reliable the output of the saliency method is. The results of the sanity checks are summarized in table 5.2.

Table 5.2   **Results of the sanity checks done on visual attribution methods**

Attribution method	Model parameter randomization test	Data randomization test
Vanilla backpropagation	PASS	PASS
Guided backpropagation	FAIL	FAIL
Integrated gradients	FAIL	FAIL
SmoothGrad	FAIL	PASS
Grad-CAM	PASS	PASS
Guided Grad-CAM	FAIL	FAIL

We can see that the methods that pass both tests are vanilla backpropagation and Grad-CAM. The saliency and activation maps produced by them are sensitive to the model and the data-generating process. They, therefore, can be used to reliably debug the model and to understand the relationship between the input images and the target label. The other techniques provide compelling images that explain the model prediction and seem acceptable from qualitative assessment. They are, however, invariant to model and label randomization and are, therefore, not adequate for model debugging and for understanding input-output relationships. The important message from these sanity checks is to be aware of confirmation bias. It is not enough for the interpretation to make sense qualitatively; it must also pass the sanity checks to be able to understand the model and input-output relationships better. The two tests proposed by the paper can be applied in practice to other interpretability techniques as well.

  In the next chapter, we will learn how to dissect the network further and understand what high-level concepts are learned by the neural network. Rather than look at pixel-level importance, we will learn about techniques that give us concept-level importance. These techniques have been shown to be sensitive to the model and the data-generating process and, therefore, pass the sanity checks discussed in this section.

Summary

- A convolutional neural network (CNN) is a neural network architecture commonly used for visual tasks such as image classification, object detection, and image segmentation.

- Fully connected DNNs do not capture pixel dependencies in an image very well and, therefore, cannot be trained to understand features in an image such as edges, colors, and gradients. CNNs, on the other hand, capture pixel dependencies or spatial dependencies in an image very well. We can also train the CNN architecture more efficiently to fit the input dataset as we reuse weights in the network.

- A CNN architecture typically consists of a sequence of convolution and pooling layers, called the feature learning layers. The objective of these layers is to extract hierarchical features from the input image. Following the feature learning convolutional layers are layers of neurons or units that are fully connected, and the purpose of these fully connected layers is to perform classification. The inputs to the fully connected layer are the high-level features learned by the convolution and pooling layers, and the output is a probability measure for the classification task.

- Various state-of-the-art CNN architectures, such as AlexNet, VGG, ResNet, Inception, and ResNeXT are implemented in popular deep learning libraries such as PyTorch and Keras. In PyTorch, you can initialize these architectures using the `torchvision` package.

- Within a CNN, as an image goes through millions of complex operations, it becomes incredibly difficult to understand how the model arrived at the final prediction. This is what makes CNNs black boxes.

- We can use visual attribution methods to interpret CNNs. These methods are used to attribute importance to parts of an image that influence the prediction made by the CNN.

- Three broad categories of visual attribution methods are available: perturbations, gradients, and activations.

- The idea behind perturbation-based methods is to perturb the input and probe its effects on the predictions made by the CNN. Techniques such as LIME and SHAP are perturbation-based methods. These techniques, however, are computationally inefficient because each perturbation requires us to perform a forward pass on the complex CNN model. These techniques can also underestimate the importance of features.

- We can use gradient-based methods to visualize the gradient of the input image with respect to the target class. Pixels with large gradient measures are considered most important, or salient, for the model. Gradient-based methods are sometimes also called backpropagation methods—the backpropagation algorithm is used to determine feature importance and saliency maps because a map of salient or important features is obtained. Popular gradient-based methods are vanilla backpropagation, guided backpropagation, integrated gradients, and SmoothGrad.

- Activation-based methods look at the feature maps or activations in the final convolutional layer and weight them based on the gradient of the target class with respect to those feature maps. The weights of the feature maps act as a proxy for the importance of the input features. This technique is called gradient-weighted Class Activation Mapping (Grad-CAM).

- Grad-CAM provides a coarse-grained activation map. To obtain more fine-grained activation maps, we can combine Grad-CAM and guided backpropagation—this technique is called guided Grad-CAM.

- The visual attribution methods that pass the model parameter randomization and data randomization tests are vanilla backpropagation and Grad-CAM. The saliency and activation maps produced by them are, therefore, more reliable for debugging the model and understanding the input-output relationships better.

Part 3

Interpreting model representations

This part of the book continues to focus on black-box models, but focuses specifically on understanding what features or representations have been learned by them.

In chapters 6 and 7, you'll learn about convolutional neural networks and neural networks used for language understanding. You will learn how to dissect the neural networks and understand what representations of the data are learned by the intermediate or hidden layers in the neural network. You'll also learn how to visualize high-dimensional representations learned by the model using techniques like principal component analysis (PCA) and t-distributed stochastic neighbor embedding (t-SNE).

Understanding
layers and units

This chapter covers

- Dissecting a black-box convolutional neural network to understand the features or concepts that are learned by the layers and units

- Running the network dissection framework

- Quantifying the interpretability of layers and units in the convolutional neural network and how to visualize them

- Strengths and weaknesses of the network dissection framework

In chapters 3, 4, and 5, we focused our attention on black-box models and how to interpret them using various techniques such as partial dependence plots (PDPs), LIME, SHAP, anchors, and saliency maps. In chapter 5, we specifically focused on convolutional neural networks (CNNs) and visual attribution methods such as gradients and activation maps that highlight the salient features that the model is focusing on. All these techniques focused on interpreting the complex processing and operations that happen within a black-box model by reducing its complexity. PDPs, for instance, are model-agnostic and show the marginal or average global effects of feature values on model prediction. Techniques like LIME, SHAP, and anchors are also model-agnostic—they create a proxy model that behaves similarly to the original black-box model but is simpler and easier to interpret. Visual attribution methods and saliency maps are weakly model-dependent and help highlight a small portion of the input that is salient, or important, for the model.

In this chapter and the next, we focus on interpreting representations or features learned by deep neural networks. This chapter specifically focuses on CNNs that are used for visual tasks such as image classification, object detection, and image segmentation. The large number of operations that happen within a CNN are organized into layers and units. By interpreting model representations, we aim to understand the role and structure of the data flowing through these layers and units. You'll specifically learn about the network dissection framework in this chapter. This framework will shed more light into the features and high-level concepts learned by the CNN. It will also help us go from visualizations like saliency maps that are typically evaluated qualitatively to more quantitative interpretations.

We will first introduce the ImageNet and Places datasets and the associated image classification task. We will then give a quick recap of CNNs and visual attribution methods, focusing on the limitations of these methods. This is to demonstrate the benefits of the network dissection framework. The remainder of the chapter will focus on this framework and how we can use it to understand the representations learned by CNNs.

6.1 Visual understanding

In this chapter, we will focus on the task of training an agent or an intelligent system to recognize real-world objects, places, and scenes. The task of this system is to perform multiclass classification. To train such an agent, we need access to large volumes of labeled data. The ImageNet dataset (http://www.image-net.org/) was created for the purpose of recognizing objects. It is a large-scale ontology of images built on the backbone of WordNet. WordNet is a lexical database of English nouns, verbs, adjectives, and adverbs that are organized into sets of synonyms, also called *synsets*. ImageNet also follows a similar structure where images are grouped by hierarchical synsets, or categories. Figure 6.1 shows an example of this structure. In this example, images of animals are organized into three categories. The highest-level category consists of images of mammals. The next level consists of images of carnivores followed by the final level, which consists of images of dogs. The full ImageNet database contains more than 14 million images grouped into 27 high-level categories. The number of synsets, or subcategories, ranges from 51 to 3,822. When it comes to building image classifiers, ImageNet is one of the most common datasets used.

For the task of recognizing places and scenes, we will use the Places dataset (http://places2.csail.mit.edu/). Knowing the place, scene, or context in which

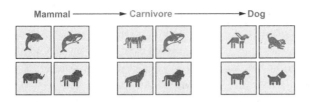

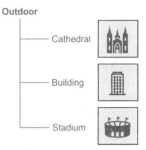

Figure 6.1   An illustration of synsets, or categories, in the ImageNet dataset

objects appear in the real world is an important aspect of building an intelligent system like a self-driving car trying to navigate a city. The Places dataset organizes images into different levels of scene categories. Figure 6.2 shows an example that illustrates the semantic structure of the dataset. The example shows a high-level scene category called Outdoor. Under this category are three subcategories called Cathedral, Building, and Stadium. In total, the Places dataset holds more than 10 million images organized into 400 unique scene categories. Using this dataset, we can train a model to learn features for various place- and scene-recognition tasks.

Figure 6.2   An illustration of categories in the Places dataset

With the ImageNet and Places datasets, we are now ready to train the intelligent system. Fortunately, we can use models for various state-of-the-art CNN architectures pretrained on the ImageNet and Places datasets. This will save us the effort, time, and money of training the models from scratch. In the next section, we will see how to leverage these pretrained models. We will also provide a recap of CNNs and the techniques that we have learned so far to interpret the output of these models.

6.2   Convolutional neural networks: A recap

In this section, we provide a quick recap of CNNs that we learned in chapter 5. Figure 6.3 illustrates a CNN architecture that can be used to classify an image in the Image-Net dataset as either being a dog or not.

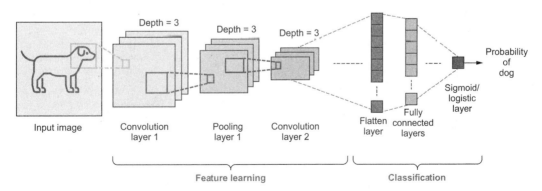

Figure 6.3   An illustration of a convolutional neural network (CNN)

The architecture consists of a sequence of layers called convolution and pooling layers, followed by a set of fully connected layers. The convolution and pooling layers combined are called the *feature-learning layers*. These layers extract hierarchical features from the input image. The first few layers extract low-level features, such as edges, colors, and gradients. Subsequent layers learn high-level features. The fully connected layers are used for classification. The features learned in the feature-learning layers are fed as inputs into the fully connected layers. The final output is a probability measure of how likely it is that the input image is of a dog.

In the previous chapter, we also learned how to initialize state-of-the-art CNN architectures using the `torchvision` package in PyTorch. We specifically focused on the ResNet architecture that was 18 layers deep, called ResNet-18. We will continue to use this architecture in this chapter as well. The ResNet-18 model can be initialized in PyTorch as follows:

```
import torchvision
model = torchvision.models.resnet18(pretrained=False)
```

Imports the torchvision package

Initializes the ResNet model with random weights

By setting the `pretrained` parameter to `False`, we initialize the ResNet model with random weights. To initialize the model pretrained on the ImageNet dataset, we have to set the `pretrained` parameter to `True`. This is shown next:

Initializes the ResNet model pretrained on the ImageNet dataset

```
imagenet_model = torchvision.models.resnet18(pretrained=True)
```

Other CNN architectures, like AlexNet, VGG, Inception, and ResNeXT, can also be initialized using `torchvision`. All the supported architectures can be found at https://pytorch.org/vision/stable/models.html.

For the Places dataset, you can find pretrained PyTorch models for various architectures at https://github.com/CSAILVision/places365. You can download the pretrained PyTorch model for use with the ResNet-18 architecture from http://mng.bz/GGmA. Because the file size is more than 40 MB, I encourage you to download it locally. Once it is downloaded, you can load the model pretrained on the Places dataset as follows:

```
import torch
places_model_file = "resnet18_places365.pth.tar"
if torch.cuda.is_available():
    places_model = torch.load(places_model_file)
else:
    places_model = torch.load(places_model_file, map_location=torch.device('cpu'))
```

Imports the PyTorch library

Sets this variable to the full path where the pretrained ResNet model has been downloaded

Loads the ResNet model pretrained on the Places dataset

We also learned various visual attribution methods that can be used to interpret CNNs, as summarized in figure 6.4. Three broad categories of visual attribution methods exist: perturbations, gradients, and activations. Techniques like LIME and SHAP are perturbation-based methods. These model-agnostic, post hoc, and local interpretability techniques use proxy models that behave similarly to the complex CNN but are easier to interpret. These techniques highlight segments, or superpixels, in the image that are important for the model prediction. These techniques are great and can be applied to any complex model. Gradient-based and activation-based methods are post hoc and local interpretability techniques. They are, however, weakly dependent on the model and highlight only a small portion of the input image that is salient or important for the model. For gradient-based methods like vanilla backpropagation, guided backpropagation, integrated gradients, and SmoothGrad, we obtain the salient pixels in the image by computing the gradient of the target class with respect to the input image. For activation-based methods like Grad-CAM and guided Grad-CAM, activations in the final convolutional layer are weighted based on the gradient of the target class with respect to the activation or feature map.

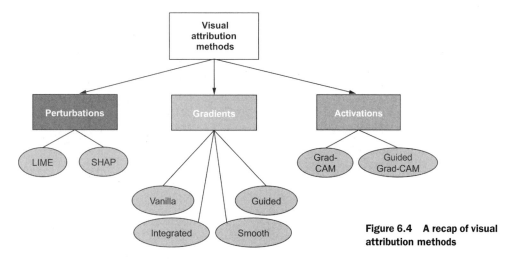

Figure 6.4   A recap of visual attribution methods

All the visual attribution methods shown in figure 6.4 highlight the important pixels or superpixels for the final model prediction. We typically assess the visualizations generated by these methods qualitatively, so the interpretations are subjective. Moreover, these techniques do not give us any information on the low-level and high-level concepts or features that are learned by the feature-learning layers and units in the CNN. In the following section, we will learn about the network dissection framework. This framework will help us dissect the CNN and come up with more quantitative interpretations. We will also be able to understand what human-understandable concepts are learned by the feature-learning layers in the CNN.

6.3   *Network dissection framework*

The network dissection framework was proposed by Zhou, Bolei, et al., researchers from MIT, in 2018 (see https://arxiv.org/pdf/1711.05611.pdf). The fundamental questions that the framework aims to answer follow:

- How does the CNN decompose the task of understanding an image?
- Does the CNN identify any features or concepts that are understandable by humans?

The framework answers these questions by finding units in the convolutional layers in the CNN that match meaningful, predefined semantic concepts. The interpretability of those units is quantified by measuring the alignment of the unit responses to those predefined concepts. Dissecting the network in this way is interesting because it makes the deep neural network less opaque. The network dissection framework consists of the following three key steps, as summarized in figure 6.5:

1 First, define a broad set of meaningful concepts that can be used to dissect the network.
2 Then, probe the network by finding units that respond to those predefined concepts.
3 Last, measure the quality or interpretability of those units to those concepts.

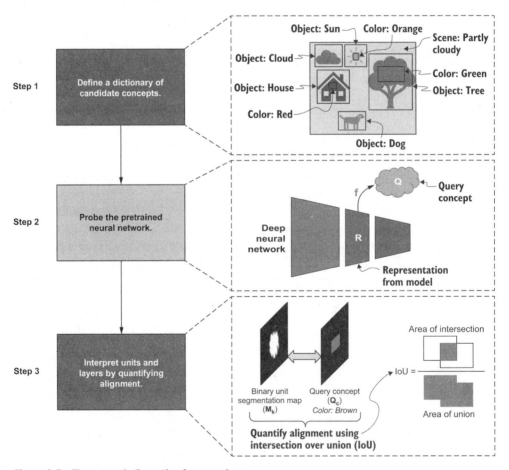

Figure 6.5   The network dissection framework

We will break down each of these steps in greater detail in the following subsections.

6.3.1   *Concept definition*

The first and most crucial step in the network dissection framework is data collection. The data must consist of images that are labeled pixelwise with concepts of different abstraction levels. The ImageNet and Places datasets, introduced in section 6.1, can be used to train models to detect real-world objects and scenes. For the purposes of network dissection, we need another independent dataset consisting of labeled concepts. We will not use this dataset for model training but rather to probe the network to understand what high-level concepts are learned by the feature-learning layers.

To dissect models trained to detect real-world objects and scenes using datasets like ImageNet and Places, Zhou, Bolei, et al. combined five different datasets to create an independent labeled dataset consisting of high-level concepts called *Broden*. Broden stands for *bro*adly and *den*sely labeled dataset. The five datasets that Broden unifies are ADE (http://mng.bz/zQD6/), Open-Surfaces (http://mng.bz/0wJE), PASCAL-Context (http://mng.bz/9KEq), PASCAL-Part (http://mng.bz/jyD8), and the Describable Textures Dataset (http://mng.bz/W7Xl). These datasets consist of annotated images of a broad range of concept categories, from low-level concept categories like colors, textures, and materials to more high-level concept categories like parts, objects, and scenes. Figure 6.6 provides an illustration of an image labeled with various concepts. In the Broden dataset, a segmented image is created for each of the concepts in an image. If we take the tree object in figure 6.6 as an example, pixels within the bounding box containing the tree have a label of 1, and pixels outside the bounding box, not containing the tree, have a label of 0. Concepts need to be labeled at the pixel level. Labels from all the five datasets are unified in the Broden dataset. Concepts with similar synonyms are also merged. Broden contains more than 1,000 visual concepts.

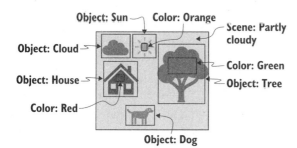

Figure 6.6   An illustration of an image with labeled concepts

Because creating a dataset with labeled concepts is a crucial step in the network dissection framework, let's take a step back and look at how to create a new dataset. We will focus specifically on the tools that we can use for this purpose and the methodology to follow to obtain consistent, high-quality labeled concepts.

We can use various tools for labeling images. LabelMe (http://mng.bz/8lE5) and Make Sense (https://www.makesense.ai/) are free web-based image-annotation tools.

In LabelMe, we can easily create an account, upload images, and label them. Through the sharing functionality, we can create annotations collaboratively as well. Images uploaded on LabelMe, however, are considered public. Make Sense is a very similar tool, but it does not allow you to collaborate and share annotations with others. The tool also does not save the state of an annotation project. Therefore, if you start a project in Make Sense, the annotations for the images in that project must be finished in one go. The tool does not allow you to save the state and start annotating from where you left off. Both LabelMe and Make Sense support multiple label types, like rectangles, lines, points, and polygons. Both tools are used mostly by researchers using datasets that are meant to be public.

For enterprise, business, or more private needs, you could host your own labeling service. The Computer Vision Annotation Tool (CVAT; https://github.com/openvinotoolkit/cvat) and Visual Object Tagging Tool (VoTT; https://github.com/microsoft/VoTT) are free, open source web services that you can deploy on your own web servers. If you do not want to deal with the hassle of hosting your own labeling service, you could also use managed services such as LabelBox (https://labelbox.com/), Amazon SageMaker Ground Truth (https://aws.amazon.com/sagemaker/groundtruth/), or the labeling services provided by Azure Machine Learning (http://mng.bz/ExgX) or Google Cloud (http://mng.bz/Nx9v). If you do not have a team of labelers who can annotate images for you, you could crowdsource the labeling effort and obtain labels using Amazon Mechanical Turk (https://www.mturk.com/).

It is also important to have a good labeling methodology to ensure high-quality and consistent labels. The protocol for the labeling task has to be clearly specified so that the labelers know the full list of concepts with clear definitions for them. The labels obtained through this process, however, can be quite noisy, especially if they are crowdsourced. To ensure consistency in the labels, take a random subset of the images and get them annotated by the same set of labelers. By doing so, you can now quantify how consistent the labels are by looking at the following three types of errors, as detailed in http://mng.bz/DxaA, which introduces the ADE20K dataset:

- *Segmentation quality*—This error quantifies the precision of the segmentation of concepts. A given concept could be segmented differently by different labelers and even by the same labeler.
- *Concept naming*—Differences in concept naming can occur where a given pixel is given a different concept name by the same labeler or a different labeler.
- *Segmentation quantity*—Some images could contain more labeled concepts than others. You can quantify this error by looking at the variance in the number of concepts in a certain image across multiple labelers.

We can circumvent the segmentation quality and quantity errors by increasing the number of labelers so that we can take a consensus or by getting the images annotated by more experienced labelers. We can avoid the concept naming error by having a clearly defined labeling protocol with precise terminology. As mentioned earlier, creating a dataset with labeled concepts is the most important step in the network dissection framework. It is also the most time-consuming and costly step. We will see the value of this dataset through the lens of interpretability in the following sections.

6.3.2 *Network probing*

Once you have a labeled dataset of visual concepts, the next step is to probe the pretrained neural network to understand how the network responds to those concepts. Let's first look at how this works for a simple deep neural network. A simplified representation of a deep neural network is shown in figure 6.7, where the number of units decreases as you go from the input layer to the output layer. A representation of the input data is learned in the intermediate layers of the network, and this is represented as R. To understand the network better, we would like to probe the network by quantifying how the representation R maps to a given query concept Q that we care about. The mapping from the representation R to query concept Q is called the *computation model* and is represented as f in the figure. Let's now define R, Q and f in the context of CNNs.

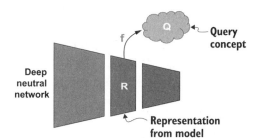

Figure 6.7 Probing a deep neural network for concepts

Figure 6.8 illustrates a CNN where layer 4 of the network is probed. In the figure, we are probing the network with an image of a dog and determining what concepts (like color and object) are learned by the units in layer 4 in the pretrained CNN. The first step, therefore, is to forward-propagate the image of the dog through the CNN. The weights of the CNN are frozen, and there is no need for training or backpropagation. Next, we pick a convolutional layer to probe (in this case, layer 4). We then obtain the output feature map or activation map after forward propagation from that layer. In general, as you go deeper into a CNN, the size of the activation map reduces. Therefore, to compare the activation map with labeled concepts in the input image, we have to up-sample, or scale, the lower-resolution activation map to the same resolution as that of the input image. This forms the representation R of convolutional layer 4 in the CNN. Repeat this process for all the images in the labeled-concepts dataset, and store the activation maps for all images. We can also repeat this process for other layers in the CNN.

Now, how do we interpret what high-level concepts are contained in these representations R? In other words, how do we map these representations R with query concepts Q? This requires us to determine a computational model f that maps R to Q. Also, how do you

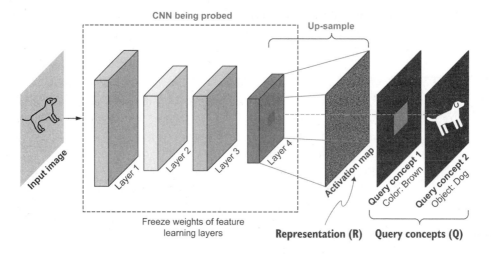

Figure 6.8 Probing layer 4 in a convolutional neural network for concepts

up-sample, or scale, the low-resolution activation map to the same resolution as the input image? This is broken down in figure 6.9.

In figure 6.9, we can see that input image *i* is forward-propagated through the CNN. For illustration purposes, suppose that we are specifically interested in unit *k* in convolutional layer *l*. The output of this convolutional layer is represented as the low-resolution activation map A_i. The network dissection framework then up-samples, or resizes, the activation map to the same resolution as the input image *i*. This is shown as the input image-resolution activation map S_i in figure 6.9. The bilinear interpolation algorithm is used in the framework. Bilinear interpolation extends linear interpolation to a two-dimensional plane. It estimates the values of new unknown pixels in the resized

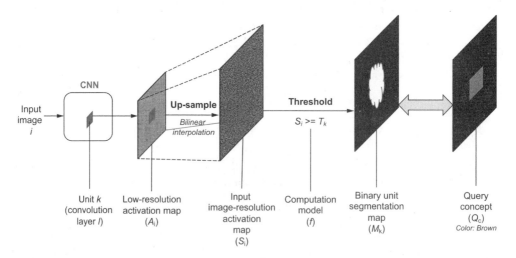

Figure 6.9 An illustration of up-sampling and how to map representation R to query concept Q

image based on known values in surrounding pixels. The estimates or interpolants are centered around each unit's response in the original activation map.

Once you have the image-resolution activation map S_i, the framework then maps this representation onto a given query concept Q_c by performing a simple thresholding. The thresholding is performed at the unit level so that the response of each unit in the convolutional layer can be compared with the query concept. In figure 6.9, the query concept Q_c is the segmented image for the color brown in the original labeled-concepts dataset. The binary unit segmentation map for unit k after thresholding is shown as M_k. The threshold used by the computation model f is T_k, where

$$M_k = S_i \geq T_k$$

The binary unit segmentation map M_k highlights all the regions for which the activation exceeds the threshold T_k. The threshold T_k is dependent on the unit that we are probing in the CNN. How do we compute this threshold? The framework looks at the distribution of the unit's activation across all the images in the labeled-concepts dataset. Let a_k be the value of a unit's activation in the low-resolution activation map A_i for a given input image i. Once you have the distribution of a_k across all the images, the threshold T_k is then computed as the top quantile level such that

$$\mathbb{P}(a_k > T_k) = 0.005$$

T_k measures the 0.005 quantile level. In other words, 0.5% of all unit activations (a_k) across all the images in the labeled-concepts dataset are greater than T_k. Once we have mapped the representation learned by the CNN to the binary unit segmentation map, the next step is to quantify the alignment of this segmentation map with all query concepts Q_c. This is detailed in the following subsection.

6.3.3 *Quantifying alignment*

After you have probed the network and obtained the binary unit segmentation map for all the units in the representation layers, the final step in the framework is to quantify the alignment of the segmentation maps with all the query concepts in the dataset. Figure 6.10 shows how to quantify the alignment for a given binary unit segmentation map M_k and query concept Q_c. The alignment is measured using the Intersection over Union (IoU) score. IoU is a useful metric for measuring the accuracy of how well a unit detects a given concept. It measures the overlap of the binary unit segmentation map with the pixelwise segmented image of the query concept. The higher the IoU score, the better the accuracy. If the binary segmentation map perfectly overlaps with the concept, we obtain a perfect IoU score of 1.

The value of IoU for a given binary segmentation map M_k and query concept Q_c is the accuracy of unit k in detecting concept c. It quantifies the interpretability of unit k by measuring how good it is at detecting concept c. In the network dissection framework, an IoU threshold of *0.04* is used, where a unit k is considered a detector of concept c if the IoU score is greater than 0.04. The value of 0.04 was picked arbitrarily by the

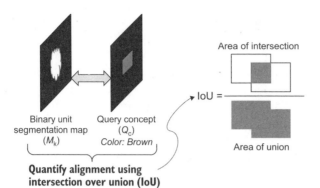

Figure 6.10   Quantifying alignment with concept

authors of the framework, and in their paper, available at https://arxiv.org/pdf/1711.05611.pdf, the authors show through human evaluation that the quality of the interpretation is insensitive to the IoU threshold. To quantify the interpretability of a convolutional layer, the framework counts the number of unique concepts aligned with units, that is, the number of unique concept detectors. With this understanding of how the network dissection framework works, let's see it in action in the following section.

6.4   *Interpreting layers and units*

In this section, we put the network dissection framework to the test by interpreting layers and units in CNN models that are pretrained on the ImageNet and Places datasets. As mentioned in section 6.2, we will focus on the ResNet-18 architecture, but the network dissection framework can be applied to any CNN model. We saw in section 6.2 how to load ResNet-18 models pretrained on the ImageNet and Places datasets. The authors of the paper have created a library called NetDissect (https://github.com/CSAILVision/NetDissect) that implements this framework. This library supports both the PyTorch and Caffe deep learning frameworks. We will, however, use an improved implementation called NetDissect-Lite (https://github.com/CSAILVision/NetDissect-Lite) that is lighter and faster than the original implementation. This library is written in PyTorch and Python 3.6. We will need to make some minor changes to the library to support later versions of Python (3.7 and above), and we will discuss this in the next subsection.

We can clone the NetDissect-Lite library to our local repository from GitHub using the following command:

```
git clone https://github.com/CSAILVision/NetDissect-Lite
```

This library is also added to the repository associated with this book as a Git submodule. If you have cloned this book's repository from GitHub, then you can pull the submodule by running the following command from the local directory where you have cloned the repository:

```
git submodule update --init -recursive
```

Once you have cloned the NetDissect-Lite repository, change into that directory locally. Then, run the following command to download the Broden dataset. The Broden dataset requires more than 1 GB of storage. Please take note of the path where this dataset is downloaded because we will need it later:

```
$>./script/dlbroden.sh
```

You can also download the ResNet-18 model pretrained on the Places dataset by running the following command from the NetDissect-Lite directory. Again, please note the path where the model is downloaded because we will need it later:

```
$>./script/dlzoo_example.sh
```

6.4.1 *Running network dissection*

In this section, we will learn how to use the NetDissect-Lite library to probe the ResNet-18 models pretrained on the ImageNet and Places datasets by using labeled concepts from the Broden dataset. We can configure the library using the settings.py file at the root of the NetDissect-Lite library. We will not be covering all the settings because for most of them, we will be using the default values provided by the library. We will, therefore, focus on the key settings, which are summarized in table 6.1.

Table 6.1 Settings for the NetDissect-Lite library

Setting	Descriptio	Possible Values
GPU	This is a Boolean setting that can be used to load the model and run network dissection on a GPU.	Possible values are `True` and `False`. If set to `True`, the GPU is used.
MODEL	This is a String setting that sets the model architecture for the pre-trained model.	Possible values are `resnet18`, `alexnet`, `resnet50`, `densenet161`, etc. In this section, we will be setting the value to `resnet18`.
DATASET	This is a string setting that lets the library know which dataset was used to train the CNN model.	Possible values are `imagenet` and `places365`. In this section, we will be using both values to compare the interpretability of the layers and units.
CATEGORIES	This setting is a list of strings that defines the high-level categories in the labeled concepts dataset.	For the Broden dataset, the list can contain the following values: `object`, `part`, `scene`, `material`, `texture`, and `color`. In this section, we will drop the `material` concept and look at the other five categories.
OUTPUT_FOLDER	This is a string setting that provides the path to the labeled concepts dataset to the library.	The default value for this setting is the path where the `./script/dlbroden.sh` script downloads the Broden dataset.
FEATURE_NAMES	This setting is a list of strings that lets the library know which feature-learning layers in the CNN to probe.	For the Resnet18 model, the list can contain the following values: `layer1`, `layer2`, `layer3`, and/or `layer4`. In this chapter, we will be using all four values to compare the interpretability of the units across all four feature-learning layers.

Table 6.1   Settings for the NetDissect-Lite library *(continued)*

Setting	Descriptio	Possible Values
`MODEL_FILE`	This string setting is used to provide the library with the path to the pre-trained model.	For the Resnet18 model pre-trained on the Places dataset, set the value of this setting to the path where the `script/dlzoo_example.sh` script downloaded the model. For models pre-trained on the ImageNet dataset, set the value to `None`. This will let the library know to load the model from the `torchvision` package.
`MODEL_PARALLEL`	This is a Boolean setting that is used to let the library know if the model was trained in multi-GPU.	Possible values are `True` and `False`.

Before running the network dissection framework, ensure that the settings.py file is updated with the right settings. To probe all the feature-learning layers in the ResNet-18 model pretrained on the ImageNet dataset, we set the key settings in the settings.py file to the following values:

```
GPU = False
MODEL = 'resnet18'
DATASET = 'imagenet'
QUANTILE = 0.005
SCORE_THRESHOLD = 0.04
TOPN = 10
CATAGORIES = ["object", "part","scene","texture","color"]
OUTPUT_FOLDER = "result/pytorch_" + MODEL + "_" + DATASET
DATA_DIRECTORY = '/data/dataset/broden1_227'
IMG_SIZE = 227
NUM_CLASSES = 1000
FEATURE_NAMES = ['layer2', 'layer3', 'layer4']
MODEL_FILE = None
MODEL_PARALLEL = False
```

Ensure that the `DATA_DIRECTORY` setting is set to the path where the Broden dataset is downloaded. Also, if you would like to use the GPU for faster processing, set the `GPU` setting to `True`. As mentioned earlier, the library provides a few subsettings. These are not explicitly set in the previous code, and you can use the default values for them.

To probe all the feature-learning layers in the ResNet-18 model pretrained on the Places dataset, we update just the following settings. The rest of the settings are the same as those for the ImageNet dataset. Ensure that the `MODEL_FILE` setting is set to the path where the ResNet-18 model pretrained on Places is downloaded:

```
DATASET = 'places365'
NUM_CLASSES = 365
MODEL_FILE = '/models/zoo/resnet18_places365.pth.tar'
MODEL_PARALLEL = True
```

Once we have set the values for the settings, we are now ready to initialize and run the framework. Run the following lines of code to probe the network and to extract the activation maps from the feature-learning layers:

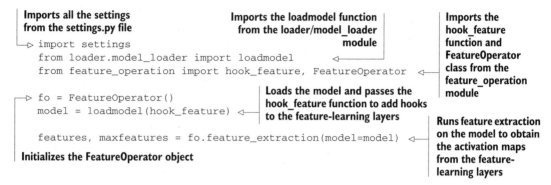

The `loadmodel` function loads the model based on the MODEL setting. The models are loaded the same way as we saw in section 6.2. The function also adds hooks to each of the feature-learning layers based on the FEATURE_NAMES setting. These hooks are used by the `FeatureOperator` object to extract the activation maps from those layers. The `FeatureOperator` class is the main class that implements steps 2 and 3 in the network dissection framework. In the previous code snippet, we are running a part of step 2 that extracts the low-resolution activation maps from the feature-learning layers using the `feature_extraction` function. This function loads the images from the Broden dataset, forward-propagates them through the model, extracts the activation maps using the hooks, and then saves them in a file called feature_size.npy. The file is saved in the OUTPUT_FOLDER path as set in settings.py. The function `feature_extraction` also returns two variables: `features` and `maxfeatures`. The `features` variable contains the activation maps for all the feature-learning layers and input images. The `maxfeatures` variable stores the maximum value activation for each image, which we will use later when generating the summary results.

Once we have extracted the low-resolution activation maps, we can run the following lines of code to calculate the threshold T_k (the 0.005 quantile level) for all the units in the feature-learning layers, up-sample the low resolution activation maps and generate the binary unit segmentation maps, calculate the IoU scores, and finally generate a summary of the results:

Imports the **generate_html_summary** function from the visualize/report module

```
from visualize.report import generate_html_summary

for layer_id, layer in enumerate(settings.FEATURE_NAMES):
    # Calculate the thresholds T_k
    thresholds = fo.quantile_threshold(features[layer_id],
        savepath=f"quantile_{layer}.npy")

    # Up-sample and calculate the IoU scores
```

Iterates through each of the feature-learning layers

Calculates the 0.005 quantile level for all units in the feature-learning layers

```
tally_result = fo.tally(features[layer_id],thresholds,
    savepath=f"tally_{layer}.csv")

# Generate a summary of the results
generate_html_summary(fo.data, layer,
                tally_result=tally_result,
                maxfeature=maxfeatures[layer_id],
                features=features[layer_id],
                thresholds=thresholds)
```

Calculates the IoU scores after up-sampling and generating the binary unit segmentation maps

Generates a summary of the results in HTML form

In this code snippet, we are iterating through each of the feature-learning layers in FEATURE_NAMES and executing the following:

- Using the quantile_threshold function in the FeatureOperator class, calculate the 0.005 quantile level (T_k) for all the units in each feature-learning layer. These quantile levels, or thresholds, are saved in a file (called quantile_{layer}.csv) for each layer in the OUTPUT_FOLDER path. The function also returns the thresholds as a NumPy array.
- Using the tally function in the FeatureOperator class, up-sample the low-resolution activation map for each feature-learning layer into the same resolution as the input image. The tally function also generates binary unit segmentation maps based on the up-sampled activation maps and thresholds calculated for each of the units. The function finally calculates the IoU scores and measures the alignment of the binary unit segmentation maps with the segmented concepts in the Broden dataset. The aggregated IoU scores for each of the high-level concepts are saved in a file (called tally_{layer}.csv) for each layer in the OUTPUT_FOLDER path. These results are also returned as a dictionary object.
- Finally, use the generate_html_summary function to create a summary of the results in HTML form.

In the following section, we will explore the results summary generated by the library and visualize the concepts learned by the units in the feature-learning layers.

Running network dissection on a custom dataset

It is important to understand the structure of the Broden dataset folder so that we can mimic that for our custom dataset and concepts. The folder at a high level consists of the following files and folder:

- *images* (folder)—Contains all the images in either JPEG or PNG format. The folder should contain the original images in {filename}.jpg format and the segmented images for each of the concepts in {filename}_{concept}.jpg format.
- *index.csv*—Contains a list of all the images in the dataset with details on the labeled concepts. The first column is image filename with the relative path to the image. This is then followed by columns that contain information on the image height and width and the segmentation height and width dimensions. This is then followed by a column for each concept containing the relative path to the segmented image for that concept.

- *category.csv*—Lists all the concept categories followed by some summary statistics on the concepts. The first column is the concept name, followed by a count of the number of labels that belong to that concept category and also the frequency of the number of images with that labeled concept.
- *label.csv*—Lists all the labels and the corresponding concept that each belongs to, followed by some summary statistics on the labels. The first column is a label number (or identifier), followed by the label name and the category that it belongs to. Summary statistics include the frequency of the number of images with that label, pixel portions or the coverage of images with that label, and the total number of images with that label.
- *c_{concept}.csv*—One file per concept category that contains all the labels, frequency of images, and coverage details.

The new dataset that you create with your own labeled concepts should follow the same structure as the Broden dataset to ensure compatibility with the network dissection framework. Once you have structured your dataset as detailed earlier, you can then update the following settings in settings.py:

- `DATA_DIRECTORY`—Points to the directory where your custom dataset is stored.
- `CATEGORIES`—Lists all the concept categories in your custom dataset, that is, in the category.csv file.
- `IMG_SIZE`—The dimension of the image in the images folder. The dimension should match the dimension in the index.csv file.

These settings will ensure that the new custom concepts dataset is loaded by the library. If you have your own pretrained model on a dataset that is different from Image-Net or Places, you will also need to update the following settings:

- `DATASET`—Set to the name of the dataset that the models have been trained on.
- `NUM_CLASSES`—Set to the number of classes or labels that the model could output.
- `FEATURE_NAMES`—Lists the feature layer names in your custom pretrained model.
- `MODEL_FILE`—Contains the full path to your pretrained model in PyTorch.
- `MODEL_PARALLEL`—If your custom model was trained in multi-GPU, this setting must be `True`.

6.4.2 *Concept detectors*

We will now analyze the results after running the network dissection framework. We will first focus on the final convolutional layer (i.e., layer 4) in the ResNet-18 model and look at the number of unique concept detectors in that layer. The number of unique detectors is a measure of the interpretability of the network and measures the number of unique concepts learned by the units in that feature-learning layer. The higher the number of unique detectors, the more diverse the trained network is in detecting human-understandable concepts.

Let's first look at the structure of the output of the results folder for the network dissection framework. The OUTPUT_FOLDER setting gives you the path to the results folder. We saw in the previous section the relevant files that are saved in that folder. Let's now process tally_layer4.csv to compute the number of unique detectors in layer 4 of the ResNet-18 model and the proportion of the units covered by those unique detectors. The following function can be used to compute the relevant statistics. The function takes in the following keyword arguments:

- network_names—A list of the models for which we need to compute the number of unique detectors. We are focusing only on the ResNet-18 model in this chapter, so this keyword argument is a list containing only one element—resnet18.
- datasets—This argument is a list of the datasets that the models are pretrained on. In this chapter, we are focusing on imagenet and places365.
- results_dir—The parent directory where the results for each of the pretrained models are stored.
- categories—A list of all the concept categories for which we need to count the number of unique detectors.
- iou_thres—The threshold for the IoU score for which we consider a unit as a detector for a concept. As we saw in section 6.3.3, the default value for this threshold is 0.04.
- layer—The feature-learning layer that we are interested in. In this case, we are focusing on the final layer, which is layer 4.

```
import os
import pandas as pd
from collections import OrderedDict

def compute_unique_detectors(**kwargs):
    network_names = kwargs.get("network_names",
                               ["resnet18"])
    datasets = kwargs.get("datasets",
                          ["imagenet", "places365"])
    results_dir = kwargs.get("results_dir", "result")
    categories = kwargs.get("categories",
                            ["object",
                             "scene",
                             "part",
                             "texture",
                             "color"])
    iou_thres = kwargs.get("iou_thres",
                           0.04)
    layer = kwargs.get("layer", "layer4")

    ud_data = []
    for network_name in network_names:
        for dataset in datasets:
            result_file = os.path.join(results_dir,
                f"pytorch_{network_name}_{dataset}/tally_{layer}.csv")
            df_result = pd.read_csv(result_file)
```

Imports the relevant modules for the function

The network_names keyword argument is the list of the models for which we need to compute the number of unique detectors

Function that computes the number of unique detectors. It takes a set of keyword arguments.

Points to the parent directory where the network dissection framework saves the results for each of the models

A list of the datasets that the models are pretrained on

A list of all the concept categories of interest

The IoU threshold to measure if a unit is a concept detector; set to 0.04 by default

Iterates through each network or model

The layer argument is set to the final layer in the ResNet-18 model by default.

Initializes an empty list to store the results of the number of unique detectors

Iterates through each dataset that the model is pretrained on

Loads the tally_{layer}.csv file as a Pandas DataFrame

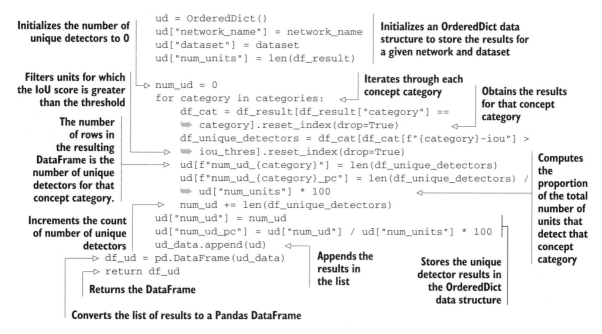

We can obtain the number of unique detectors for the final layer of the ResNet-18 model pretrained on ImageNet and Places by running the following line of code. Note that no keyword arguments are provided to the function because the default values for the arguments will compute the stats for the ResNet-18 model pretrained on ImageNet and Places for the final feature-learning layer:

```
df_ud = compute_unique_detectors()
```

If we wanted to compute the statistics for, say, the third feature-learning layer, we could call the function as follows:

```
df_ud = compute_unique_detectors(layer="layer3")
```

Once we have obtained the number of unique detectors as a Pandas DataFrame, we use the following function to plot the results:

```
def plot_unique_detectors(df_ud, **kwargs):
    categories = kwargs.get("categories",
                            ["object",
                             "scene",
                             "part",
                             "texture",
                             "color"])
    num_ud_cols = [f"num_ud_{c}" for c in categories]
    num_ud_pc_cols = [f"num_ud_{c}_pc" for c in categories]
```

Dictionary to rename the column names to the capitalized concept category names

```
num_ud_col_rename = {}
num_ud_pc_col_rename = {}
for c in categories:
    num_ud_col_rename[f"num_ud_{c}"] = c.capitalize()
    num_ud_pc_col_rename[f"num_ud_{c}_pc"] = c.capitalize()
```

Indexes the DataFrame by the network name and dataset

```
df_ud["network_dataset"] = df_ud.apply(lambda x: x["network_name"] + "_"
    + x["dataset"], axis=1)
df_ud_num = df_ud.set_index("network_dataset")[num_ud_cols]
df_ud_num_pc = df_ud.set_index("network_dataset")[num_ud_pc_cols]

df_ud_num = df_ud_num.rename(columns=num_ud_col_rename)
df_ud_num_pc = df_ud_num_pc.rename(columns=num_ud_pc_col_rename)
```

Renames the column names to the capitalized concept category names

Creates a Matplotlib figure with two subplot rows

```
f, ax = plt.subplots(2, 1, figsize=(8, 10))
df_ud_num.plot(kind='bar', stacked=True, ax=ax[0])
ax[0].legend(loc='center left', bbox_to_anchor=(1, 0.5))
ax[0].set_ylabel("Number of Unique Detectors")
ax[0].set_xlabel("")
ax[0].set_xticklabels(ax[0].get_xticklabels(), rotation=0)
df_ud_num_pc.plot(kind='bar', stacked=True, ax=ax[1])
ax[1].get_legend().remove()
ax[1].set_ylabel("Proportion of Unique Detectors (%)")
ax[1].set_xlabel("")
ax[1].set_xticklabels(ax[1].get_xticklabels(), rotation=0)
```

On the first subplot, visualizes the number of unique detectors as a stacked bar plot

Returns the Matplotlib figure and axis

```
return f, ax
```

On the second subplot, visualizes the proportion of unique detectors as a stacked bar plot

Plot the number of unique detectors and proportions as follows. The resulting figure is shown in figure 6.11:

```
f, ax = plot_unique_detectors(df_ud)
```

The top row in figure 6.11 shows the absolute number of unique detectors in the final feature-learning layer for the two ResNet-18 models pretrained on the ImageNet and the Places datasets. The bottom row shows the count as a proportion of the total number of units in the final layer. The total number of units in the final feature-learning layer in ResNet-18 is 512. We can see that the ImageNet model has 302 unique detectors, and this accounts for roughly 59% of the total units. The Places model, on the other hand, has 435 unique detectors, and this accounts for roughly 85% of the total units. Overall, it looks like the model trained on the Places dataset has a much more diverse set of concept detectors than ImageNet. Places are typically composed of multiple scenes. This is why we see a lot more scene detectors emerging in the model trained on the Places dataset than on the ImageNet dataset. The ImageNet dataset consists of a lot more objects. This is why we see a lot more object detectors emerging on the ImageNet model. We can also observe a lot more high-level concepts like objects and scenes emerging in the final feature-learning layer than low-level concepts like colors, textures, and parts.

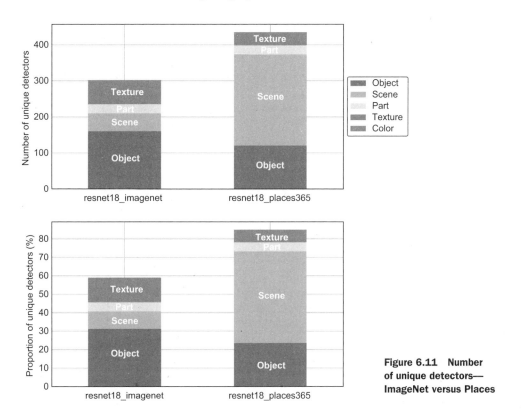

Figure 6.11 Number of unique detectors— ImageNet versus Places

Let's now extend the `compute_unique_detectors` function to compute unique detectors for all the feature-learning layers in the ResNet-18 model. This is so that we can observe what concepts are learned by all the layers in the network. As an exercise, I encourage you to update the function and use a `layers` keyword argument that represents a list of feature-learning layers. Also add a nested `for` loop to iterate through all the layers to compute the number of unique detectors for each layer. The solution to this exercise can be found in the GitHub repository associated with this book at http://mng.bz/KBdZ.

Once you have obtained the DataFrame with the number of unique detectors for all the layers, you can use the following helper function to plot the statistics as a line graph:

Plots the proportion of unique detectors for all the layers in the network

Plots the proportion of unique detectors for all the layers in a network pretrained on a given dataset

Extracts the statistics for all the concept categories

```
def plot_ud_layers(df_ud_layer):
    def plot_ud_layers_dataset(df_ud_layer_dataset, ax):
        object_uds = df_ud_layer_dataset["num_ud_object_pc"].values
        scene_uds = df_ud_layer_dataset["num_ud_scene_pc"].values
        part_uds = df_ud_layer_dataset["num_ud_part_pc"].values
        texture_uds = df_ud_layer_dataset["num_ud_texture_pc"].values
        color_uds = df_ud_layer_dataset["num_ud_color_pc"].values
```

Displays the legend

Labels the x-ticks for all the layers in the network

Filters rows from the source DataFrame for the network pretrained on the Places dataset

Creates a Matplotlib figure with two subplot rows

Plots the statistics as a line chart

Labels the y-axis

Filters rows from the source DataFrame for the network pretrained on the ImageNet dataset

Plots the statistics for all the layers in the first subplot row for the ImageNet dataset

Plots the statistics for all the layers in the second subplot row for the Places dataset

Returns the figure and axis

```
ax.plot(object_uds, '^-', label="object")
ax.plot(scene_uds, 's-', label="scene")
ax.plot(part_uds, 'o-', label="part")
ax.plot(texture_uds, '*-', label="texture")
ax.plot(color_uds, 'v-', label="color")
ax.legend()
ax.set_xticks([0, 1, 2, 3])
ax.set_xticklabels(["Layer 1", "Layer 2", "Layer 3", "Layer 4"])
ax.set_ylabel("Proportion of Unique Detectors (%)")
df_ud_layer_r18_p365 = df_ud_layer[(df_ud_layer["network_name"] ==
    "resnet18") &
                                    (df_ud_layer["dataset"] ==
    "places365")].reset_index(drop=True)
df_ud_layer_r18_imgnet = df_ud_layer[(df_ud_layer["network_name"] ==
    "resnet18") &
                                    (df_ud_layer["dataset"] ==
    "imagenet")].reset_index(drop=True)
f, ax = plt.subplots(2, 1, figsize=(8, 10))
plot_ud_layers_dataset(df_ud_layer_r18_imgnet, ax[0])
ax[0].set_title("resnet18_imagenet")
plot_ud_layers_dataset(df_ud_layer_r18_p365, ax[1])
ax[1].set_title("resnet18_places365")

return f, ax
```

We can obtain the plot in figure 6.12 by running the following line of code:

```
f, ax = plot_ud_layers(df_ud_layer)
```

The top row in figure 6.12 shows the proportion of unique detectors across all the layers in the ResNet-18 model pretrained on the ImageNet dataset. The bottom row shows the same statistics for the model trained on the Places dataset. We can see that for both models, low-level concept categories like colors and textures emerge in the lower feature-learning layers, and high-level concept categories like parts, objects, and scenes emerge in the higher or deeper layers. This means that more high-level concepts are learned at the deeper layers. We can see that the representational ability of the network increases with the layer depth. Deeper layers have more capacity to learn complex visual concepts like objects and scenes. In the following section, we will dissect the network further by looking at specific labels and concepts that are learned by each of the units in the network.

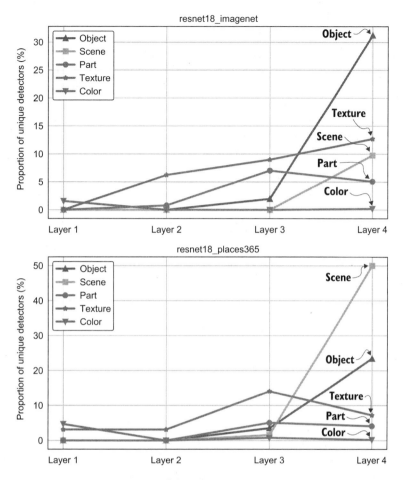

Figure 6.12   Number of unique detectors by layers—ImageNet versus Places

6.4.3   *Concept detectors by training task*

In the previous section, we visualized the number of unique detectors for all the high-level concept categories. Let's now dig deeper and visualize the number of unique detectors for each concept or label in the Broden dataset. We will focus on the final feature-learning layers and three top-ranked concept categories in terms of the number of unique detectors: textures, objects, and scenes.

We will need to extend the `compute_unique_detectors` function developed in section 6.4.2 to compute the statistics per concept or label. As an exercise, I highly encourage you to do this because it will give you a better understanding of the format of the tally_{layer}.csv file generated by the NetDissect-Lite library. You can pass in a new keyword argument that lets the function know whether to aggregate by concept category or by concept or label. For aggregating by concept or label, you will need to group by both `category` and `label` and count the number of units for which the category IoU score is greater than the threshold. The solution to this exercise can be found in the GitHub repository associated with this book. Invoke the new function and store the result in a DataFrame called `df_cat_label_ud`.

We will first look at the texture concept category. Extract the DataFrames for the texture concept category using the following code snippet:

Extracts the statistics for the ResNet-18 model pretrained on ImageNet and sorts the IoU scores in descending order

```
df_r18_imgnet_texture = df_cat_label_ud[(df_cat_label_ud["network_name"] ==
    "resnet18") &
                            (df_cat_label_ud["dataset"] == "imagenet") &
                            (df_cat_label_ud["category"] == "texture")].\
            sort_values(by="unit", ascending=False).reset_index(drop=True)

df_r18_p365_texture = df_cat_label_ud[(df_cat_label_ud["network_name"] ==
    "resnet18") &
                            (df_cat_label_ud["dataset"] == "places365") &
                            (df_cat_label_ud["category"] == "texture")].\
            sort_values(by="unit", ascending=False).reset_index(drop=True)
```

Extracts the statistics for the ResNet-18 model pretrained on Places and sorts the IoU scores in descending order

You can now visualize the number of unique detectors for the various texture concepts using the following code. The resulting figure is shown in figure 6.13:

```
import seaborn as sns        # Imports the Seaborn library

f, ax = plt.subplots(1, 2, figsize=(16, 10))    # Creates a Matplotlib figure with two subplot columns
sns.barplot(x="unit", y="label", data=df_r18_imgnet_object,
    ax=ax[0])
ax[0].set_title(f"resnet18_imagenet : {len(df_r18_
    imgnet_object)} objects")
ax[0].set_xlabel("Number of Unique Detectors")
ax[0].set_ylabel("")
sns.barplot(x="unit", y="label", data=df_r18_
    p365_object, ax=ax[1])
ax[1].set_title(f"resnet18_places365 : {len
    (df_r18_p365_object)} objects")
ax[1].set_xlabel("Number of Unique Detectors")
ax[1].set_ylabel("");
```

Plots the number of unique detectors for all the texture concepts learned by the ImageNet model

Plots the number of unique detectors for all the texture concepts learned by the Places model

In the previous section (see figure 6.11), we observed that the ImageNet model has more unique detectors in the final layer for the texture concept category than the model trained on the Places dataset. But how diverse are the concepts learned by the units in this layer? Figure 6.13 aims to answer this. We can see that the ImageNet model covers 27 texture concepts, whereas the Places model covers 21. The top three textures for the ImageNet model account for 19 unique detectors. They are striped, waffled, and spiraled. The top three textures for the Places model, on the other hand, account for 10 unique detectors. They are interlaced, checkered, and stratified. Although the number of textures learned by the units in the final layer are less for the Places model, we see a higher proportion of unique detectors for this model in the lower feature-learning layers (as seen in figure 6.12).

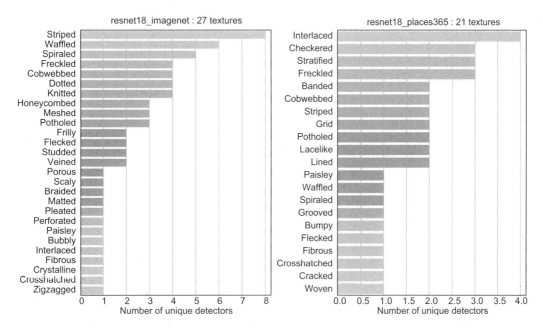

Figure 6.13   Number of unique texture detectors—ImageNet versus Places

Let's now visualize the number of unique detectors for various object and scene concepts. As an exercise, extend the code written for the textures concept category to objects and scenes. The resulting figure for the object concept category is shown in figure 6.14. Because the model trained on the Places dataset detects a lot more scenes in the final layer, the visualization for the scene concept category has been split into two separate figures. Figure 6.15 shows the number of scene detectors for the ImageNet model, and figure 6.16 shows the number of scene detectors for the Places model.

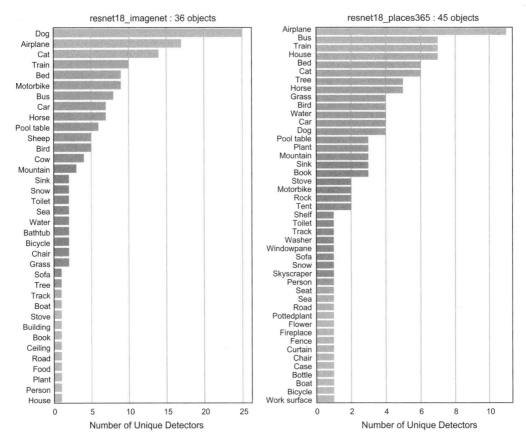

Figure 6.14   Number of unique object detectors—ImageNet versus Places

Let's first look at figure 6.14. In the previous section, we observed that the ImageNet model has a higher proportion of unique detectors for the high-level objects category because the ImageNet dataset has a lot more objects in it. If we look at how diverse the concepts learned are, however, we can see that many more objects emerge in the model trained on the Places dataset. The Places model detects 45 objects as opposed to the 36 objects detected by the ImageNet model in the final feature-learning layer. The top object detected by the ImageNet model is dog, which accounts for 25 unique detectors—a high proportion of labeled images of dogs are present in the ImageNet dataset. The top object detected by the Places model is airplane, which accounts for 11 unique detectors.

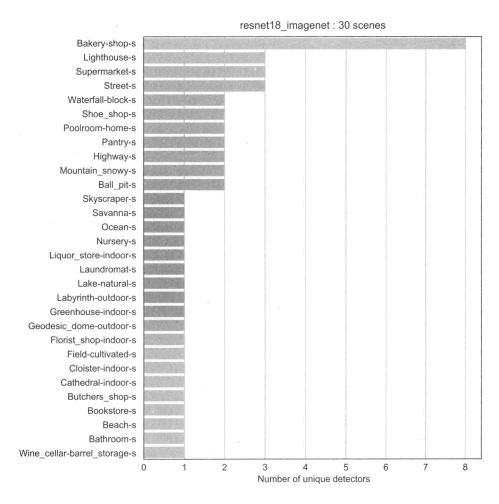

Figure 6.15   Number of unique scene detectors—ImageNet dataset

If we now compare figures 6.15 and 6.16, we can see that the model trained on the Places dataset is able to identify a much more diverse set of scenes than the ImageNet model (119 versus 30). This is expected because the Places dataset contains a lot of labeled places, which are typically made up of a lot of scenes. Note that in figure 6.16, although the model trained on the Places dataset is able to identify 119 scenes in total, the figure is only showing the top 40 scenes to make it easier to read the figure.

By going deeper and visualizing the number of unique detectors for each concept, we can ensure that the dataset used to train the model is diverse enough and has good coverage of the concepts of interest. We can also use these visualizations to understand what concepts the units are focusing on in each layer of the neural network.

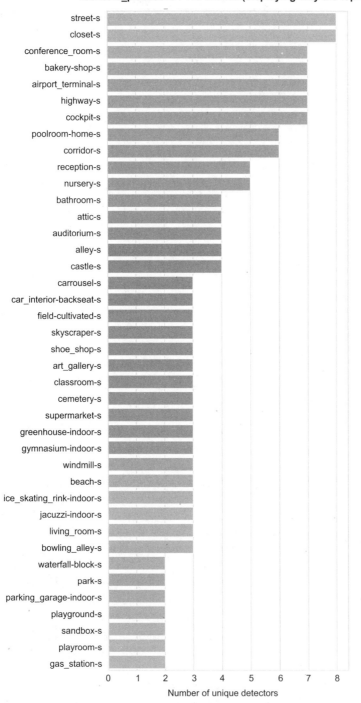

resnet18_places365 : 119 scenes (displaying only the top 40)

Figure 6.16   Number of unique scene detectors—Places dataset

Transfer learning

Transfer learning is a technique whereby a model trained for a particular task is used as a starting point for another task. For example, let's say we have a model trained on the ImageNet dataset that is great at detecting objects. We would like to use this model as a starting point to detect places and scenes. To do this, we can load the weights of the ImageNet model and use those weights as a starting point before training and fine-tuning them to the Places dataset. The general idea behind transfer learning is that features learned in one domain can be reused in another domain, provided there is some overlap between the two domains. When a pretrained network in one domain is trained for a task in another domain, the training time is typically faster and yields more accurate results.

The authors of the network dissection framework analyzed how the interpretability of units evolves during transfer learning in their paper, available at https://arxiv.org/pdf/1711.05611.pdf. They used the AlexNet model pretrained on the ImageNet dataset and fine-tuned it to the Places dataset. The authors observed that the number of unique detectors increased for the model pretrained on ImageNet but fine-tuned to Places. Units that detected dogs initially evolved to other objects and scenes like horse, cow, and waterfall. A lot of the places in the Places dataset contain those animals and scenes. If the model pretrained on Places is fine-tuned to the ImageNet dataset, the authors observed a drop in the number of unique detectors. For the Places-to-ImageNet network, a lot of the units evolve to dog detectors because the proportion of labeled data for dogs is much higher in ImageNet.

6.4.4 Visualizing concept detectors

In the previous sections, we quantified the interpretability of the units in each feature-learning layer in the CNN by looking at the number of unique detectors for each concept category and individual concepts. In this section, we will visualize the binary unit segmentation maps generated for each of the units in the feature-learning layers by the NetDissect library. The library will overlay the binary unit segmentation maps on the original images and generate JPG files for us. This is useful if we want to visualize the specific pixels in the original image that the unit is focusing on for a given concept.

Due to lack of space, we cannot visualize all the images generated for all the units and models. We will, therefore, focus on the model pretrained on the Places dataset, as well as specific units with the maximally activated images for certain concepts. The following function can be used to obtain the binary segmented images generated by the library:

Imports the mpimg module provided by Matplotlib to load and display images

Gets the binary unit segmentation map overlayed on the image and the associated stats for a given unit

Obtains the network name, dataset, results directory, feature-learning layer, and unit of interest

```
import matplotlib.image as mpimg

def get_image_and_stats(**kwargs):
    network_name = kwargs.get("network_name",
                             "resnet18")
    dataset = kwargs.get("dataset",
                         "places365")
```

```
                    results_dir = kwargs.get("results_dir", "result")     Obtains the network name,
                    layer = kwargs.get("layer", "layer4")                  dataset, results directory, feature-
                    unit = kwargs.get("unit", "0000")                      learning layer, and unit of interest

                    result_file = os.path.join(results_dir,                          Loads the tally
                                                                                     results file as a
                       f"pytorch_{network_name}_{dataset}/tally_{layer}.csv")        Pandas DataFrame
                    df_result = pd.read_csv(result_file)

                    image_dir = os.path.join(results_dir,
                                          f"pytorch_{network_name}_{dataset}/html/image")
                    image_file = os.path.join(image_dir,                   Loads the binary unit
                                          f"{layer}-{unit}.jpg")           segmented map overlaid
                    img = mpimg.imread(image_file)                         on the original image

                    df_unit_stats = df_result[df_result["unit"] == int(unit)+1]
                    stats = None
                    if len(df_unit_stats) > 0:
                        stats = {
                            "category": df_unit_stats["category"].tolist()[0],
                            "label": df_unit_stats["label"].tolist()[0],
                            "iou": df_unit_stats["score"].tolist()[0]
                        } #H
                    return img, stats
```

Filters the DataFrame to obtain statistics for the layer and unit of interest

Initializes the stats variable to None

If there are results for the layer and unit of interest, extracts the category, label, and IoU from the DataFrame and stores them in dict

Returns the image and associated statistics for the layer and unit of interest

We will now focus on units 247 and 39, which detect the airplane object. We saw in the previous section (see figure 6.14) that the airplane object has the most unique detectors among all the objects in the Places model. The units are zero-indexed and are saved as four-digit strings by the NetDissect library. We, therefore, need to pass the strings "0246" and "0038" for units 247 and 39, respectively, as the unit keyword argument in the get_image_and_stats function. The following code snippet will obtain the image and associated statistics and visualize them in Matplotlib. The resulting plot is shown in figure 6.17:

Extracts the image and statistics for unit 39

Extracts the image and statistics for unit 247

Creates a Matplotlib figure with two subplot rows

Displays the image for unit 247 on the top row and displays the stats in the title

```
img_247, stats_247 = get_image_and_stats(unit="0246")
img_39, stats_39 = get_image_and_stats(unit="0038")
f, ax = plt.subplots(2, 1, figsize=(15, 4))
ax[0].imshow(img_247, interpolation='nearest')
ax[0].grid(False)
ax[0].axis(False)
ax[0].set_title(f"Unit: 247, Label: {stats_247['label']}, Category:
  {stats_247['category']}, IoU: {stats_247['iou']:.2f}",
            fontsize=16)
ax[1].imshow(img_39, interpolation='nearest')
ax[1].grid(False)
ax[1].axis(False)
ax[1].set_title(f"Unit: 39, Label: {stats_39['label']}, Category:
  {stats_39['category']}, IoU: {stats_39['iou']:.2f}",
            fontsize=16);
```

Displays the image for unit 39 on the bottom row and displays the stats in the title

Unit: 247, Label: airplane, Category: object, IoU: 0.19

Unit: 39, Label: airplane, Category: object, IoU: 0.06

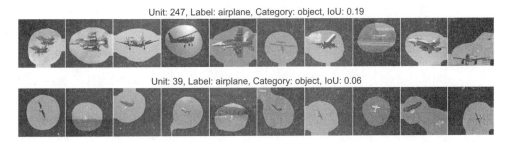

Figure 6.17   Visualization of object concept detector—airplane

The top row in figure 6.17 shows the segmentation generated for the 10 maximally activated Broden images for unit 247. The average IoU is 0.19. Because the binary unit segmentation map is overlaid on the original image, the pixels that are activated are those where $S_i >= T_k$. The pixels that are not activated are shown as black. From the images, we can see that the unit is focusing on airplanes and not on any other random object. The bottom row in figure 6.17 shows the segmentation generated for the 10 maximally activated Broden images for unit 39. The average IoU is 0.06 and is lower in this case. From the images, we can see that the unit activated on airplanes as well as on general concepts like birds, flight, sky, and the color blue.

Figure 6.18 shows the binary segmented images generated for three objects, namely, train (top row), bus (middle row), and track (bottom row). The specific units are 168, 386, and 218, respectively. For the train concept detector, we can see the activated pixels highlighting engines and railway tracks. The average IoU is high in this case, at 0.27. For the bus concept detector, the activated pixels seem to highlight buses and general concepts like any vehicle with large windows and a relatively flat front. The average IoU in this case is 0.24. The track concept detector is interesting. The activated pixels seem to highlight images with two parallel tracks, which include railway tracks, bowling alley lanes, and a sushi conveyor belt. The average IoU is 0.06.

Unit: 168, Label: train, Category: object, IoU: 0.27

Unit: 386, Label: bus, Category: object, IoU: 0.24

Unit: 218, Label: track, Category: object, IoU: 0.06

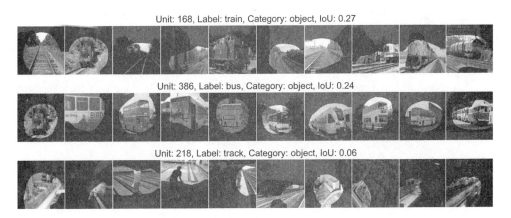

Figure 6.18   Visualization of object concept detector—train, bus, and track

Finally, figure 6.19 shows the segmented images for scenes that are not directly represented in the training set. We are specifically focusing on units 379 and 370, which highlight the highway and nursery scenes, respectively. The top row shows the highway scene, and the bottom row shows the nursery scene. We can see that the model trained on the Places dataset is learning these high-level scene concepts really well.

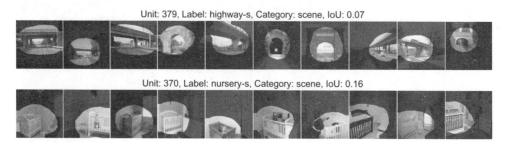

Figure 6.19   Visualization of scene concept detector—highway and nursery

6.4.5   *Limitations of network dissection*

The network dissection framework is a great tool that helps us open up black-box neural networks. It overcomes the limitations of visual attribution methods by coming up with quantifiable interpretations. We can see how a CNN decomposes the task of identifying an image by visualizing the features or concepts learned by each of the units in the feature-learning layers. The network dissection framework, however, has the following limitations, as highlighted in the original paper by the authors of the framework:

- The framework requires a labeled dataset of concepts at the pixel level. This is the most crucial step in the framework and can be quite time-consuming and costly. Moreover, concepts that are not expressed in the dataset will not show up when interpreting the units, even if the network has learned them.
- The framework cannot identify groups of units that jointly represent one concept.
- The interpretability of units is quantified by the "number of unique detectors" metric. This metric favors larger and deeper networks that have the capacity to learn more high-level concepts.

Dissecting neural network is an active area of research, and the research community is exploring many promising avenues, such as automatic identification of concepts and using concept scores to identify adversarial attacks on neural networks.

Summary

- The visual attribution methods we learned in the previous chapter have some limitations. They are typically assessed qualitatively and are quite subjective. These techniques do not give us any information on the low-level and high-level concepts or features that are learned by the feature-learning layers and units in a convolutional neural network (CNN).

- The network dissection framework discussed in this chapter overcomes the limitations of visual attribution methods by coming up with more quantitative interpretations. By using the framework, we will also be able to understand what human-understandable concepts are learned by the feature-learning layers in the CNN.

- The framework consists of three key steps: concept definition, network probing, and alignment measurement. The concept definition step is the most crucial step because it requires us to collect a labeled dataset of concepts at the pixel level. The network probing step is about finding units in the network that respond to those predefined concepts. Finally, the alignment measurement step quantifies how well the unit activation aligns with those concepts.

- We learned how to run the network dissection framework using the NetDissect library on PyTorch models trained on the ImageNet and Places datasets. We used the Broden dataset for the concepts.

- We learned how to quantify the interpretability of the units by using the "number of unique detectors" metric and visualized the interpretability of units for various concept categories and individual concepts.

- We also learned how to visualize the binary unit segmented images generated by the library to see what pixels a unit is focusing on for a particular concept.

- The network dissection framework is a great tool that helps us open up black-box neural networks. It suffers from a few limitations, however. Creating a labeled dataset of concepts can be quite time-consuming and costly. The framework cannot identify groups of units that jointly represent one concept. The "number of unique detectors" metric favors larger and deeper networks, which have the capacity to learn more high-level concepts.

Understanding
semantic similarity

7

This chapter covers

- Learning dense word representations that capture semantic meaning

- Visualizing semantic similarity of high-dimensional word embeddings using dimensionality-reduction techniques like PCA and t-SNE

- Strengths and weaknesses of PCA and t-SNE

- Validating visualizations generated by PCA and t-SNE qualitatively and quantitatively

In the previous chapter, we switched our focus from interpreting the complex processing and operations that happen within a black-box model to interpreting the representations or features learned by the model. We specifically looked at the network dissection framework to understand what concepts are learned by the feature-learning layers in a convolutional neural network (CNN). The framework consisted of three key steps: concept definition, network probing, and alignment measurement. The concept definition step is all about data collection, specifically collecting a labeled dataset of concepts at the pixel level. This is the most time-consuming and crucial step. The next step is to probe the network and determine what units in the CNN respond to those predefined concepts. The final step involves quantifying how well the units' responses align with the concepts. The framework overcame the limitations of visual attribution methods by coming up with quantitative interpretations in the form of human-understandable concepts.

In this chapter, we will continue with the topic of interpreting representations learned by deep neural networks but will switch our focus to natural language processing (NLP). NLP is a subfield in machine learning that deals with natural language. So far, we have been dealing with inputs in the form of images or in tabular form with numeric features. In NLP, we will deal with inputs in the form of text. We will specifically focus on how to represent text in a dense and semantically meaningful form and how to interpret words that are similar in meaning—that is, those that have semantic similarity—learned by those representations.

We will first introduce a concrete example of analyzing sentiment in movie reviews. We will then learn about neural word embedding, an interesting branch of deep learning that is widely used to represent text in a semantically meaningful form. These word representations can then be used as inputs to a model for predicting the sentiment. The remainder of the chapter will focus on interpreting and visualizing semantic similarity from the word representations. We will specifically learn about linear and nonlinear dimensionality-reduction techniques such as principal component analysis (PCA) and t-distributed stochastic neighbor embedding (t-SNE).

7.1 Sentiment analysis

In this chapter, we are tasked by a movie website called Internet Movie Repository to determine the sentiments of reviews of movies. The objective is to determine whether a review is associated with a positive or negative emotion. This is illustrated in figure 7.1, where we have two movies and a couple of reviews for each of them. The ratings for both movies are shown purely for illustrative purposes. Based on the words or sequence of words in each review, we want to determine whether a review expresses a positive emotion or opinion or a negative one.

The goal is to build an AI system that, given a review as input, determines whether the review conveys a positive or negative emotion. Given this information, we can formulate the problem as a binary classification problem. It will be similar to the binary classifiers that we saw in chapters 4 and 5, but rather than dealing with tabular data with numeric features or images, we are dealing with a sequence of words, as shown in figure 7.2. The input to the model is a sequence of words representing the review, and the output is a score that represents the probability that the sentiment of the review is positive.

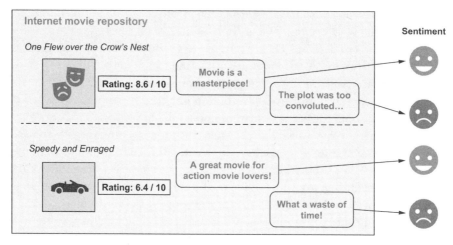

Figure 7.1   Sentiment analysis of movie reviews

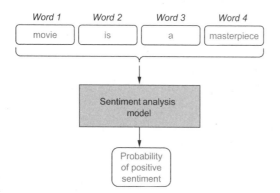

Figure 7.2   Sentiment binary classifier

The sentiment analysis model in figure 7.2 is shown as a black box. We'll cover the specifics of the model in section 7.3.4. Before we jump into how to build the model, we want to answer the following two key questions:

1   How do we represent a word in a form that the model can process?
2   How do we model a sequence of words and build a classifier based on that?

The main focus of this book is on answering the first question. We will learn about deep learning models that can be used to represent words in a dense and semantically meaningful form and how to interpret them. Once we have a good way of representing words, answering the second question—how to build a model that processes a sequence of words—becomes more straightforward. Although this is not the main focus of this book, we will briefly look at sequence modeling and how to interpret such models using techniques that we have learned in the previous chapters. Before we jump into word representations, let's explore the dataset of movie reviews first and figure out why we need a good representation of the words to be able to build the sentiment classifier.

7.2 *Exploratory data analysis*

In this section, we'll explore the movie review dataset and determine whether we can engineer any numeric features to train a simpler logistic regression or tree-based model. The main objective is to determine the need for coming up with semantically meaningful word representations and to model sequences of words. We will be using the `torchtext` package provided by PyTorch to load and process the dataset. The `torchtext` package is similar to `torchvision` in that it provides various data-processing utilities, popular datasets, and models for NLP. We can install the package using `pip` as follows:

```
$> pip install torchtext
```

In addition to `torchtext`, we will also install spaCy, a popular NLP library that we will use for string tokenization. Tokenization is the process of splitting a string of text into discrete components or tokens, such as words and punctuations. A naive tokenization method is to split a string of text on spaces, but this method does not take into account punctuation. The `spaCy` library provides more sophisticated ways of tokenizing strings in various languages. We will focus on the English language in this chapter and, therefore, use a model called `en_core_web_sm` for string tokenization. The spaCy library and the model can be installed as follows:

```
$> pip install spacy
$> python -m spacy download en_core_web_sm
```

With all the libraries in place, we can now load the movie review dataset as follows:

Imports PyTorch and the relevant utilities from torchtext

```
import torch
from torchtext.legacy import data, datasets
TEXT = data.Field(tokenize='spacy',
                  tokenizer_language='en_core_web_sm')
LABEL = data.LabelField(dtype=torch.float)
train_data, test_data = datasets.IMDB.splits(TEXT, LABEL)
```

Initializes the Field class with the tokenizer for the movie review text

Initializes the LabelField class to load the sentiment labels as float

Loads the movie review dataset and splits it into train and test sets

Let's now look at some key summary statistics from this dataset, such as the number of reviews in the train and test sets, the proportion of positive and negative reviews, and the number of words in each review, as summarized in table 7.1. In the interest of space, we will not show the source code for this, but you can obtain it from the GitHub repository associated with this book.

From table 7.1, we can observe that the train and test sets have an equal number of movie reviews—25,000 each. The reviews are equally split between positive and negative reviews for both sets. We can also observe that the summary statistics of the

Table 7.1 Key statistics from the movie review dataset

Statistics		Train set	Test set
Number of reviews		25,000	25,000
Proportion of positive reviews		50%	50%
Proportion of negative reviews		50%	50%
Number of words in positive reviews	Minimum	14	11
	Median	202	198
	Maximum	2789	2640
Number of words in negative reviews	Minimum	11	5
	Median	203	203
	Maximum	1827	1290

number of words in a review are similar across both train and test sets. We can see some differences between positive and negative reviews, especially the minimum and maximum number of words per review. Besides understanding the dataset, the reason for looking at some of these key summary statistics is to determine whether we can engineer certain numeric features and build a simple logistic regression or tree-based classifier for sentiment analysis.

In that vein, let's look at the distribution of the number of words per review, comparing positive and negative sentiments. Are there any differences in the number of words for positive and negative reviews? And if so, are negative reviews usually longer or shorter than positive reviews? We can answer these questions by looking at figure 7.3. You can find the source code to generate this plot in the GitHub repository associated with this book.

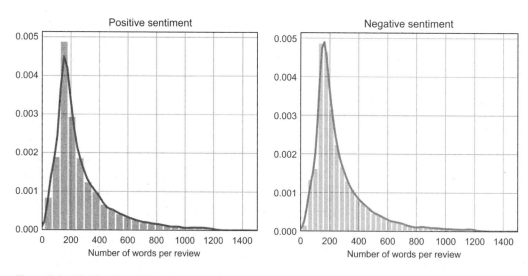

Figure 7.3 Distribution of the number of words per review—positive versus negative

In figure 7.3, we can see no glaring differences between positive and negative reviews in terms of the number of words. Looking at the number of words, therefore, does not accurately predict whether a review is positive or negative.

Figure 7.4 Word cloud for positive reviews

How about the frequency or occurrences of words? Are any words more common in positive or negative reviews? Figure 7.4 shows a word cloud of all the common words in positive reviews. The word cloud was generated after some data cleaning where very common words such as *a, the, is, at, which,* and *on* (also called stop words) and punctuation have been removed. You can access the code to remove all the stop words and clean the data in the GitHub repository associated with this book. In a word cloud, the larger the word, the more frequently it occurs in the reviews. We can see that for positive reviews, the most frequently occurring words are words like *film, movie, one,* and *character.* We also see words that convey positive sentiment like *love, great, good,* and *wonderful.*

Figure 7.5 shows the word cloud for negative reviews. At first glance, we do see some of the same words as those in positive reviews—such as *film, movie, one,* and *character*—also commonly occurring in negative reviews. We also see some words that

Figure 7.5   Word cloud for negative reviews

convey negative sentiment, such as *bad*, *unfortunately*, *poor*, and *stupid*. If we compare figures 7.4 and 7.5, there aren't any glaring differences in word counts between positive and negative reviews. We could, however, find more signal from this word count feature by cleaning the dataset further using human knowledge and heuristics. We could, for instance, remove some of the neutral words such as *film*, *movie*, *one*, and *character*, just to name a few. As you can imagine, this supervised way of engineering features using some background knowledge of the language (identifying neutral words, for instance) and heuristics is quite time-consuming and not guaranteed to extend easily to other languages. We need a better way of representing words in a language, which will be the focus of the next section.

7.3   *Neural word embeddings*

In the previous section, we saw how difficult it is to come up with numeric features to train a sentiment analysis model. We will now learn how to represent words in a numeric form that encodes as much of the meaning as possible. We can then use these word representations to train a sentiment analysis model. Before we jump in, let's get the terminology out of the way. Dense representations of words that encode semantic meaning are called *word embeddings, word vectors,* or *distributed representations.* Representations or word embeddings learned by neural networks are called *neural word embeddings.* We will focus on neural word embeddings in this chapter.

We need to be aware of a few more NLP terms. We will use the term *corpus* to refer to the body of text that we will be processing. For the movie review example, the corpus would be all of the movie reviews in the dataset. We will use the term *vocabulary* to refer to the words within the text corpus.

7.3.1 One-hot encoding

Now let's look at a naive way of representing words that shows the need for word embeddings. This exercise highlights the need to come up with more sophisticated ways of representing words in a dense, semantically meaningful form. Assume we have a corpus of text consisting of *V* words in its vocabulary. The vocabulary size *V* is typically quite large. Let's look at the example shown in figure 7.6. In the figure, we can see the words in the corpus listed in the table on the left. From the table, we can see that the corpus consists of more than 10,000 words. Each word in the corpus is assigned an index in the table.

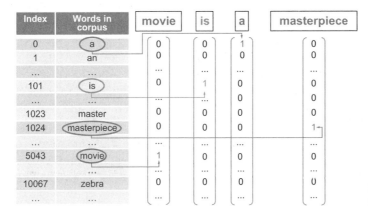

Figure 7.6 An illustration of one-hot encoded vectors

A naive way of representing words in the corpus is to use a vector with a size equal to the vocabulary size *V*, where each entry in the vector corresponds to a word in the corpus. In figure 7.6, we can see representations for words in the phrase "movie is a masterpiece." A naive presentation for the word *this* consists of a vector where the entries for each of the other words is 0 and the value at the position or index for the word *this* is 1. Similarly, for the other words in the sentence, we can see a vector of all zeros, except at the index for the word where the value is 1. This sort of representation is called *one-hot encoding.*

As we can see in the figure, one-hot encoding uses an extremely sparse representation for the words where the vectors are mostly zeros, with only a single 1. It does not encode any semantic information about a word. Words that occur frequently together or that are similar in meaning are hard to identify using this representation. The size of the vector is also large. We will need a vector as large as the vocabulary to represent words. Processing such vectors would be extremely inefficient in terms of computing and storage.

Note that the representation in figure 7.6 is indeed a very naive representation. We have ways of improving the representation by removing the stop words. This should reduce the size of the one-hot-encoded word vector used to represent each word. Another alternative is to use the *bag of words* (*BoW*) model. The BoW model essentially maps each word to a number that represents how frequently it occurs in the corpus. In a BoW representation, stop words would typically have larger numeric values because they frequently occur in the language. We could either remove these stop words, or we could use another representation called *term frequency inverse document frequency* (*TF-IDF* for short). The TF-IDF model essentially weights inversely the frequency of occurrence of each word in the corpus of reviews with the number of reviews that contain that word. This model is a good way of filtering out stop words because they will be associated with a lower numeric value. The numeric value is lower because such words occur frequently across reviews. Both BoW and TF-IDF are efficient ways of representing words, but they still do not encode the semantic information about a word.

7.3.2 *Word2Vec*

We can overcome the limitations of one-hot encoding and other more efficient representations like BoW and TF-IDF by using *Word2Vec* (short for Word to Vector) embeddings. The key idea behind Word2Vec is to look at words in context. We can encode meaning by looking at words that typically occur together. Let's look at an example and come up with some notation. In figure 7.7, we can see the same phrase as before, "movie is a masterpiece." The figure also shows a context with a window size equal to 3, that is, a context consisting of three tokens or words: *movie*, *is*, and *a*. The window size is equivalent to the number of tokens or words in the context. We denote the center word in the context as w_t, the word immediately to the left as w_{t-1}, and the word immediately to the right as w_{t+1}. Words to the left and right of the center word are also called *surrounding words* or *context words*.

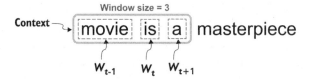

Figure 7.7 An illustration of context, window size, surrounding words, and center word

We can use two key neural network architectures to come up with Word2Vec embeddings: continuous bag of words (CBOW) and skip-gram, as shown in figure 7.8.

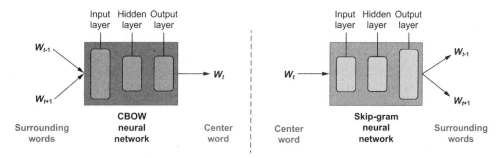

Figure 7.8 An illustration of CBOW and skip-gram neural word embedding models for window size = 3

As seen in the figure, the idea behind the CBOW architecture is to predict the center word given the surrounding, or context, words. The underlying neural network architecture is the fully connected neural network consisting of an input layer, a hidden layer, and an output layer. The skip-gram architecture, on the other hand, predicts the surrounding or context words given the center word. The underlying neural network architecture is similar to that of CBOW. Both CBOW and skip-gram models are also similar in the sense that they try to predict neighboring words or words that typically occur together. But they differ in some respects. The skip-gram model has been shown to work well with small amounts of data and also represents less frequently occurring words well. The CBOW model, on the other hand, is faster to train and has been shown to come up with better representations for more frequently occurring words. The training processes for both models are equivalent. So, to keep things simple, let's focus on one of them and take a closer look at the skip-gram training process.

The first step in training the skip-gram word embedding is to come up with a training dataset. Given the corpus of text, the idea is to come up with a dataset consisting of center words as input and the corresponding surrounding, or context, words as output. We need to know the window size for the context prior to generating the dataset because the window size is an important hyperparameter for the training process. Let's stick with the same window size of 3, as in the earlier model, and look at a concrete example, shown in figure 7.9. In the figure, we are using the same example sentence as before. We set the context window at the start of the text (shown as context 1 in the figure) and identify the center word and surrounding words. We then come up with a training data table consisting of the center word as input and the surrounding words as output. In the table for context 1, the word *is* is associated with the two neighboring words, *movie* and *a*.

We then continue this process by sliding the window to the right by one word, as shown as context 2 in figure 7.9. We will then add another entry to the training data table for the new center word and surrounding words. We repeat this process for all the text in the corpus. Once we have the training dataset consisting of input and output words, we are ready to train the skip-gram neural network. We can further simplify the training process by reformulating the problem as a binary classification problem as

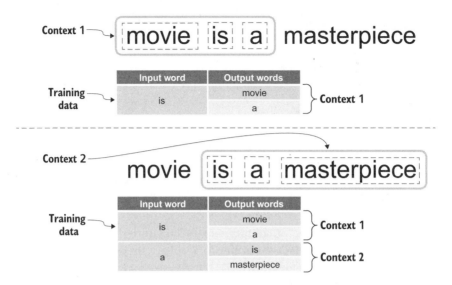

Figure 7.9   Training data preparation for the skip-gram model

follows: instead of predicting the surrounding words given a center word, we predict whether a given pair of words are neighbors. A pair of words are neighbors if they occur within the context. We can use the training data table that we generated in figure 7.9 to come up with positive labels for this new binary classification formulation. This is shown in the top half of figure 7.10 where the table of input and output (surrounding or context) words is transformed into a table of word pairs with a positive label (i.e., label = 1). The positive label denotes that the pair of words are neighbors.

Positive label identification

Input word	Output word
is	movie
is	a
a	is
a	masterpiece

Input word 1	Input word 2	Label
is	movie	1
is	a	1
a	is	1
a	masterpiece	1

Negative label Identification

Input word	Random word
is	are
is	have
a	an
a	the

Input word 1	Input word 2	Label
is	are	0
is	have	0
a	an	0
a	the	0

Figure 7.10   Training data preparation with negative sampling

How do we determine the negative labels, that is, the pairs of words that are not neighbors? We can do this using a process called *negative sampling*. For each word in the training data table from figure 7.9, we randomly sample a new word from the vocabulary. The choice of window size is important. If the window size is relatively small when compared to the number of words in the vocabulary, random sampling will ensure that the likelihood of the selected word being outside the context for the input word is small. This is shown in the bottom half of figure 7.10. For each pair of input word and random word, we assign a negative label (i.e., label = 0). These correspond to pairs of words that are not neighbors.

Once we have the training dataset for the new binary classification formulation, we are ready to train the skip-gram model. We will call the neural network model with this new formulation as skip-gram with negative sampling. The input words will be represented as one-hot-encoded vectors. Although the model is trained to determine whether two words are neighbors, the end objective of the training process is to learn neural word embeddings or dense representations for the words. This is the purpose of the hidden layer in the architecture. For the hidden layer, we will need to initialize the two matrices shown in figure 7.11: one embedding matrix and one context matrix. The embedding matrix consists of one row for each word in the vocabulary. The number of columns corresponds to the size of the word embedding or word vector used to represent the word. This is shown as N in figure 7.11.

We also need to determine another hyperparameter, the embedding size, before training. The choice of embedding size determines how dense we want the representation to be. It also determines how much semantic information is captured in the representation. The context matrix is also of the same size as the embedding matrix. Both matrices are initialized with random values. The values in these matrices are parameters in the neural network that we aim to learn using the training dataset that we have generated in figure 7.10.

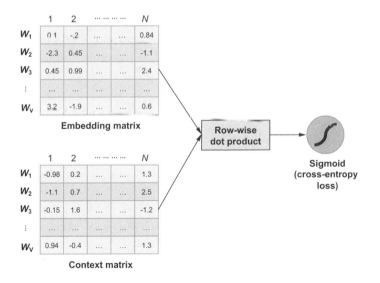

Figure 7.11 Skip-gram with negative sampling

Let's now take a closer look at the learning process. Figure 7.11 shows the two matrices and a row-wise dot-product operation being performed on them. The row-wise dot product essentially measures the similarity between two pairs of words. If we then pass the resulting vector through a sigmoid function, we will get a similarity, or probability, measure between 0 and 1. We can then compare these scores with the true label for pairs of words in the training data and update the parameters accordingly. The parameters can be updated through backpropagation, as we learned in chapters 4 and 5.

Once the learning process is complete, we can discard the context matrix and use the embedding matrix as a mapping of words to their corresponding neural word embeddings. We can obtain the mapping as follows: each row in the embedding matrix is a representation for a given word in the vocabulary. For instance, the first row in the matrix corresponds to the representation for word w_1. The second row is a representation for word w_2, and so on.

7.3.3 GloVe embeddings

The skip-gram with negative sampling model is a great way of coming up with a dense representation of words that captures the similarity between pairs of words that occur within a local context. The model does not do a great job of identifying stop words, however. Stop words, like *is, a, the*, and *this*, will be flagged as words similar to words like, say, *masterpiece* because they occur together in a local context. We can identify such stop words by looking at global statistics of words, that is, how frequently pairs of words occur within the whole corpus of text. The *global vectors* (also called *GloVe*) *model* is an improvement to skip-gram that captures both global and local statistics. Going forward, we will use pretrained GloVe word embeddings.

We will not be training GloVe word embeddings from scratch using the movie review dataset but instead will use pretrained GloVe embeddings trained on a much larger corpus of text. A common corpus of text used to train word embeddings is Wikipedia. We have the following two ways of loading GloVe embeddings pretrained on the Wikipedia corpus:

1   Using the `torchtext` package provided by PyTorch
2   Using `gensim`, a common open source Python library used for NLP

The first approach of loading GloVe embeddings using `torchtext` is useful if we have to train another downstream model, like sentiment classification, that makes use of these embeddings as features in PyTorch. The second approach of loading GloVe embeddings using `gensim` is useful for analyzing the word embeddings because a lot of utility functions come right out of the box. We will use the former approach for training the sentiment classifier and the latter approach for interpreting the word embeddings. We can load the word embeddings using `torchtext` as follows:

Initializes the GloVe class with the model pretrained
on six billion words from the Wikipedia corpus

```
import torchtext.vocab    ◁─── Imports the vocab module in torchtext

glove = torchtext.vocab.GloVe(name='6B',
                              dim=100)   ◁──── Loads the GloVe embedding with size 100
```

Note that the GloVe embeddings pretrained on six billion words from the Wikipedia corpus is loaded. The embedding size of the pretrained model is 100.

If you have not installed `gensim` on your machine, you can do so by running the following command:

```
$> pip install --upgrade gensim
```

We can then load the GloVe embeddings as follows:

```
from gensim.models import KeyedVectors                              Imports the relevant
from gensim.scripts.glove2word2vec import glove2word2vec            modules and classes
from gensim.test.utils import datapath, get_tmpfile                from gensim

path_to_glove = 'data/glove.6B/glove.6B.100d.txt'   ◁──   Initializes the path to the
                                                          pretrained GloVe embedding file
glove_file = datapath(path_to_glove)
word2vec_glove_file = get_tmpfile(glove_file)                      Initializes the
model = KeyedVectors.load_word2vec_format(word2vec_glove_file)     GloVe embedding
```

Note that with `gensim`, we need to download the pretrained GloVe embedding file. You can download the embedding pretrained on six billion words from Wikipedia with an embedding size of 100 from the GloVe project website (https://nlp.stanford .edu/projects/glove/).

7.3.4 *Model for sentiment analysis*

In section 7.1, we posited the following two key questions for building the sentiment analysis model:

1 How do we represent a word in a form that the model can process?
2 How do we model a sequence of words and build a classifier based on that?

We have already answered the first question in the previous section by learning about neural word embeddings. The key focus of this chapter is on word embeddings and how to interpret them. For the sake of completeness, we answer the second question by providing a high-level overview of how to model a sequence of words to build a sentiment classifier.

The high-level architecture for the sentiment classifier is shown in the top half of figure 7.12. It consists of two neural network architectures that are chained together. The first neural network is called a recurrent neural network (RNN), and the second neural network is a fully connected neural network, which we learned about in chapter 4. Let's take a closer look at RNNs, shown in the bottom half of figure 7.12.

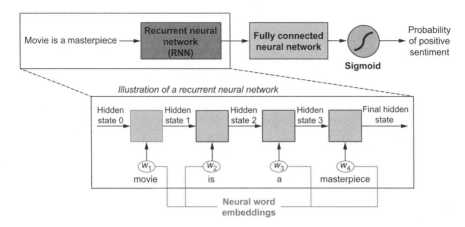

Figure 7.12   **Sequence modeling and sentiment analysis using recurrent neural networks (RNNs)**

RNNs are typically used in analyzing sequences, like a sequence of words, as in the sentiment analysis problem, or time-series analysis, like weather forecasting. For the sentiment analysis problem, the RNN takes the sequence of words one at a time and produces a hidden state for each word, which is the representation of the previous inputs. The words are fed into the RNN using the neural word embedding representation learned in the previous section. Once all of the words have been fed into the RNN, the final hidden state is then used to train the feed-forward neural network for sentiment classification. We are glossing over a lot of detail here because this is not meant to be the primary focus of this chapter and the book. A great resource for learning more about RNNs and language models is the online course on NLP with deep learning from Stanford University (http://web.stanford.edu/class/cs224n/).

Transformer networks

A recent breakthrough in NLP has been *transformer networks*, proposed by a team at Google Research in 2017 in their seminal paper "Attention Is All You Need" (https://arxiv.org/abs/1706.03762). Like RNNs, transformer networks or trans- formers are used to model sequential data. As we saw in section 7.3.4, RNNs process the input one word at a time in order. The output of the current word, or timestep— that is, the hidden state—is required before we can process the next word. It is hard to parallelize the training process, and, therefore, training RNNs is quite time- consuming. Transformers overcome this limitation by adopting the attention mechanism and do not require us to feed the input of words in order. Intuitively, the attention mechanism is similar to the convolution-based approach in convolutional neural networks (CNNs) where the interactions of words that occur closer together in sequences are modeled at lower layers and interactions of words that occur farther apart in sequences are modeled at higher layers. All the words are fed into the network at once, together with information on their relative and absolute positions.

We are glossing over a lot of detail here—an entire chapter is required to do justice to this topic, but, unfortunately, that's beyond the scope of this book. A great resource for learning more about transformers, with video lectures and lecture notes, is the online course on NLP with deep learning from Stanford University (http://web .stanford.edu/class/cs224n/). Developments in the transformer network architecture include systems such as bidirectional encoder representations from transformers (BERT) and generative pretrained transformer (GPT). Pretrained word embeddings learned by transformers can be loaded in PyTorch using the popular open-source library provided by Hugging Face (https://huggingface.co/transformers/). The interpretability techniques that you will learn in the subsequent sections to understand semantic similarity learned by GloVE word embeddings can be extended to embeddings learned by transformer networks as well. The techniques are model-agnostic.

7.4   *Interpreting semantic similarity*

In the previous section, you learned how to obtain dense representation of words that encode semantic meaning using neural word embeddings. Now we will focus on understanding and interpreting semantic similarity from those learned word embeddings. You will learn how to measure semantic similarity and also how to visualize similarity between high-dimensional word embeddings in two dimensions.

Before we start measuring and interpreting semantic similarity, the first step is to identify a few words where the meanings are varied and nuanced and we have a good understanding of the semantic similarity between them and other words that would be similar to them. This is similar to the concept definition step in the network dissection framework in chapter 6 in that we need a good human understanding of what specifically we want to measure and interpret. In the context of semantic similarity in neural word embeddings, we need an understanding or taxonomy of words to verify whether the neural word embeddings have learned the semantic meanings properly.

We will look at two different sets of words to interpret semantic similarity. The first set of words is not necessarily related to the movie review or sentiment classification problem. The words are, however, meant to verify whether certain nuances of words are captured by the word embeddings. The first set (referred to as set 1) of words follows:

- *Basketball*
- *Lebron*
- *Ronaldo*
- *Facebook*
- *Media*

The meaning or link between these words can be obtained from the taxonomy, shown in figure 7.13. In the figure, the words in the set are highlighted. We can see that within the category Sport, we have *Basketball* and *Football/Soccer*. A Sport also has personalities— *Lebron* and *Ronaldo* fall under the categories Sport and Personality. There is also a link

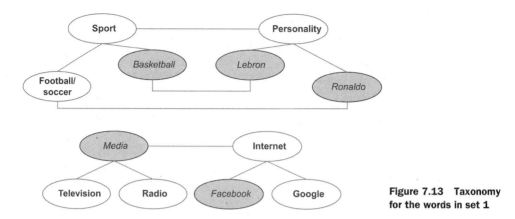

Figure 7.13   Taxonomy for the words in set 1

between the sport personalities and their respective sports. *Lebron*, for instance, is linked with the sport *Basketball* and *Ronaldo* is linked with the sport *Football/Soccer*. Also, within the category Media, we have different types of media, such as *Television*, *Radio*, and *Internet*. Within the Internet category, there are companies like *Facebook* and *Google*. Figure 7.13 serves as a map of how words are linked, and we can use this to interpret semantic meaning in word embeddings.

The second set (referred to as set 2) of words is related to movie reviews. We will look at the following set of movies to see how they are related:

- *Godfather*
- *Goodfellas*
- *Batman*
- *Avengers*

The taxonomy for the second set of words is shown in figure 7.14.

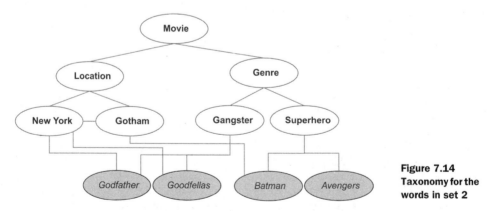

Figure 7.14 Taxonomy for the words in set 2

The movies in the set are highlighted. We have categorized the movies based on their genre and the location of shoot. Movies like *Godfather* and *Goodfellas* belong to the Gangster genre, and they are both shot in the location New York. Movies like *Batman* and *Avengers* are Superhero movies. *Batman* is based in the location *Gotham*, which is a fictitious place loosely based on *New York*. It is worth highlighting that such nuances and meanings for words are language- and context-dependent, and, therefore, we need a good understanding of this before we set out to interpret semantic meaning.

7.4.1 *Measuring similarity*

Now that we have the words of interest, how do we quantify similarity between them? We are specifically interested in measuring similarity between representations of words or word embeddings. For ease of visualization, let's first consider a simple example of word embeddings of size 2. Suppose that we have two words, *Basketball* and *Football*, in this word embedding space, as shown in figure 7.15. These two words are represented in the figure as vectors W_1 and W_2, respectively.

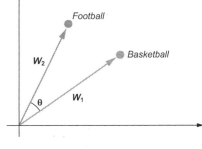

Figure 7.15   An illustration of measuring similarity between word embeddings in 2-D space

One way of measuring similarity between the word vectors W_1 and W_2 is to look at how close they are in the 2-D embedding space. The similarity measure should have the property that if the word vectors are close together, then they are more similar. If they are further apart, then they are less similar. A good metric that has this property is the cosine of the angle between the two vectors—$\cos(\theta)$. This measurement is called cosine similarity. The mathematical formula for cosine similarity given word vectors W_1 and W_2 is shown next:

$$\text{Cosine Similarity} = \frac{\mathbf{w}_1 . \mathbf{w}_2}{||\mathbf{w}_1||\,||\mathbf{w}_2||}$$

It is essentially the dot product of the word vectors divided by the product of the Euclidean norm, or magnitude, of the two vectors.

Using `gensim`, we can easily obtain the words that are most similar to a given word as follows. In section 7.3.3, we saw how to load the GloVe word embedding using `gensim`. Once the embeddings have been initialized, we can obtain the top five most similar words for the first set of words using the following code:

We are interested in the top five most similar words.

Initializes an array with the first set of words

```
words = ['basketball', 'lebron', 'ronaldo', 'facebook', 'media']
topn = 5
```

Initializes an array to store the most similar words

```
sim_words_scores = []
for word in words:
    sim_words = model.most_similar(word, topn=topn)
```

Iterates through each word

Gets the top five most similar words from the gensim model

```
print(f"Words similar to: {word}")
for sim_word in sim_words:
    sim_words_scores.append((word, sim_word[0], sim_word[1]))
    print(f"\t{sim_word[0]} ({sim_word[1]:.2f})")
```

Stores the similar words in array and print the results

The output of this code is summarized in table 7.2. The top row consists of the words in the set. Each column in the table shows the top five words that are similar to the words in the topmost row of that column. The cosine similarity measure is also shown in parenthesis for the similar words. We can see from the table that the GloVe word embedding has indeed learned words that are semantically similar in meaning. The first column, for instance, shows all the words that are similar to *basketball*, and they are all sports. The second column shows all the words that are similar to *Lebron*, and they are all sports personalities that play basketball. The third column shows all sports personalities that play football or soccer. The fourth column shows companies that are similar to *Facebook*, that is, internet or web-based social media companies. The last column shows all the words that are similar to *Media*. As an exercise, do a similar analysis for the second set of words. The solution can be found in the GitHub repository associated with this book.

Table 7.2   Top five similar words for the words in set 1

Basketball	Lebron	Ronaldo	Facebook	Media
Football (0.86)	Dwyane (0.79)	Ronaldinho (0.86)	Twitter (0.92)	News (0.77)
Hockey (0.8)	Shaquille (0.75)	Rivaldo (0.85)	MySpace (0.9)	Press (0.75)
Soccer (0.8)	Bosh (0.72)	Beckham (0.84)	YouTube (0.81)	Television (0.75)
NBA (0.78)	O'Neal (0.68)	Cristiano (0.84)	Google (0.75)	TV (0.73)
Baseball (0.76)	Carmelo (0.68)	Robinho (0.82)	Web (0.74)	Internet (0.72)

Let's now also visualize the cosine similarity between the words in the first set. The following code shows how to compute the cosine similarity between pairs of words and how to visualize them:

Imports the cosine_similarity helper function from Scikit-Learn

Imports Pandas to store the cosine similarity of word pairs in a DataFrame

```
from sklearn.metrics.pairwise import cosine_similarity

import pandas as pd

import matplotlib.pyplot as plt
import seaborn as sns

words = ['basketball', 'lebron', 'ronaldo', 'facebook', 'media']
word_pairs = [(a, b) for idx, a in enumerate(words) for b
    in words[idx + 1:]]
```

Imports the visualization-related libraries

Initializes the first set of words

Creates an array with word pairs based on the initialized set of words

```
cosine_sim_word_pairs = []
for word_pair in tqdm(word_pairs):
    cos_sim = cosine_similarity([model[word_pair[0]]],
                                [model[word_pair[1]]])[0][0]
    cosine_sim_word_pairs.append([str(word_pair), "glove",
    ➡ cos_sim])
```
Computes the cosine similarity for word pairs and stores it in an array

```
df_sim = pd.DataFrame(cosine_sim_word_pairs,
                      columns=['Word Pairs',
                               'Embedding',
                               'Cosine Similarity'])
```
Creates a DataFrame with the results

```
f, ax = plt.subplots()
sns.barplot(x="Word Pairs", y="Cosine Similarity",
            data=df_sim[df_sim['Embedding'] == 'glove'],
            ax=ax)
plt.xticks(rotation=90);
```
Uses the DataFrame to plot a bar chart

The resulting plot is shown in figure 7.16. We can observe from the figure that *Basketball* and *Lebron* are much more similar to each other than to any other word. Also, the word *Basketball* is more similar to *Ronaldo* than to *Facebook* and *Media*, because we know from our taxonomy in figure 7.13 that *Basketball* and *Ronaldo* are linked to the category Sport. Using the taxonomy, we can make similar observations for the other pairs of words as well. The word *Facebook*, for instance, is much more similar to the word *Media* than any other word, because Facebook is a social media company.

As an exercise, write the code to visualize the cosine similarity for the pairs of movies in the second set. You can access the source code from the GitHub repository associated with this book, and the resulting plot is shown in figure 7.17. We can observe

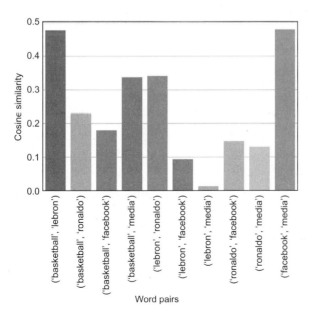

Figure 7.16   Visualization of cosine similarity of GloVe embeddings for word pairs in set 1

from the figure that the two gangster movies, *Godfather* and *Goodfellas*, are more similar to each other than they are to the superhero movies *Batman* and *Avengers*. Similarly, the Superhero movies are closer together than they are to the Gangster movies. We can also see that *Godfather* and *Goodfellas* are more similar to *Batman* than *Avengers*. This could be because the movies are based in locations that are connected, as we established in our taxonomy in figure 7.14.

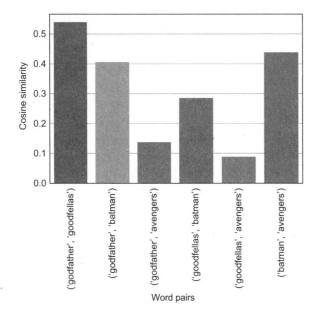

Figure 7.17   Visualization of the cosine similarity of GloVe embeddings of various movie pairs in set 2

We now have a way of measuring similarity between word embeddings, using the cosine similarity measure. Using a specific set of words for evaluation and their corresponding taxonomy, we have also validated that the GloVe word embeddings with 100 dimensions capture the semantic meaning of words really well. Let's now see how we can come up with a visualization of the word embeddings in 2-D space, similar to the one illustrated in figure 7.15, without losing any of the semantic meaning. This is going to be the focus of the next two sections. You will specifically learn about two techniques: principal component analysis (PCA) and t-distributed stochastic neighbor embedding (t-SNE).

7.4.2   *Principal component analysis (PCA)*

Principal component analysis (PCA) is a powerful technique for reducing the dimensionality of a dataset. Because we are dealing with word embeddings with 100 dimensions, we want to reduce the dimensionality to 2 so that we can easily visualize the dataset. We want to reduce the dimensionality and, at the same time, capture as much of the variation or the semantic information as possible. Let's see PCA in action by looking at a simple example. For the sake of illustration, we will look at word embeddings of size 2 and see how we can use PCA to reduce the dimensionality from 2 down to 1. Figure 7.18 shows four words placed on a 2-D plane. For ease of visualization, we are assuming that the embedding size is 2. The goal is to visualize the word embeddings in one dimension—on a 1-D line. We can see that words 1 and 2 (*Doctor* and *Nurse*) are semantically similar because they are closer together in the 2-D space. Words 3 and 4 (*Athletics* and *Athlete*) are also semantically similar. Word pairs 1 and 2, however, are further away from word pairs 3 and 4 because they are not semantically similar.

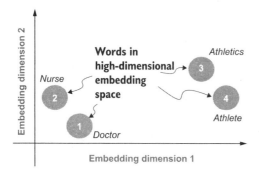

Figure 7.18 An illustration of four words in an embedding space of size 2

The first step of PCA is to take the mean of the words across all dimensions and subtract the mean from the word embeddings. This is shown in figure 7.19, where the mean is represented by a large cross. The purpose of this transformation is to center the words around the mean, that is, place the mean of the data at the origin. By centering the word embeddings on the mean, we still preserve the distances between the words in 2-D space and, therefore, their semantic meaning.

Because we are interested in visualizing the word embeddings on a line, the next step of PCA is to fit a line through the word embeddings. The line of best fit is the one

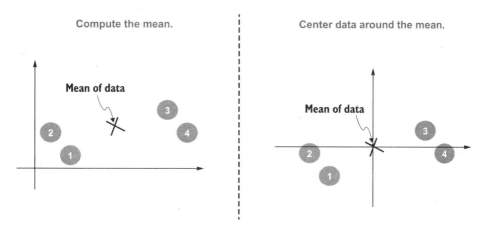

Figure 7.19 An illustration of computing the mean and centering the words around the mean

that minimizes the perpendicular distance between each word and the line. In other words, the goal is to minimize the projected distance between the words and the line or maximize the distance between the origin and the projection of each word on the line. Maximizing the distance between the projections on the origin will ensure that as much of the variation in the data is preserved as possible. This is shown in figure 7.20. The line of best fit is also called the principal component. We are interested only in visualizing the words in 1-D, so there will be one only principal component.

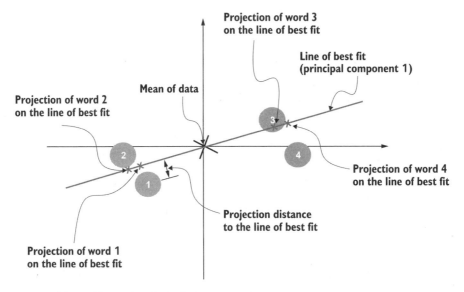

Figure 7.20   An illustration of principal component

The final step is to project each word onto the principal component. This will serve as our visualization of the word embeddings in 1-D, as shown in figure 7.21.

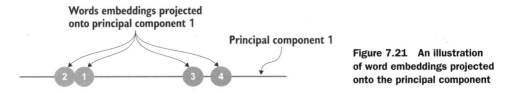

Figure 7.21   An illustration of word embeddings projected onto the principal component

Now that we have an intuition of how PCA works, let's extend the technique to multiple dimensions. Let's represent all the word embeddings by the matrix X where the number of rows is equal to the number of words in the vocabulary and the number of columns is equal to the embedding size. Let's represent the embedding size as n. The goal is to reduce the dimension of the words to size k, where for the purposes of visualization is typically 2 or 3.

As we've seen through the visual example, the first step is to center the data to the mean. This is shown by the following equation, where the mean is subtracted from the embedding matrix X. The mean center data is represented by matrix U:

$$U = X - \bar{X}$$

The next step is to compute the covariance of matrix U. This is shown by the next equation where the covariance matrix is represented by matrix V. The purpose of computing the covariance of matrix U is to estimate the variance across each of the embedding dimensions in the mean-centered data:

$$V = U^T U$$

Once you have the estimate of the variance, the next step is to compute the eigenvalues and eigenvectors for matrix V by solving the following characteristic equation. By solving for λ, we can obtain the roots for the equation, which will give us the eigenvalues. Note that in the next equation, "det" stands for determinant and the matrix I is the identity matrix. Once we have the eigenvalues, we can obtain the corresponding eigenvectors:

$$\det (V - \lambda I) = 0$$

The eigenvectors essentially give us the principal components. The magnitude of the eigenvalue gives us an estimate of the amount of variation captured by each of the principal components. We should then sort the vectors in descending order of eigenvalues and pick the top k principal components to project our data to. The top k principal components will capture as much of the variation in the data as possible. Let's represent the matrix with the top k principal components (or eigenvectors) as W. The final step is to project the original word embeddings in n-dimensional space to the k-dimensional space by applying the following equation:

$$Y = W^T X$$

Let's now see PCA in action on the GloVe word embeddings. The first step is to prepare the data where we extract the word embeddings for the words that we are interested in visualizing. This is shown in the next code snippet where we extract the word embeddings for the words in set 1 and their corresponding top five similar words:

```
viz_words = [sim_word_score[1] for sim_word_score in
    sim_words_scores]
main_words = [sim_word_score[0] for sim_word_score in
    sim_words_scores]
```
Creates lists with main words and similar words to visualize

```
word_vectors = []
for word in tqdm(viz_words):
    word_vectors.append(model[word])
word_vectors = np.array(word_vectors)
```
Extracts the word embeddings for words to visualize

Once we have prepared the data, we can run PCA and obtain the projections of the word embeddings in the lower-dimensional space. For ease of visualization, we will set the number of principal components to 2. We can use the PCA implementation provided by the Scikit-Learn library. The following code shows how to obtain the principal components and then project the data onto them:

Imports the PCA class from Scikit-Learn

Initializes the PCA class with two principal components

```
from sklearn.decomposition import PCA

pca_2d = PCA(n_components=2,
             random_state=24).fit(word_vectors)
pca_wv_2d = pca_2d.transform(word_vectors)

pca_kwv_2d = {}
for idx, word in enumerate(viz_words):
    pca_kwv_2d[word] = pca_wv_2d[idx]
```

Sets the random state and obtains the best fit for the word vectors

Projects the word vectors onto the principal components

Creates a dictionary mapping from each word to its PCA word embeddings

Once we have the projections of the word embeddings in 2-D space, we can easily visualize it using the Matplotlib and Seaborn libraries, as shown next:

```
df_pca_2d = pd.DataFrame(pca_wv_2d, columns=['y', 'x'])
df_pca_2d['text'] = viz_words
df_pca_2d['word'] = main_words

f, ax = plt.subplots(figsize=(10, 8))
sns.scatterplot(data=df_pca_2d,
                x="x", y="y",
                hue="word", style="word", s=50, ax=ax)

ax.legend()
for i, row in df_pca_2d.iterrows():
    ax.text(row['x']+.05, row['y']-0.02, str(row['text']),
            size=size)
```

Creates a DataFrame with 2-D PCA coordinates for each word

Creates a scatterplot

Adds a legend and annotations for the scatterplot

The resulting plot is shown in figure 7.22. The main words in set 1 are shown in the legend, and their top five most similar words are illustrated using the symbol corresponding to each word. The word *Basketball*, for instance, is represented by a circle, and the word *Media* is represented by a diamond. Let's take a moment to admire the output of the PCA technique. We are now able to visualize the original 100-dimensional word embeddings in two dimensions! But does the PCA representation still preserve the semantic meaning captured in 100 dimensions? In figure 7.22, we do see the words similar to the main word clustered together, except for the word, *lebron*. Some basketball personalities like *bosh*, *dwyane*, and *carmelo* are closer to the football personalities than to their basketball peers.

This is expected because we may not be capturing as much of the variation in the original dataset in just two dimensions. We can easily check this by running the following line of code:

```
print(pca_2d.explained_variance_ratio_)
```

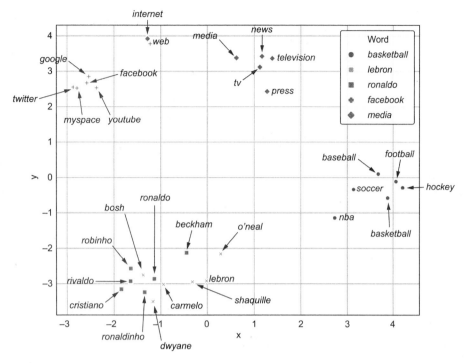

Figure 7.22 Visualizing semantic similarity of GloVe word embeddings for words in set 1 using PCA

This code outputs the percentage of variation captured in each of the principal components. If we sum them up, we get roughly 49%. This means that by projecting the word embeddings to just two principal components, we are able to capture 49% of the variation in the data. As an exercise, try training a PCA with three principal components to see if a major chunk of the variance in the data can be captured. If so, try visualizing the embeddings in 3-D to see if the issues observed in 2-D are resolved.

Although PCA is a powerful technique, it does suffer from some a major drawback. It assumes that the dataset or the word embeddings can be modeled linearly. This may not be the case for most of the datasets that we deal with. In the next section, we will learn about an even more powerful and popular technique called t-SNE that can generalize to nonlinear structures.

7.4.3 t-distributed stochastic neighbor embedding (t-SNE)

t-SNE falls under the broad class of machine learning techniques called *manifold learning*, where the objective is to learn nonlinear structures from higher-dimensional data in lower dimensions. This technique is one of the most popular choices for visualizing higher-dimensional data. Let's see it in action using a simple two-dimensional dataset where the goal is to visualize it in one dimension. In figure 7.23, we see the familiar example of four words in 2-D space on the left. The first step is to construct a similarity table for all pairs of words. This similarity table will give us a measure of similarity, or the probability of pairs of words being neighbors in the high-dimensional embedding space. Another way to look at it is to calculate the joint probability distribution for words in the high-dimensional embedding space. We will see how to do this mathematically in a bit.

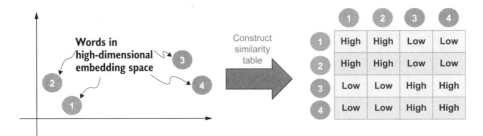

Figure 7.23   Constructing a similarity table for word embeddings in high-dimensional space

The next step is to randomly place all the words on a line, because we are interested in visualizing the word embeddings in 1-D space. This is shown on the left in figure 7.24. Once we have placed the words randomly on the line, we should construct a similarity table for the words randomly represented on that 1-D space. This is shown on the right in figure 7.24. The entries in the table that are different from the higher-dimensional joint probability distribution are highlighted. We will see how to mathematically compute this joint probability distribution for the lower-dimensional space shortly.

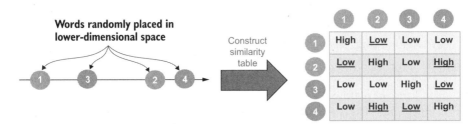

Figure 7.24   Randomly placing words in the lower dimension and the corresponding similarity table

The final step is the t-SNE learning process, as shown in figure 7.25. We must feed the joint probability distributions of the random lower-dimensional representation and the higher-dimensional representation into the learning algorithm. The objective of the learning algorithm is to update the lower-dimensional representation such that both probability distributions are similar. This will then give us a lower-dimensional visualization that preserves the probability distributions, or similarities, from the higher-dimensional space.

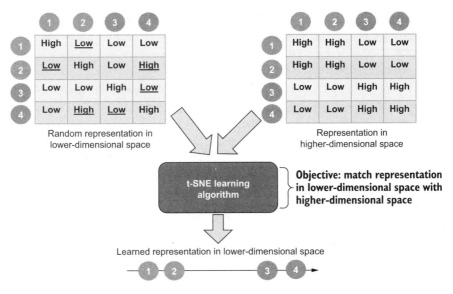

Figure 7.25 t-SNE learning algorithm

Let's now look at it mathematically. The first step is to construct a similarity table, or joint probability distribution, for the words in the higher-dimensional embedding space. For each word, we can project a Gaussian distribution centered on that word such that words that are closer to it have a higher probability and words that are further away from it have a lower probability. This is shown in the following equation, which computes the probability of a word x_j being close to x_i. The numerator is the Gaussian distribution centered on the word x_i with a standard deviation of σ. The standard deviation σ is a hyperparameter for t-SNE, and we will see how to set this hyperparameter shortly. The denominator is a normalization factor to ensure that the probabilities are of a similar range for clusters of words with different densities:

$$p_{j|i} = \frac{\exp(-\|x_i - x_j\|^2/2\sigma^2)}{\sum_{k \neq i} \exp(-\|x_i - x_k\|^2/2\sigma^2)}$$

Using this equation, we have a risk of the probability of word x_j being a neighbor of word x_i being different from the probability of word x_i being a neighbor of x_j, because the two conditional probabilities come from different distributions. To ensure that the similarity measure is commutative, we will compute the final probability of two words x_i and x_j being neighbors as follows:

$$p_{ij} = \frac{p_{j|i} + p_{i|j}}{2n}$$

Once you have computed the joint probability distribution for the higher-dimensional embedding space, the next step is to place the words randomly on the lower-dimensional space. We should then compute the joint probability distribution for the lower-dimensional representation using the following equation. The equation essentially computes the probability that two words in the lower dimension represented as y_i and y_j are neighbors:

$$q_{ij} = \frac{(1 + \|y_i - y_j\|^2)^{-1}}{\sum_{k \neq l}(1 + \|y_k - y_l\|^2)^{-1}}$$

Note that a different distribution is used for the lower-dimensional representation. The numerator in the equation essentially is a t-distribution, hence the name t-SNE. Figure 7.26 shows the difference between the Gaussian distribution and the t-distribution. We can see that the t-distribution has a heavier tail (where the probability scores are not negligible for extreme values) on the right than the Gaussian distribution. We are exploiting this property of the t-distribution for the lower-dimensional space to ensure that points that may be moderately spaced in the higher dimension are not clumped together in the lower dimension.

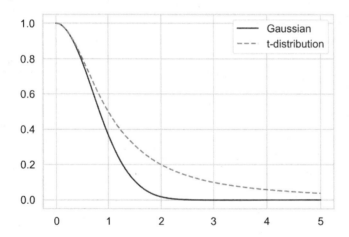

Figure 7.26   A Gaussian distribution vs. t-distribution

Once we have the joint distributions for both the higher-dimensional and lower-dimensional representations, the last step is to train an algorithm to update the lower-dimensional representation such that both distributions are similar. This optimization can be done by quantifying the gap between both the distributions. We can use the Kullback–Leibler (KL) divergence metric for this purpose.

The KL divergence is a measure of the entropy, or difference, between two distributions. The higher the value, the greater the difference. To be more precise, the KL divergence could range from 0 for identical distributions to infinity for vastly different distributions. The KL divergence metric can be computed as follows:

$$D_{KL}(P||Q) = \sum_i \sum_j \left(p_{ij} \log \frac{p_{ij}}{q_{ij}} \right)$$

The objective of the learning algorithm is to determine the distribution for the lower-dimensional representation such that the KL divergence metric is minimized. We can do this optimization by applying gradient descent and iteratively updating the lower-dimensional representation. The entire t-SNE algorithm has been implemented in the Scikit-Learn library.

Before jumping into the code, there is one detail that we glossed over. Note that when computing the joint probability distribution for the higher-dimensional representation, we fit a Gaussian centered on each word with a standard deviation of σ. This standard deviation is an important hyperparameter for t-SNE. It is referred to as *perplexity*, which is a rough estimate of the number of close neighbors each word has. As we will see later, the choice of perplexity will drastically change the visualization of the word embeddings and is, therefore, an important hyperparameter. We can train t-SNE on the GloVE word embeddings using the next code. We are using the words from set 1 and their associated top five most similar words:

```python
from sklearn.manifold import TSNE
```
⟵ **Imports the TSNE class from Scikit-Learn**

```python
perplexity = 10
learning_rate = 20
iteration = 1000
```
Initializes the t-SNE hyperparameters

```python
tsne_2d = TSNE(n_components=2,
               random_state=24,
               perplexity=perplexity,
               learning_rate=learning_rate,
               n_iter=iteration).fit(word_vectors)
```
Initializes the TSNE class and trains the model using the word vectors

Obtains the t-SNE word embeddings in 2-D space

```python
tnse_wv_2d = tsne_2d.fit_transform(word_vectors)
```

```python
tsne_kwv_2d = {}
for idx, word in enumerate(viz_words):
    tsne_kwv_2d[word] = tnse_wv_2d[idx]
```
Creates a mapping from each word to its t-SNE embeddings

Note that we have set the perplexity to 10. We can reuse the code from the previous section on PCA to visualize the lower-dimensional t-SNE embeddings. The resulting figure is shown in figure 7.27.

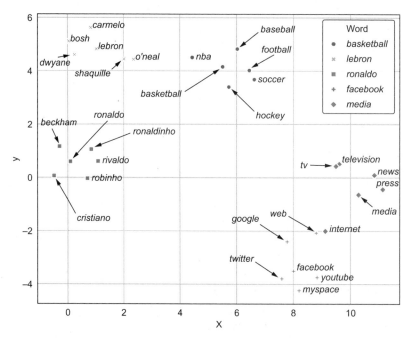

Figure 7.27   Visualizing semantic similarity of GloVe word embeddings for words in set 1 using t-SNE

The visualization shown in figure 7.27 does look better qualitatively than PCA. We do see the basketball personalities clustered together and distinct from the football personalities cluster. This is still a qualitative assessment, and we will see how to validate these visualizations quantitatively in the following section.

Let's see what happens when we set the perplexity to a large value, say, 100. As an exercise, retrain the t-SNE model using a perplexity of 100 and visualize the resulting word embeddings. You can see the code in the GitHub repository associated with this book. The resulting plot is shown in figure 7.28.

We can see that the words are clustered in a random order, and all the words seem to be placed roughly in a circle. The authors of the t-SNE algorithm recommend the perplexity be set between 5 and 50. The guideline is to use a higher perplexity value for denser datasets where there are dense clusters of words in the higher-dimensional space.

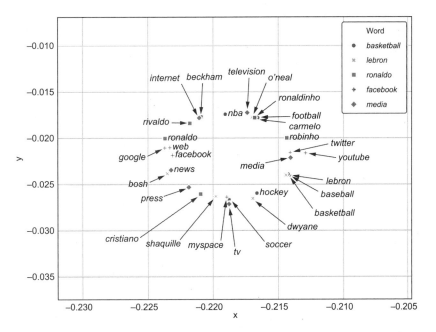

Figure 7.28   t-SNE visualization with high perplexity

7.4.4   *Validating semantic similarity visualizations*

We have learned two techniques to visualize higher-dimensional word embeddings, namely, PCA and t-SNE. We evaluated each visualization qualitatively, but is there a way of validating them quantitatively? To validate the plots quantitatively, we can measure the cosine similarity between word pairs in the lower-dimensional representation and compare that with the higher-dimensional representation. We have already done this for the higher-dimensional representation in section 7.4.1 (see figure 7.16). As an exercise, extend the code in section 7.4.1 to also visualize the embeddings generated by PCA and both the t-SNE models (perplexity = 10 and perplexity = 100). The resulting plot is shown in figure 7.29. You can check out the solution in the GitHub repository associated with this book.

We can see that the PCA representation is not consistent with the original GloVe representation. For instance, *basketball* and *lebron* have lower similarity than *basketball* and *facebook* in the PCA representation. We can, however, see that the representation learned by t-SNE with a perplexity of 10 preserves as much of the similarity captured by the original GloVe embedding. The t-SNE with a perplexity of 100 shows all word pairs with similar meaning and is clearly the worst representation among the three. This sort of validation will be easier to do at scale than to qualitatively assess a 2-D visualization generated by PCA and t-SNE for all the words of interest.

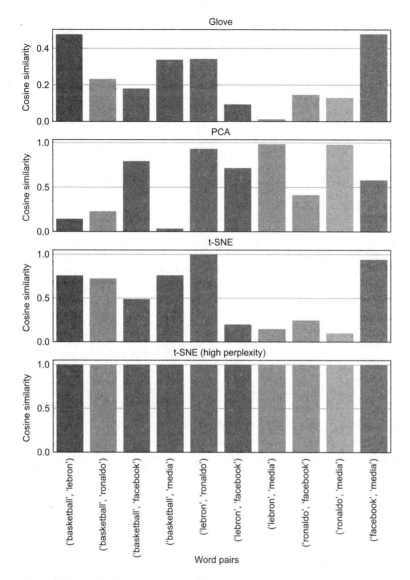

Figure 7.29   Validating visualizations of semantic similarity

Summary

- In this chapter, we focused on the field of natural language processing (NLP), specifically on the topic of representing words in a form that captures semantic meaning. We also learned how to interpret and visualize semantic similarity from these word representations using dimensionality-reduction techniques like PCA and t-SNE.

- A naive way of representing words is using one-hot encoding. However, this representation is sparse and computationally inefficient and does not encode any semantic meaning.
- Dense representations of words that encode semantic meaning are called word embeddings, word vectors, or distributed representations. Representations or word embeddings learned by neural networks are called neural word embeddings.
- Dense representations of words can be learned using neural network architectures like continuous bag of words (CBOW), skip-gram, and global vectors (GloVe).
- In the context of interpreting and visualizing semantic similarity in neural word embeddings, we need an understanding or taxonomy of words to verify whether the neural word embeddings have learned the semantic meanings properly.
- We can measure semantic similarity using the cosine similarity metric. The metric has a property where word embeddings that are closer together have a larger score than word embeddings that are further apart.
- We can visualize higher-dimensional word embeddings in lower dimensions using dimensionality-reduction techniques such as principal component analysis (PCA) and t-distributed stochastic neighbor embedding (t-SNE).
- Although PCA is a powerful technique, it does suffer from a major drawback: it assumes that the dataset or the word embeddings can be modeled linearly. This may not be the case for most of the datasets that we deal with.
- t-SNE falls under the broad class of machine learning techniques called manifold learning, where the objective is to learn nonlinear structures from higher-dimensional data in lower dimensions. The technique is one of the most popular choices for visualizing higher-dimensional data.
- We can quantitatively validate the visualizations generated by PCA and t-SNE by computing the cosine similarity for different pairs of words and checking to see if the degree of similarity is consistent with the original higher-dimensional representation.

Part 4

Fairness and bias

Great job making it this far into the book! You now have various interpretability techniques in your toolkit, and you should be well equipped to build robust AI systems! This final part focuses on fairness and bias and paves the way for explainable AI.

In chapter 8, you will learn about various definitions of fairness and how you can check whether your model is biased. You'll also learn about techniques to mitigate bias and a standardizing approach of documenting datasets using datasheets that help improve transparency and accountability with the stakeholders and users of the AI system.

In chapter 9, we'll pave the way for explainable AI by discussing how to build such systems, and you'll also learn about contrastive explanations using counterfactual examples.

Fairness and mitigating bias

This chapter covers

- Identifying sources of bias in datasets
- Validating whether machine learning models are fair using various fairness notions
- Applying interpretability techniques to identify the source of discrimination in machine learning models
- Mitigating bias using preprocessing techniques
- Documenting datasets using datasheets to improve transparency and accountability and to ensure compliance with regulation

You have learned a lot so far and have added a lot of interpretability techniques to your toolkit, ranging from those that you can use to interpret model processing (chapters 2 to 5) to those for interpreting representations learned by a machine learning model (chapters 6 and 7). We will now employ some of these techniques to address an important problem when building systems driven by machine learning models, which is tackling the problem of bias. This problem is important for multiple reasons. We must build systems that do not discriminate against individuals or users of the system. If businesses use AI for decision-making, such as providing opportunities to users or for some quality of service or information, biased decisions can incur a huge cost to the business by damaging the business's reputation or by having a negative impact on their customers' trust. Certain regions, like the United States and Europe, have laws that prohibit discriminating against individuals based on protected attributes, such as gender, race, ethnicity, sexual orientation, and so on. Some regulated industries, such as financial services, education, housing, employment, credit, and health care, prohibit or restrict the use of protected attributes in decision-making, and AI systems need to provide certain fairness guarantees.

Before we jump into the problem of bias and fairness, let's recap the process that we used to build a robust AI system that addresses common issues, such as data leakage, bias, regulatory noncompliance, and concept drift, as shown in figure 8.1. The learning, testing, and understanding phases are done offline and are all about training the model based on historical labeled data, evaluating it, and understanding it using various interpretability techniques. Once the model is deployed, it goes online and starts to make predictions on live data. This model is also monitored to ensure there is no concept drift, which happens when the distribution of the data in the production environment deviates from that in the development and testing environments. There is also a feedback loop where new data is added back to the historical training dataset for continuous training, evaluation, and deployment.

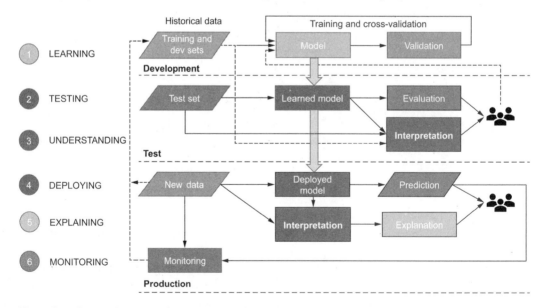

Figure 8.1   Recap of how to build a robust AI system

What may be the sources of bias in this system? One source, as shown in figure 8.2, is the historical training dataset where there may be bias in the labeling process or bias in the sampling or data-collection process. Another source is the model itself, where the algorithm may be favoring certain individuals or groups of individuals over others. If the model is training on a dataset that is itself biased, then the bias is further amplified. Another source of bias is the feedback loop from the production environment back to the development and test environments. If the initial dataset or model is biased, then the deployed model in production will continue to make biased predictions. If the data based on these predictions is fed back as training data, then these biases are further reinforced and amplified.

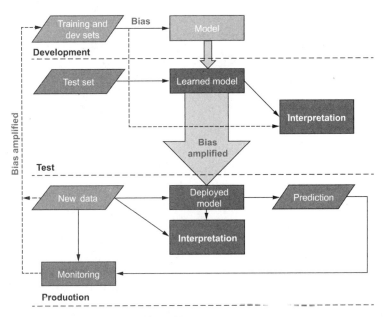

Figure 8.2   Sources of bias in the AI system

Where does interpretability fit into the problem of bias and fairness? As seen in figure 8.2, we can use interpretability techniques during training and testing to expose issues with the historical dataset or the model. We have already seen this in action in chapter 3 where biases in ethnicity were exposed in the high school student grade-prediction problem using partial dependency plots (PDPs). Once the model has been deployed, we can use interpretability techniques to ensure that the model predictions continue to be fair.

In this chapter, we will delve deeper into the topic of bias and fairness using another concrete example of predicting the income of adults. We will then come up with formal definitions for various notions of fairness and use them to determine whether the model is biased. We will then use interpretability techniques to measure and expose fairness issues. We will also discuss techniques to mitigate bias. Lastly, we will look at a standardizing approach of documenting datasets using datasheets that will help improve transparency and accountability with the stakeholders and users of the AI system.

8.1   *Adult income prediction*

To contextualize the problem of fairness, let's look at a concrete example. You are tasked by the Census Bureau to build a model to predict the income of adults in the United States. The prediction problem is shown in figure 8.3.

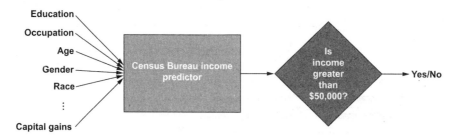

Figure 8.3   Income predictor for the Census Bureau

As we can see in figure 8.3, we are given various inputs for income prediction, such as level of education, occupation, age, gender, race, capital gains earned, and so on. We are tasked with building the income predictor shown as the rectangular box that takes these inputs and outputs a yes or no answer to the question, "Does the adult earn more than $50,000 per year?" This problem can, therefore, be formulated as a binary classification problem because we are interested in a binary answer: yes or no. We will treat the answer "yes" as the positive label and the answer "no" as the negative label.

We are given a historical dataset from the Census Bureau consisting of 30,940 adults. The input features are summarized in table 8.1. From the table, we can see a mixture of continuous and categorical variables. Most of the datasets that we have dealt with in this book consisted of continuous features where the feature values are real numbers. We have seen how to deal with categorical features in chapter 3. To recap, categorical features are features whose values are discrete and finite. We need to encode them into numerical values, and we have also seen how to do that in chapter 3 using label encoders.

Table 8.1   Input features for income prediction

Feature name	Description	Type	Is protected attribute?
age	Age of the adult	Continuous	Yes
workclass	Class of worker	Categorical	No
fnlwgt	Final weight assigned by the Census Bureau	Continuous	No

Table 8.1 Input features for income prediction

Feature name	Description	Type	Is protected attribute?
education	Level of education	Categorical	No
marital-status	Marital status	Categorical	No
occupation	Occupation	Categorical	No
gender	Male or female	Categorical	Yes
race	White or Black	Categorical	Yes
capital-gain	Capital gains	Continuous	No
capital-loss	Capital losses	Continuous	No
hours-per-week	Number of working hours per week	Continuous	No
native-country	Country of origin	Categorical	No

In addition, table 8.1 also shows whether a given feature is a protected attribute. Protected attributes are attributes that cannot be used to discriminate against an individual according to legislation largely shared by many countries. In the United States, for instance, the Civil Rights Act of 1964 protects individuals from discrimination on the basis of attributes like gender, race, age, color, creed, national origin, sexual orientation, and religion. In the United Kingdom, individuals with the same attributes are protected from discrimination according to the Equality Act of 2010.

In this dataset, we are dealing with three protected attributes: age, gender, and race. Age is a continuous feature, and gender and race are categorical. We will primarily focus on gender and race in this chapter, but we will learn how to extend the fairness notions and techniques to a continuous protected attribute like age as well. As for gender and race, we are dealing with two genders, male and female, and two races, white and Black, in this dataset. We unfortunately cannot include more gender or race groups because they are not properly represented in this dataset.

Finally, the target variable in this dataset is binary, where 1 is used to indicate that the adult earns more than $50,000 per year and 0 is used to indicate that the salary is less than or equal to $50,000 per year. Let's now explore this dataset, specifically focusing on the distribution of salary overall and for the two protected attributes of interest: gender and race.

8.1.1   Exploratory data analysis

Figure 8.4 shows the overall split of salary, gender, and race in the 30,940 adults in the dataset provided by the Census Bureau. We can see that the dataset is indeed skewed or biased. Around 75% of the population earns a salary that is less than or equal to $50K, and the rest earn a salary greater than $50K. In terms of gender, male adults are more represented in this dataset than female adults, where around 65% of the population is male. Similarly for race, we do see a bias toward white adults, in that around 90% of the adults in the dataset are white. Note that you can find the source code used for exploratory data analysis in the GitHub repository associated with this book.

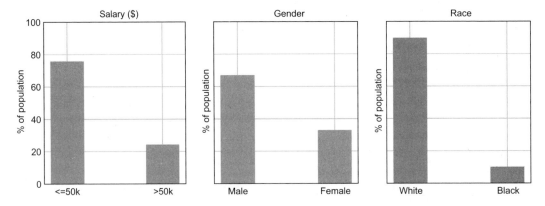

Figure 8.4   Salary, gender, and race distributions

Let's now look at the distribution of salary for various protected gender and race groups to determine whether there is any bias there. This is shown in figure 8.5. If we look at gender, we can see that a higher proportion of male adults than female adults earn more than $50K. We can also make the same observation for race, where a higher proportion of white adults than Black adults earns more than $50K.

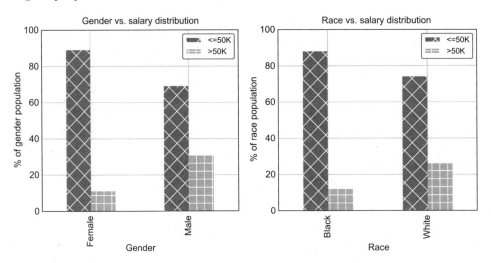

Figure 8.5   Distributions of salary vs. gender and salary vs. race

Finally, let's look at the representation of gender for the two races in this dataset, shown in figure 8.6. We can see that among Black adults, the split between male and female is pretty even, at around 50%. For white adults, on the other hand, more white male adults are represented than white females. This analysis is useful to determine the main cause of the bias in terms of salary. Because 70% of the white adults are male, the bias in salary for white adults may be better explained by the gender protected group where male users may be earning more than female users in the dataset. For Black adults, on the other hand, because the split between male and female is pretty even, the main source of bias for Black adults may be the race itself.

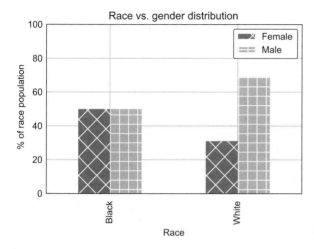

Figure 8.6   Gender vs. race distribution

It is important to understand the root cause of these biases in the dataset before we proceed to build the model. We are not sure how the dataset was collected and, hence, cannot be certain of the root cause. We can, however, hypothesize that the sources of bias could be the following:

- Sampling bias, where the dataset does not properly represent the true population.
- Labeling bias, where biases may exist in the way that salary information is recorded for various groups in the population.
- Systemic bias in society. If there is systemic bias, then that bias will be reflected in the dataset.

As we already discussed in chapter 3, the first problem can be solved by collecting more data that is representative of the population. In this chapter, we will also learn about properly documenting the data-collection process using datasheets for improved transparency and accountability. These datasheets can also be used to determine the root cause of biases in the dataset. Labeling bias can be fixed by improving the data-collection process. We will also learn about another technique to correct for label bias in this chapter. The last problem is much harder to solve, requiring better policies and laws, and this is beyond the scope of this book.

8.1.2 Prediction model

From our exploratory analysis, we found some biases in our dataset, the root causes of which are unfortunately unknown. In the interest of measuring model fairness, we will now build a model for predicting the income of adults. We will use a random forest model for this purpose. As you learned in chapter 3, a random forest is a way of combining decision trees, specifically using the bagging technique. An illustration of this model is shown in figure 8.7. The training data is fed in tabular or matrix form into the random forest model. Note that the categorical features are encoded into numerical values. Using random forest, we can train multiple decision trees in parallel on separate random subsets of the training data. Predictions are made using these individual decision trees, and all of them are combined to come up with the final prediction. Majority voting is typically used as a way of combining the individual decision tree predictions into a final one.

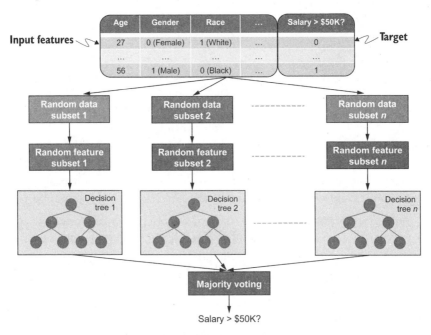

Figure 8.7   An illustration of a random forest model for income prediction

As an exercise, write the code to train a random forest model on the adult income dataset. You can use the code examples from chapter 3 as a reference. Note that you can use the `LabelEncoder` class provided by Scikit-Learn to encode the categorical features into numerical values. Also, you can try the `RandomForestClassifier` class provided by Scikit-Learn to initialize and train the model. You can find the solution to this exercise in the GitHub repository associated with this book.

For the remainder of this chapter, we will use a random forest model trained using 10 estimators or decision trees with a maximum depth of 20 for each decision tree.

The performance of this model is summarized in table 8.2. We will consider four metrics for model evaluation, namely, accuracy, precision, recall, and F1. These metrics were introduced in chapter 3, and we have repeatedly used them in previous chapters. We will also consider a baseline model that always predicts the majority class to be 0, that is, the income of the adult is always less than or equal to $50K. The performance of the random forest model is compared with this baseline. We can see that the random forest model outperforms the baseline on multiple metrics, achieving an accuracy of about 86% (+10% compared to the baseline), a precision of about 85% (+27% compared to the baseline), a recall of about 86% (+10% compared to the baseline), and an F1 of about 85% (+19% compared to the baseline).

Table 8.2 Performance of the income-prediction random forest model

	Accuracy (%)	Precision (%)	Recall (%)	F1 (%)
Baseline	76.1	57.9	76.1	65.8
Random forest	85.8	85.3	85.8	85.4

Let's now interpret the random forest model in a couple of ways. First, let's look at the importance of the input features as deemed by the random forest model. This will help us understand the importance of some of the protected group features, as shown in figure 8.8. You can review the source code used to generate the plot in the GitHub repository associated with this book. We can see that age (a protected group) is the most important feature, followed by capital gains. Race and gender, however, seem to have low importance. It could be that race and gender are encoded in some of the other features. We can check this by looking at the correlations between the features. We can also understand how race and gender may interact with some of the other features using partial dependence plots (PDPs), as we saw in chapter 3.

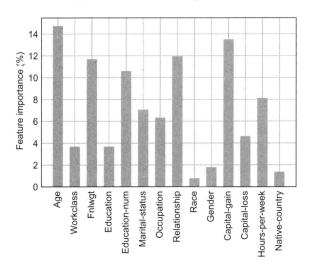

Figure 8.8 The importance of features learned by the random forest model

Next, we can use the SHAP technique to determine how the model makes a single prediction. As we learned in chapter 4, SHAP is a model-agnostic local interpretability technique that uses game-theoretic concepts to quantify the impact of features on a single model prediction. Figure 8.9 shows the SHAP explanation for an adult who earns more than $50K per year. Note that this data point was not used for training. We can see how each feature value pushes the model prediction from the base value to a score of 0.73 (i.e., 73% likelihood that the adult earns more than $50K). The most important feature values for this instance are capital gains, level of education, and hours worked per week in descending order.

Figure 8.9   SHAP explanation for a single prediction where salary is greater than $50K

We will revisit SHAP and dependency plots in the context of fairness again in section 8.3. We will also discuss how to use other interpretability techniques that we have learned in this book, like network dissection and t-SNE. But before that, let's learn about various notions of fairness.

8.2   *Fairness notions*

In the previous section, we trained a random forest model to make salary predictions. The objective of the model was to determine for each adult a binary outcome: whether or not they earn more than $50K. But were these predictions fair for various protected groups like gender and race? To formalize the definitions of various notions of fairness, let's look at a simple illustration of the predictions made by the model and the relevant measurements required for fairness. Figure 8.10 depicts an illustration of the predictions made by the model projected on a two-dimensional plane. The random forest model splits the 2-D plane into two halves that separate the positive predictions (on the right half) from the negative predictions (on the left half). The actual labels of 20 adults have been projected onto this 2-D plane as well. Note that the position of the actual labels on the 2-D plane is irrelevant. What matters is whether the labels fall on the left half (where the model predicts negative, i.e., 0) or on the right half (where the model predicts positive, i.e., 1). The actual positive labels are shown as circles and the actual negative labels are shown as triangles.

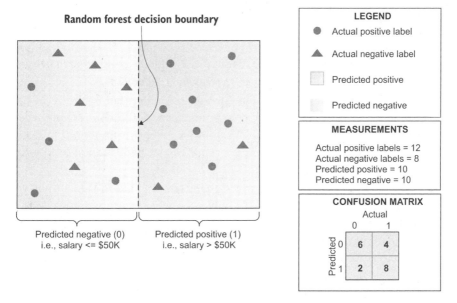

Figure 8.10 An illustration of model predictions and measurements relevant for fairness notions

Based on the illustration in figure 8.10, we can now define the following basic measurements:

- *Actual positive labels*—Data points for which the ground truth label in the dataset is positive. In figure 8.10, adults who earn more than $50K per year in the dataset are shown as circles. If we count the circles, the number of actual positive labels is equal to 12.

- *Actual negative labels*—Data points for which the ground truth label in the dataset is negative. In figure 8.10, adults who earn less than or equal to $50K per year in the dataset are shown as triangles. The number of actual negative labels is, therefore, 8.

- *Predicted positive*—Data points for which the model predicts a positive outcome. In figure 8.10, data points that fall in the right half of the 2-D plane have a positive prediction. There are 10 data points that fall in that region. Hence, predicted positive measurement is 10.

- *Predicted negative*—Data points for which the model predicts a negative outcome. In figure 8.10, these are points that fall in the left half of the 2-D plane. The predicted negative measurement is also 10.

- *True positive*—In figure 8.10, the true positives are the circles that fall in the right half of the 2-D plane. They are essentially data points for which the model predicts positive, and the actual label is also positive. There are eight such circles, and, therefore, the number of true positives is 8. We can also obtain this from the confusion matrix as well, where true positives are the cases where the model predicts 1 and the actual label is 1.

- *True negative*—The true negatives, on the other hand, are the triangles that fall in the left half of the 2-D plane. They are data points for which the model predicts negative, and the actual label is also negative. In figure 8.10, we can see that the number of true negatives is 6. From the confusion matrix, these are cases where the model predicts 0 and the actual label is 0.
- *False positive*—The false positives are triangles that fall in the right half of the plane in figure 8.10. They are data points for which the model predicts positive, but the actual label is negative. From the figure, the number of false positives is 2. From the confusion matrix, these are cases where the model predicts 1, but the actual label is 0.
- *False negative*—The false negatives are circles that fall in the left half of the 2-D plane. They are essentially data points for which the model predicts negative, but the actual label is positive. Since there are four circles in the left half of figure 8.10, the number of false negatives is 4. From the confusion matrix, these are cases where the model predicts 0, but the actual label is 1.

With these basic measurements in place, let's now define various notions of fairness.

8.2.1   Demographic parity

The first notion of fairness that we will consider is called *demographic parity*. The demographic parity notion is sometimes also called *independence, statistical parity*, and, legally, *disparate impact*. It asserts that for the model, parity exists in the positive prediction rates for different protected groups. Let's look at the example illustrated in figure 8.11. In the figure, the 20 adults—as we saw in figure 8.10—have been separated into two groups, A and B, one for each of the protected gender groups. Group A consists of male adults and has 10 data points in its 2-D plane. Group B consists of female adults with 10 data points in its 2-D plane.

Based on the illustration in figure 8.11, we can now calculate the basic measurements described earlier. For male adults, there are six actual positives, four actual negatives, five predicted positives, and five predicted negatives. For female adults, we can

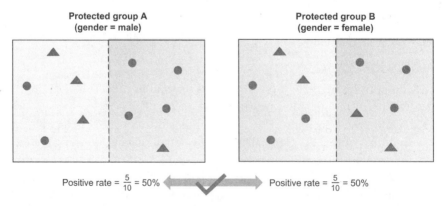

Figure 8.11   An illustration of demographic parity for two protected gender groups

see that the actual positives/negatives and predicted positive/negatives are the same as for male adults. The positive rate for both male and female adults is the proportion of adults in each group for which the model predicts positive. We can see from figure 8.11 that the positive rates for both male and female users are the same—equal to 50%. We can, therefore, assert that there is demographic parity between the two groups.

Let's look at this from a practical standpoint. Assume that the model predictions are used to allocate a scarce resource, say, a housing loan. Let's also assume that adults who earn more than $50K are more likely to be able to afford a house and pay off the loan. If a decision like a housing loan application is made based on the model prediction, where loans are granted to adults who earn more than $50K, then demographic parity will ensure that the loans are granted at an equal rate for both male and female adults. Demographic parity asserts that the model predicts that the salary of male and female adults is greater than $50K with equal likelihood.

Let's now define demographic parity more formally and use this definition to check whether our random forest model is fair using this notion. Let's represent the model predictions as $\hat{y}$ and the protected group variable as z. The gender protected group can have two possible values for the variable z:: 0 for female adults and 1 for male adults. For the race protected group as well, the variable z can have two possible values: 0 for Black adults and 1 for white adults. Demographic parity requires that the probability that the model predicts positive for one protected group is similar or equal to the probability that the model predicts positive for the other protected group. The probability measures are similar if their ratio is between thresholds τ_1 and τ_2, where the thresholds are typically 0.8 and 1.2, respectively. The thresholds are 0.8 and 1.2, to closely follow the 80% rule in legal literature for disparate impact, as shown by the next equation. The probability measures are equal if the ratio is 1:

$$\tau_1 \leq \frac{\mathbb{P}\left(\hat{y}=1|z=0\right)}{\mathbb{P}\left(\hat{y}=1|z=1\right)} \leq \tau_2$$

Now, how would we use this definition for a protected group feature that is categorical but with more than two values? In this example, we considered only two races: white and Black. What if there were more races in the dataset? Note that individuals could be multiracial, where they identify with multiple races. We will treat them as a separate race to ensure there is no discrimination toward individuals who identify as multiple races. In such a scenario with more than two races, we would define the demographic parity ratio metric for each race and take a one-vs.-all strategy, where $z = 0$ represents the race of interest and $z = 1$ represents all the other races. Note that individuals who are multiracial could belong to multiple groups. We will then need to ensure that the demographic parity ratio is similar for every race when compared to all other races. How about for a protected group feature that is continuous, like age? In this case, we would need to split the continuous feature into discrete groups and then apply the one-vs.-all strategy.

With the definition now in place, let's see if the random forest model is fair. The following code snippet evaluates the model using the demographic parity notion:

Loads the indices for female adults in the test set where the encoded gender = 0

Loads the indices for male adults in the test set where the encoded gender = 1

Loads the indices for white adults in the test set where the encoded race = 1

Loads the indices for Black adults in the test set where the encoded race = 0

```
male_indices_test = X_test[X_test['gender'] == 1].index.values
female_indices_test = X_test[X_test['gender'] == 0].index.values
white_indices_test = X_test[X_test['race'] == 1].index.values
black_indices_test = X_test[X_test['race'] == 0].index.values

y_score = adult_model.predict_proba(X_test)

y_score_male_test = y_score[male_indices_test, :]
y_score_female_test = y_score[female_indices_test, :]
y_score_white_test = y_score[white_indices_test, :]
y_score_black_test = y_score[black_indices_test, :]

dem_par_gender_ratio = np.mean(y_score_female_test
  [:, 1]) / np.mean(y_score_male_test[:, 1])
dem_par_race_ratio = np.mean(y_score_black_test
  [:, 1]) / np.mean(y_score_white_test[:, 1])
```

Gets the model predictions for all the adults in the test set

Obtains the model predictions for the two gender groups

Obtains the model predictions for the two race groups

Computes the demographic parity ratio for the two gender groups

Computes the demographic parity ratio for the two race groups

Note that in this code snippet, we are using the label-encoded dataset and the model trained in section 8.1.2. The label-encoded input features are stored in the X_test data frame, and the random forest model is named adult_model. Note that you can obtain the code used for data preparation and model training from the GitHub repository associated with this book. We are computing the demographic parity ratio as the ratio of average probability scores for predicting the positive class of one of the groups (female/Black adults) to its counterpart groups (male/white adults). Once we have computed the demographic parity ratios for the gender and race groups, we can plot the metric using the following code snippet:

```
def plot_bar(values, labels, ax, color='b'):
    bar_width = 0.35
    opacity = 0.9
    index = np.arange(len(values))
    ax.bar(index, values, bar_width,
            alpha=opacity,
            color=color)
    ax.set_xticks(index)
    ax.set_xticklabels(labels)
    ax.grid(True);

threshold_1 = 0.8
threshold_2 = 1.2
```

Helper function called plot_bar used to plot the bar chart

Sets the thresholds for the demographic parity ratio

```
f, ax = plt.subplots()
plot_bar([dem_par_gender_ratio, dem_par_race_ratio],
         ['Gender', 'Race'],
         ax=ax, color='r')
ax.set_ylabel('Demographic Parity Ratio')
ax.set_ylim([0, 1.5])
ax.plot([-0.5, 1.5],
        [threshold_1, threshold_1], "k--",
        linewidth=3.0)
ax.plot([-0.5, 1.5],
        [threshold_2, threshold_2], "k--",
        label='Threshold',
        linewidth=3.0)
ax.legend();
```

Initializes a Matplotlib plot

Plots the demographic parity ratios for gender and race as bar charts

Sets the label for the y-axis

Plots threshold_1 as a horizontal line

Limits the y-axis to values between −0.5 and 1.5

Plots threshold_2 as a horizontal line

Displays the legend for the plot

The resulting plot is shown in figure 8.12. We can see that the demographic parity ratios are 0.38 and 0.45, respectively, for gender and race. They are not within the threshold and, therefore, the random forest model is not fair for both protected groups using the demographic parity notion. We will see how to mitigate bias and train a fair model in section 8.4.

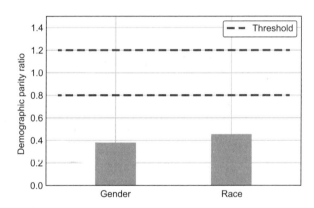

Figure 8.12 Demographic parity ratios for gender and race

8.2.2 *Equality of opportunity and odds*

The demographic parity notion is useful for scenarios where we want to ensure parity in the treatment of all protected groups, irrespective of their prevalence in the population. It ensures that the minority group is treated the same way as the majority group. In some scenarios, we might want to consider the distribution of the actual label for all protected groups. For example, if we are interested in employment opportunities, one group of individuals may be more interested in and qualified for certain jobs than other groups. We may not want to ensure parity in such a scenario because we may want to ensure that job opportunities are given to the right group of individuals who are more interested in and qualified for it. We can use the equality of opportunity and odds fairness notion in such a scenario.

Let's go back to the illustration used for demographic parity to build up our intuition. In figure 8.13, the separation of the 20 adults in groups A (male) and B (female) is the same as what we saw for demographic parity in figure 8.11. For equality of opportunity and odds, we are interested in measurements that take into account the distribution of the actual label for each of the protected groups. These measurements are computed in figure 8.13 as the true positive rate and the false positive rate. The true positive rate measures the probability that an actual positive is predicted positive and is computed as the ratio of the number of the true positives to the sum of the number of true positives and false negatives. In other words, the true positive rate measures the percentage of actual true cases that the model got right, also called recall. For group A (male), the true positive rate is about 66.7%, and for group B (female), the true positive rate is 50%. We say there is equality of opportunity when parity exists in the true positive rates between the groups. Because the true positive rates do not match in the toy example illustrated in figure 8.13, we can say that we have not achieved equality of opportunity for the gender protected group.

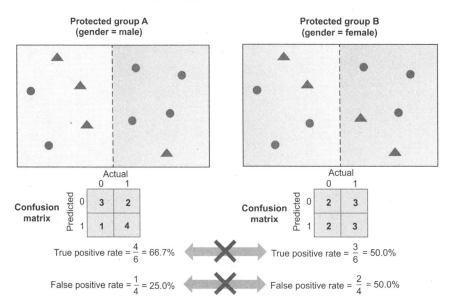

Figure 8.13   An illustration of equality of opportunity and odds for two protected gender groups

Equality of odds extends the definition of equality of opportunity to another symmetric measurement called false positive rate. False positive rate measures the probability that an actual negative event is predicted as positive. It is computed as the ratio of the number of false positives to the sum of the number of false positives and true negatives. We can assert that equality of odds exists when there is parity in the true positive rates and false positive rates between the protected groups. In the toy example illustrated in figure 8.13, there is no parity in the true positive rates between groups A and B, so we cannot say equality of odds exists. Moreover, the false positive rates also do not match between the two groups.

We can define equality of opportunity and odds more formally using the equations that follow. The first equation essentially computes the difference in the true positive rates between the two groups. The second equation computes the difference in the false positive rates between the two groups. Parity is present when the difference is equal to or close to 0. This notion is different from the demographic parity notion in that it considers the distribution of the actual label—positive for the true positive rate and negative for the false positive rate. In addition, the demographic parity notion compares the probabilities as a ratio rather than additively, closely following the "80% rule" in the legal literature:

$$\mathbb{P}\left(\hat{y} = 1 | z = 0, y = 1\right) - \mathbb{P}\left(\hat{y} = 1 | z = 1, y = 1\right)$$

$$\mathbb{P}\left(\hat{y} = 1 | z = 0, y = 0\right) - \mathbb{P}\left(\hat{y} = 1 | z = 1, y = 0\right)$$

Now let's see if our random forest model is fair using this notion. We can compare the true positive rate and false positive rate using the receiver operator characteristic (ROC) curve. The ROC curve essentially plots the true positive rate against the false positive rate. For equality of opportunity and odds, we can then use the area under the curve (AUC) as an aggregate measure of performance to easily compare the performance of the model for each of the protected groups. We can look at the difference in the AUC between the groups to see how fair the model is. The next code snippet shows how to compute the true/false positive rates and the AUC:

Imports the roc_curve and auc helper functions from Scikit-Learn

Defines a helper function to compute the ROC and AUC for each of the protected groups

```
from sklearn.metrics import roc_curve, auc

def compute_roc_auc(y_test, y_score):
    fpr = dict()
    tpr = dict()
    roc_auc = dict()
    for i in [1]:
        fpr[i], tpr[i], _ = roc_curve(y_test,
            y_score[:, i])
        roc_auc[i] = auc(fpr[i], tpr[i])
    return fpr, tpr, roc_auc

fpr_male, tpr_male, roc_auc_male = compute_roc_auc(y_male_test,
                                        y_pred_proba_male_test)
fpr_female, tpr_female, roc_auc_female = compute_roc_auc(y_female_test,
                                        d_proba_female_test)
fpr_white, tpr_white, roc_auc_white = compute_roc_auc(y_white_test,
                                        y_pred_proba_white_tes
fpr_black, tpr_black, roc_auc_black = compute_roc_auc(y_black_test,
                                        y_pred_proba_black_test)
```

Defines dictionaries for the true/false positive rates and AUC to store the metrics for each of the classes in the dataset

Returns the dictionaries to the caller of the function

For the actual label, computes the true/false positive rates and AUC and stores them in dictionaries

Uses the helper function to compute the metrics for male adults

Uses the helper function to compute the metrics for female adults

Uses the helper function to compute the metrics for white adults

Uses the helper function to compute the metrics for Black adults

Once the metrics have been computed for each of the protected groups, we can use the following code snippet to plot the ROC curve:

Sets the line width for the line chart

```
lw = 1.5
f, ax = plt.subplots(1, 2, figsize=(15, 5))
ax[0].plot(fpr_male[1], tpr_male[1],
        linestyle='-', color='b',
        lw=lw,
        label='Male (Area = %0.2f)' % roc_auc_male[1])
ax[0].plot(fpr_female[1], tpr_female[1],
        linestyle='--', color='g',
        lw=lw,
        label='Female (Area = %0.2f)' % roc_auc_female[1])
ax[1].plot(fpr_white[1], tpr_white[1],
        linestyle='-', color='c',
        lw=lw,
        label='White (Area = %0.2f)' % roc_auc_white[1])
ax[1].plot(fpr_black[1], tpr_black[1],
        linestyle='--', color='r',
        lw=lw,
        label='Black (Area = %0.2f)' % roc_auc_black[1])
ax[0].legend()
ax[1].legend()
ax[0].set_ylabel('True Positive Rate')
ax[0].set_xlabel('False Positive Rate')
ax[1].set_ylabel('True Positive Rate')
ax[1].set_xlabel('False Positive Rate')
ax[0].set_title('ROC Curve (Gender)')
ax[1].set_title('ROC Curve (Race)')
```

Initializes the Matplotlib plot consisting of one row and two columns

In the first column, plots the ROC curve for male adults

In the first column, plots the ROC curve for female adults

In the second column, plots the ROC curve for white adults

In the second column, plots the ROC curve for Black adults

Annotates and labels the plot

The resulting plot is shown in figure 8.14. The first column in the plot compares the ROC curves for the two gender groups: male and female. The second column compares the ROC curves for the two race groups: white and Black. The area under the curve is shown in the legend for both plots. We can see that the AUC is 0.89 for male adults and 0.92 for female adults. The difference is roughly 3% skewed toward female adults. The AUC for white adults, on the other hand, is 0.9 and for Black adults, 0.92. The difference is roughly 2% skewed toward Black adults. Unlike demographic parity, unfortunately, no guidelines from the legal or research communities exist on what thresholds to use for the AUC difference metric to consider a model fair. In this chapter, if the difference is statistically significant, we will treat the model as unfair using the equality of opportunity and odds notion. We will see if these differences are significant using confidence intervals in section 8.3.1.

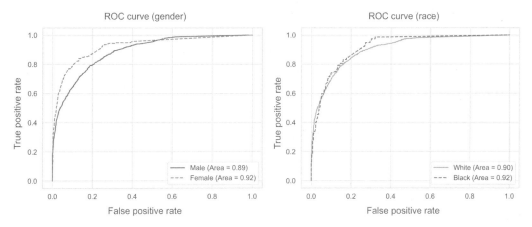

Figure 8.14   Received operator characteristic (ROC) curve for gender and race

8.2.3   *Other notions of fairness*

The most commonly used notions of fairness are demographic parity and equality of opportunity/odds. But, for awareness, let's also look at the following other notions of fairness:

- *Predictive quality parity*—No difference exists in the prediction quality between different groups. The prediction quality can be either the accuracy of the model or any other performance metric, like F1.
- *Treatment equality*—The model treats the groups equally, whereby parity exists in the false prediction rate. The false prediction rate is quantified as the ratio of the false negatives to the false positives.
- *Fairness through unawareness*—Fairness can be achieved by not explicitly using the protected attributes as features for prediction. In an ideal world, the other features used by the model are not correlated with the protected attributes, but this is almost always not the case. Hence, achieving fairness through unawareness is not guaranteed. We will see this in action in section 8.4.1.
- *Counterfactual fairness*—A model is fair to an individual if it makes the same prediction if that individual belongs to another protected group in a counterfactual world.

We can divide all the notions of fairness into two categories—*group fairness* and *individual fairness*. Group fairness ensures that the model is fair for different protected groups. For the adult income dataset, protected groups are gender, race, and age. Individual fairness, on the other hand, ensures that the model makes similar predictions for similar individuals. For the adult income dataset, individuals can be similar based on their level of education, country of origin, or hours worked per week, to name a few examples. Table 8.3 shows which category the different notions of fairness belong to.

Table 8.3   Group and individual fairness notion

Fairness notion	Description	Category
Demographic parity	Parity in the positive prediction rates for different protected groups	Group
Equality of opportunity and odds	Parity in the true positive rates and false positive rates for different protected groups	Group
Predictive quality parity	Parity in the prediction quality for different protected groups	Group
Treatment equality	Parity in the false prediction rates for different protected groups	Group
Fairness through unawareness	Fairness achieved by not explicitly using protected attributes as features for prediction	Individual
Counterfactual fairness	Similar prediction for an individual if that individual belonged to another protected group in a counterfactual world	Individual

8.3   *Interpretability and fairness*

In this section, we will learn how to use interpretability techniques to detect the source of discrimination due to the model. The source of discrimination can be broadly categorized into the following two groups:

- *Discrimination via input features*—Fairness issues that can be traced back to the input features.
- *Discrimination via representation*—Fairness issues that are hard to trace back to the input features, especially for deep learning models that process inputs like images and text. For such cases, we could instead trace the source of discrimination to deep representations learned by the model.

8.3.1   *Discrimination via input features*

Let's first look at discrimination via input features. When we looked at the various fairness notions in section 8.2, we saw by processing the model output that the random forest model is not fair using the demographic parity and equality of opportunity/odds fairness measures. How can we explain these measures of fairness by tracing back to the inputs? We can make use of SHAP for this purpose. As we saw in chapter 4 and in section 8.1.2, SHAP decomposes the model output into Shapley values for each of the inputs. These Shapley values are of the same unit as the model output—if we sum up the Shapley values for all the features, we will get a value that matches the model output that measures the probability of predicting a positive outcome. We saw an illustration of this in section 8.1.2. Because the Shapley values for the input features sum up to the model output, we can attribute differences in the model output (and, in turn, the fairness measures) between protected groups back to differences in the Shapley values for each of the inputs. This is how you would trace any discrimination or fairness issues back to the inputs.

Let's see this in action using code. The following code snippet defines a helper function to generate SHAP differences between protected groups and can be used to generate visualizations for differences in the model output traced back to the input:

Helper function to generate the SHAP group difference plot that takes six inputs. Input 1: DataFrame of feature values

Input 2: Vector of target values

Input 3: SHAP values generated for the input features

Input 4: Fairness notion that can be demographic_parity of equality_of_opportunity

Input 5: Protected group that can be either gender or race

Input 6: Flag to indicate whether to trace the source of discrimination to the inputs

Returns None for fairness notions and protected groups that are not supported

Sets the label for the demographic parity notion

Sets the label and processes only the actual positives for the equality of opportunity notion

Sets the label and mask for the gender protected group

Sets the label and mask for the race protected group

Sets the label for visualization

Restricts the visualization to xmin and xmax

Creates visualization when trace_to_input is set to True

Creates visualization when trace_to_input is set to False

```python
def generate_shap_group_diff(df_X,
                             y,
                             shap_values,
                             notion='demographic_parity',
                             protected_group='gender',
                             trace_to_input=False):
    if notion not in ['demographic_parity',
        'equality_of_opportunity']:
        return None
    if protected_group not in ['gender', 'race']:
        return None
    if notion == 'demographic_parity':
        flabel = 'Demographic parity difference'
    if notion == 'equality_of_opportunity':
        flabel = 'Equality of opportunity difference'
        positive_label_indices = np.where(y == 1)[0]
        df_X = df_X.iloc[np.where(y == 1)[0]]
        shap_values = shap_values[np.where(y == 1)[0],:]
    if protected_group == 'gender':
        pg_label = 'men v/s women'
        mask = df_X['gender'].values == 1
    if protected_group == 'race':
        pg_label = 'white v/s black'
        mask = df_X['race'].values == 1
    glabel = f"{flabel}\nof model output for {pg_label}"
    xmin = -0.8
    xmax = 0.8
    if trace_to_input:
        shap.group_difference_plot(shap_values,
                             mask,
                             df_X.columns,
                             xmin=xmin,
                             xmax=xmax,
                             xlabel=glabel,
                             show=False)
    else:
        shap.group_difference_plot(shap_values.sum(1),
                             mask,
                             xmin=xmin,
                             xmax=xmax,
                             xlabel=glabel,
                             show=False)
```

We'll first use the helper function to check the demographic parity difference in the model output for the gender protected group, as shown in the next code sample. Note that we are looking at model predictions only in the test set. The shap_values variable contains the Shapley values for all the inputs and adults in the dataset. We generated this in section 8.1.2, and you can find the source code in the GitHub repository associated with this book:

```
test_indices = X_test.index.values                Extracts the indices of
                                                   the inputs in the test set
generate_shap_group_diff(X_test,
                         y_test,
                         shap_values[1][test_indices,:]    Invokes the helper function
                         notion='demographic_parity',      to generate the SHAP plot
                         protected_group='gender',         with the appropriate inputs
                         trace_to_input=False)
```

The resulting visualization is shown in figure 8.15. Note that the difference can be positive or negative. If the difference is positive, then the model is biased toward male adults, and if the difference is negative, then the model is biased toward female adults. We can see in figure 8.15 that the random forest model is skewed toward male adults where it predicts positive (i.e., salary > \$50K) more for male adults.

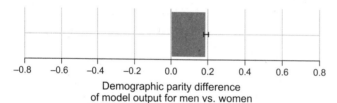

Demographic parity difference
of model output for men vs. women

Figure 8.15   SHAP
demographic parity difference
in model output for gender

To determine what is causing the demographic parity difference between male and female adults, we can trace it back to the input features using the following code snippet:

```
generate_shap_group_diff(X_test,
                         y_test,
                         shap_values[1][test_indices,:]    Invokes the helper function with
                         notion='demographic_parity',      the same inputs as before but
                         protected_group='gender',         with trace_to_input set to True
                         trace_to_input=True)
```

The resulting plot is shown in figure 8.16. We can see that the bias is primarily coming from three features: relationship, gender, and marital status. By identifying the features that are causing the model to violate the demographic parity fairness notion, we can take a closer look at the data to understand what the cause of the bias is for these features, as we discussed in section 8.1.1.

As an exercise, use the helper function to determine whether a difference exists in the equality of opportunity fairness measure and trace it back to the inputs. You can set the `notion` input parameter to `equality_of_opportunity` so that the function will look only at the difference in model outputs and Shapley values for the actual positives in the dataset.

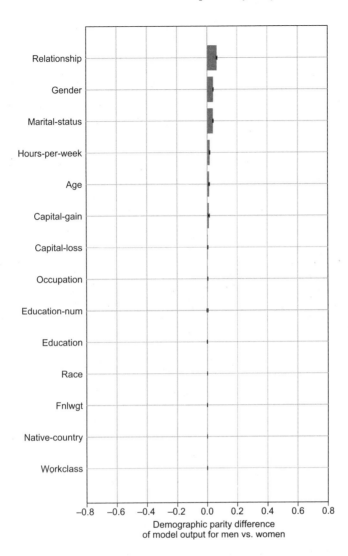

Figure 8.16 SHAP demographic parity difference for gender traced back to the inputs

Figure 8.17 shows the resulting visualization for the model output. We can see that the difference in true positive rates between male and female adults is statistically significant where the model is skewed toward male adults when predicting a positive outcome. We can say, therefore, that the model is unfair using the equality of opportunity notion. You can trace the bias back to the inputs by setting the `trace_to_input` parameter to `True`.

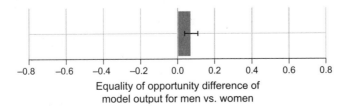

Figure 8.17 SHAP equality of opportunity difference for gender

8.3.2   *Discrimination via representation*

In some cases, it is hard to trace the discrimination issue or differences in fairness measures back to the inputs. For example, if the input is an image or a text, it will be hard to trace differences in fairness measures back to pixel values or values in word representations. In such cases, a better option would be to detect any bias in the representations learned by the models. Let's look at a simple example where the objective is to train a model to detect whether an image contains a doctor. Let's suppose that we have trained a convolutional neural network (CNN) that predicts whether an image contains a doctor. If we want to check whether this model is biased toward any protected group like gender, we can make use of the network dissection framework that we learned in chapter 6 to determine whether the model has learned any concepts specific to the protected attribute. The high-level process is shown in figure 8.18.

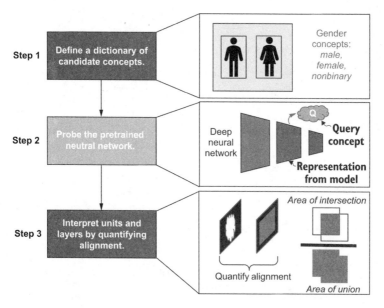

Figure 8.18   A high-level illustration of how to use the network dissection framework to check for bias in the learned representations

In figure 8.18, we focus on the gender protected attribute. The first step is to define a dictionary of gender-specific concepts. The figure shows an example where an image has been labeled at the pixel level for the various gender concepts such as male, female, and nonbinary. The next step is to probe the pretrained network followed by quantifying the alignment of each unit and layer in the CNN with the gender-specific concepts. Once we have quantified the alignment, we can check how many unique detectors exist for each of the gender concepts. If one of the genders has more unique detectors, we can say that the model seems to have learned a representation that is biased to that gender.

Let's now look at an example where the input to the model is in the form of text. We learned in chapter 7 how to come up with dense and distributed representations of words that convey semantic meaning. How can we check whether the representations learned by the model are biased toward a protected group? If we look at the doctor example, is the word *doctor* gender neutral or biased toward any gender? We can check this by using of the t-distributed stochastic neighbor embedding (t-SNE) technique that we learned in chapter 7. We will, however, first need to come up with a taxonomy for words so that we know which words are gender neutral and which words are associated with a particular gender, like *male* or *female*. Once we have the taxonomy, we can use t-SNE to visualize how close the word *doctor* is to other words in the corpus. If the word *doctor* is closer to other gender-neutral words like *hospital* or *healthcare*, the representation learned by the model for *doctor* is not biased. If, on the other hand, the word *doctor* is closer to gender-specific words like *man* or *woman*, then the representation is biased.

8.4 Mitigating bias

We have the following three broad ways of mitigating bias in a model:

- *Preprocessing*—We apply these methods before training the model in an aim to mitigate bias in the training dataset.
- *In-processing*—We apply these methods during model training. The fairness notion is explicitly or implicitly incorporated into the learning algorithm such that the model optimizes not just for performance (like accuracy) but also for fairness.
- *Postprocessing*—We apply these methods after model training to the predictions made by the model. The model predictions are calibrated to ensure that the fairness constraint is met.

We will focus on two preprocessing methods in this section.

8.4.1 Fairness through unawareness

One common preprocessing method is to remove any protected features from the model. In certain regulated industries like housing, employment, and credit, it is forbidden by law to use any protected features as inputs to a model used for decision-making. For the random forest model that we've trained for adult income prediction, let's try to remove the two protected features of interest—gender and race—and see if the model is fair using the equality of opportunity/odds notion. As an exercise, remove the label-encoded gender and race features from the random forest model and retrain the model using the same hyperparameters as earlier. Check out the solution in the GitHub repository associated with this book.

The performance of the retrained model in terms of the ROC curve is shown in figure 8.19. As we saw in section 8.2.2, the ROC curve was used to plot the true positive rate against the false positive rate, and we can use the AUC obtained from this ROC curve to check whether the model is fair given the equality of opportunity and odds notion. For the previous random forest model that used gender and race as input features, the AUC difference was 3% between gender groups and 2% between race groups. By using fairness through unawareness, the difference between the race groups has reduced to 1%, but with no change to the difference between the gender groups. Fairness through unawareness, therefore, does not provide any fairness guarantees. Other features could be highly correlated with these protected groups and could act as a proxy for gender and race. Moreover, we also see a degradation in model performance for all the groups where the AUC has reduced when compared to the previous random forest model. As we mentioned earlier, certain regulated industries require us to use fairness through unawareness by law. Even though the model is not guaranteed to be fair, the law requires that such industries not use any protected features in the model.

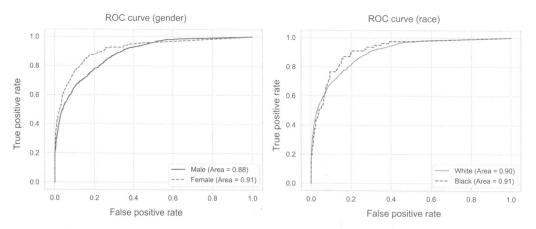

Figure 8.19   ROC curve for gender and race: fairness through unawareness

8.4.2   *Correcting label bias through reweighting*

Heinrich Jiang and Ofir Nachum proposed another preprocessing technique in 2019 that provides fairness guarantees. In the research paper published by the authors, available at https://arxiv.org/abs/1901.04966, they provide a mathematical formulation of biases that could arise in the training dataset. They assume that biases could occur in the observed labels in the dataset (also called label bias), and this could be corrected by iteratively reweighting the data points in the training dataset without changing the observed labels. They provide theoretical guarantees for this algorithm for a variety of fairness notions, such as demographic parity and equality of opportunity/odds. You can refer to the original paper to learn more about the mathematical formulation and the proofs. In this section, we will provide an overview of the algorithm and use the implementation provided by the authors at http://mng.bz/Ygjj.

The algorithm for correcting bias through reweighting is hinged on a key assumption. The labels observed in the dataset are based on an underlying true and unbiased set of labels that is unknown. The observed dataset is biased due to a labeler or process that is introducing the bias. The key assumption is that the source of this bias is unintentional and potentially due to unconscious or inherent biases. Based on this assumption, the authors of the paper mathematically prove that it is possible to build an unbiased classifier that is potentially trained on the unknown, unbiased dataset through reweighting of the features in the observed, biased dataset. This is illustrated in figure 8.20.

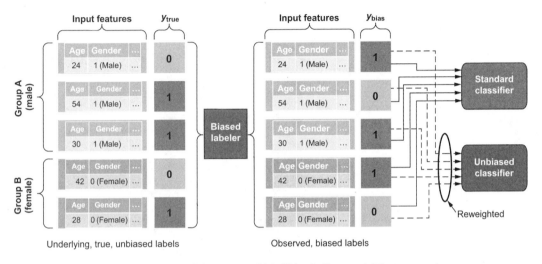

Figure 8.20 Underlying assumption of the source of label bias in the reweighting approach

The label bias reweighting algorithm is iterative and is summarized in figure 8.21. Let's assume that there are K protected groups in the dataset and N features. For the adult income dataset, the number of protected groups that are considered are four (two gender groups and two race groups). The dataset contains 14 features. Before running the algorithm, we need to initialize coefficients for each of the protected groups with a value of 0. We also need to initialize weights for each of the features with a value of 1.

With the coefficient and weights initialized, the next step is to train a model using these weights. Because we are considering the random forest model in this chapter, the model trained in this step will be identical to the model trained in section 8.1.2. The next step is to compute the fairness violations for this model for each of the K protected groups. The fairness violation is dependent on the specific notion that we are interested in. If the fairness notion is demographic parity, then the fairness violation for a protected group is the difference in the overall average positive rate for the model and the average positive rate for that specific protected group. If the fairness notion is equality of opportunity, then we need to consider the difference in the overall average true positive rate and the average true positive rate for the specific protected group. Once we have computed the fairness violations, the next step is to update the coefficients for each of the protected groups. The objective of the algorithm is to minimize the fairness violation, so we update the coefficients by subtracting the fairness violations from it. The final step is to then update the weights for each of the features using the coefficients for the protected groups. The formula for updating the weights is shown in figure 8.21, and you can see the derivation of this formula in the original paper published by the authors of this algorithm. The steps in this paragraph are then repeated T times where T is a hyperparameter that represents the number of iterations for which we want to run the algorithm.

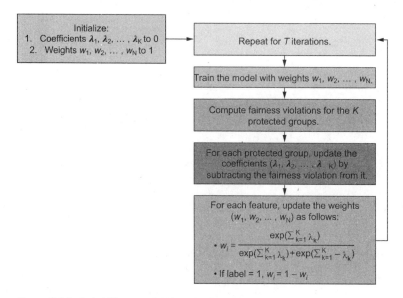

Figure 8.21   Label bias reweighting algorithm

Now let's apply this algorithm to the adult income dataset the model trained earlier. But before running the algorithm, we first need to prepare the data using the following code snippet. The idea is to convert the label-encoded gender and race features into one-hot encoded features where there is one column for each of the four protected groups (male, female, white, and Black adults) and a value of 0 or 1 to indicate whether the adult belongs to that specific protected group:

**Imports the partial function provided
by the Python functool library**

**Helper function to prepare
the dataset for the label bias
reweighting algorithm**

**Creates a
copy of the
original
DataFrame
and makes
changes to
the copy**

**Helper function that
maps each feature to
its encoded value**

```
from functools import partial
def prepare_data_for_label_bias(df_X, protected_features,
                                protected_encoded_map):
    df_X_copy = df_X.copy(deep=True)
    def map_feature(row, feature_name, feature_encoded):
        if row[feature_name] == feature_encoded:
            return 1
        return 0
```

```
colname_func_map = {}
for feature_name in protected_features:
    protected_encoded_fv = protected_encoded_map
    ➥ [feature_name]
    for feature_value in protected_encoded_fv:
        colname = f"{feature_name}_{feature_value}"
        colname_func_map[colname] = partial
        ➥ (map_feature,
            feature_name=feature_name,
            feature_encoded=protected_encoded_fv[feature_value])

for colname in colname_func_map:
    df_X_copy[colname] = df_X_copy.apply
    ➥ (colname_func_map[colname],
        axis=1)
df_X_copy = df_X_copy.drop(columns=protected_features)
return df_X_copy
```

Loops through all the protected features and creates separate columns for each group with their corresponding binary-encoded value

Drops the original protected feature columns from the copy of the DataFrame

Returns the copy of the DataFrame with the new columns

You can then use this helper function to prepare the dataset as follows. Note that a mapping of each protected group to its corresponding label-encoded value is created before invoking the helper function:

```
protected_features = ['gender', 'race']
protected_encoded_map = {
    'gender': {
        'male': 1,
        'female': 0
    },
    'race': {
        'white': 1,
        'black': 0
    }
}
df_X_lb = prepare_data_for_label_bias(df_X,
                            protected_features,
                            protected_encoded_map)
X_train_lb = df_X_lb.iloc[X_train.index]
X_test_lb = df_X_lb.iloc[X_test.index]
PROTECTED_GROUPS = ['gender_male', 'gender_female', 'race_white', 'race_black']
protected_train = [np.array(X_train_lb[g]) for g
➥ in PROTECTED_GROUPS]
protected_test = [np.array(X_test_lb[g]) for g
➥ in PROTECTED_GROUPS]
```

List of protected features to process

Mapping of each protected group to its corresponding label-encoded value

Invokes a helper function to prepare the dataset for the label bias reweighting algorithm

Splits the new dataset into train and test sets

Extracts the columns for the protected groups

Once you have prepared the dataset, you can easily plug it into the label bias reweighting algorithm. You can find the source code for this algorithm in the GitHub repository (http://mng.bz/Ygjj) published by the authors of the paper. In the interest of space, we will not rehash that code in this section. As an exercise, run through the algorithm and determine the weights for each of the data points in the training dataset. Once you have determined the weights, you can then retrain the unbiased random forest model by using the following code snippet:

Uses the helper function learned in chapter 3 to create the random forest model

```
model_lb = create_random_forest_model(10, max_depth=20)
model_lb.fit(X_train_lb,
             y_train,
             weights)
```

Invokes the fit method and passes in the prepared dataset and the weights obtained using the label bias reweighting algorithm

The performance of the retrained model in terms of the ROC curve is shown in figure 8.22. We can see that the differences in AUC between the gender groups and race groups are both 1%. This model is, therefore, fairer in terms of equality of opportunity and odds than the previously trained random forest model with gender and race as features and the model trained without those features.

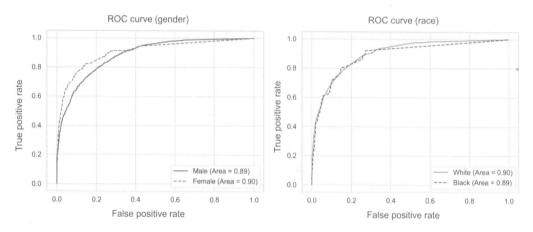

Figure 8.22   ROC curve for gender and race after correcting for label bias

8.5   *Datasheets for datasets*

While exploring the adult income dataset in section 8.1.1, we noticed that some protected groups (such as female and Black adults) were not properly represented, and biases existed in the labels for these groups. We identified a few sources of bias, namely, sampling bias and label bias, but we could not identify the root cause of the bias. The primary reason for this is that the data-collection process for this dataset is unknown. In a paper published by Timnit Gebru and other researchers at Google and Microsoft in 2020, a standardized process was proposed to document datasets. The idea is for data creators to come up with a datasheet that answers key questions regarding the motivation, composition, data-collection process, and uses of a dataset. Some of the key questions are highlighted next, but a more thorough study of this can be found in the original research paper at https://arxiv.org/pdf/1803.09010.pdf:

- Motivation
  - For what purpose was the dataset created? The goal of this question is to understand whether the dataset is meant for a specific task or to address a specific gap or need.
  - Who created the dataset? The goal is to identify an owner for the dataset, which could be an individual, team, company, organization, or institution.
  - Who funded the creation of the dataset? The goal is to understand whether the dataset is associated with a research grant or any other source of funding.
- Composition
  - What does the dataset represent? The goal is to understand whether the data represents documents, photos, videos, people, countries, or any other representation.
  - How many examples in the dataset? This question is self-explanatory and is meant to understand the size of the dataset in terms of the number of data points or examples.
  - Does the dataset contain all possible examples, or is it a sample from a larger dataset? The goal is to understand whether the dataset is a sample from a larger dataset or population. This will help us check whether any sampling bias exists.
  - Is the dataset labeled? The goal is to check whether the dataset is raw or labeled.
  - Does the dataset rely on external sources? The goal is to identify whether there is any external source or dependency for the dataset such as websites, tweets on Twitter, or any other dataset.
- Collection process
  - How was the data acquired? This question helps us understand the data-collection process.
  - What was the sampling strategy used, if applicable? This is an extension of the sampling question in the Composition section and helps us check whether any sampling bias exists.
  - Over what timeframe was the data collected?
  - Was the data collected from individuals directly or through a third party?
  - If the data is related to people, was their consent obtained for data collection? If the dataset is related to people, it is important that we work with experts in other domains like anthropology. The answer to this question is also essential to determine whether the dataset is compliant with regulations like the General Data Protection Regulation (GDPR) in the European Union (EU).
  - Does a mechanism for individuals exist to revoke consent in the future? This is also essential to determining whether the dataset is compliant with regulations.

- Uses
  - What will the dataset be used for? The goal is to identify all the possible tasks or uses for the dataset.
  - Should the dataset not be used for any tasks? The answer to this question will help us ensure that the dataset is not used for tasks that it isn't intended for.

Datasheets for datasets have already been adopted by research and industry. Some examples are the QuAC dataset used for question answering (https://quac.ai/datasheet.pdf), the RecipeQA dataset consisting of cooking recipes (http://mng.bz/GGnA), and the Open Images dataset (https://github.com/amukka/openimages). Although datasheets for datasets add additional overheard for dataset creators, they improve transparency and accountability, help us determine sources of bias if there are any, and ensure that we are compliant with regulations such as GDPR in the EU.

Summary

- Various sources of bias could occur in a dataset, such as sampling bias and label bias. Sampling bias occurs when the dataset does not properly represent the true population. Labeling bias occurs when bias exists in the way that labels are recorded for various groups in the population.
- Various fairness notions include demographic parity, equality of opportunity and odds, predictive quality parity, fairness through unawareness, and counterfactual fairness. Commonly used fairness notions are demographic parity and equality of opportunity and odds.
- Demographic parity is sometimes also called independence or statistical parity and is legally known as disparate impact. It asserts that a model contains parity in the positive prediction rates for different protected groups. The demographic parity notion is useful for scenarios where we want to ensure parity in the treatment of all protected groups, irrespective of their prevalence in the population. It ensures that the minority group is treated the same way as the majority group.
- For scenarios where we want to consider the distribution of the actual label for all protected groups, we can use the equality of opportunity and odds fairness notions. We say that equality of opportunity exists when parity is present in the true positive rates between the groups. Equality of odds extends the definition of equality of opportunity to another symmetric measurement called false positive rate.
- We can categorize all the notions of fairness into two sets: group fairness and individual fairness. Group fairness ensures that the model is fair for different protected groups. Individual fairness, on the other hand, ensures that the model makes similar predictions for similar individuals.
- We can use the interpretability techniques that we have learned in this book to detect a source of discrimination due to the model. The source of discrimination can be broadly categorized into two types: discrimination via input features and discrimination via representation.

- Discrimination via input traces the discrimination or fairness issues back to the input features. We can use the SHAP interpretability technique to trace fairness issues back to the input.

- These types of fairness issues are hard to trace back to the input features, especially for deep learning models that process inputs like images and text. For such cases, we could instead trace the source of discrimination to deep representations learned by the model. We can trace the source of discrimination to representations learned by the model using the network dissection framework and the t-SNE technique learned in chapters 6 and 7, respectively.

- Examples of two techniques that we can use to mitigate bias are fairness through unawareness and a reweighting technique to correct label bias. Fairness through unawareness does not guarantee fairness, but the reweighting technique does provide fairness guarantees.

- A standardized process exists to document datasets using datasheets. Datasheets aim to answer key questions regarding the motivation, composition, data-collection process, and uses of a dataset. Although datasheets for datasets add additional overheard for dataset creators, they improve transparency and accountability, help us determine sources of bias if there are any, and ensure that we are compliant with regulation such as GDPR in the EU.

Path to explainable AI

9

This chapter covers

- A recap of interpretability techniques learned in this book
- Understanding the properties of an explainable AI system
- Common questions asked of an explainable AI system and applying interpretability techniques to answer them
- Using counterfactual examples to come up with contrastive explanations

We are now approaching the end of our journey through the world of interpretable AI. Figure 9.1 provides a map of this journey. Let's take a moment to reflect on and to summarize what we have learned. Interpretability is all about understanding the cause and effect within an AI system. It is the degree to which we can consistently estimate what the underlying models in the AI system will predict given an input, understand how the models came up with the prediction, understand how the prediction changes with modifications to the input or algorithmic parameters, and finally understand when the models have made a mistake. Interpretability is becoming increasingly important because machine learning models are proliferating in various industries such as finance, healthcare, technology, and legal, to name a few. Decisions made by such models require transparency and fairness. The techniques that we have learned in this book are powerful tools to improve transparency and ensure fairness.

We looked at two broad classes of machine learning models in this book—white-box and black-box models—that fall on the spectrum of interpretability and predictive power. White-box models are inherently transparent and are straightforward to interpret. However, they have low to medium predictive power. We specifically focused on linear regression, logistic regression, decision trees, and generalized additive models (GAMs) and learned how to interpret them by understanding the internals of the model. Black-box models are inherently opaque and are harder to interpret, but they offer much higher predictive power. We focused most of our attention in this book on interpreting black-box models such as tree ensembles and neural networks.

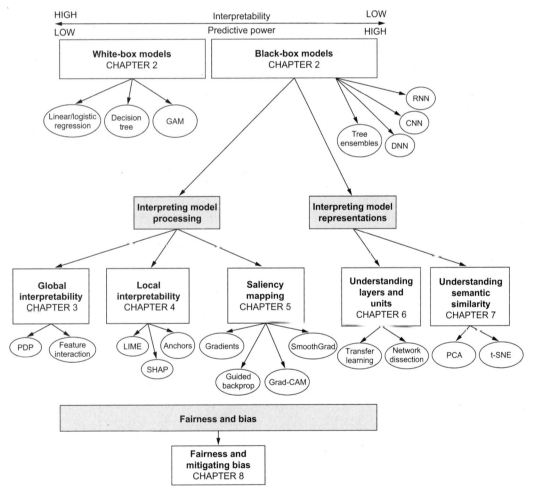

Figure 9.1 Map of our journey through the world of interpretable AI

We have two ways of interpreting black-box models. One is to interpret model processing—that is, understand how the model processes the inputs and arrives at the final prediction. The other way, interpreting model representations, is applicable only to deep neural networks. To interpret model processing, we learned about post hoc model-agnostic methods such as partial dependence plots (PDPs) and feature interaction plots to understand the global effects of the input features on the model's predictions. We also learned about post hoc model-agnostic methods that are local in scope, such as local interpretable model-agnostic explanations (LIME), SHapley Additive exPlanations (SHAP), and anchors. We can use these methods to explain how the model arrived at individual predictions. We also used visual attribution methods, such as saliency maps, to understand what input features or image pixels were important for neural networks used for visual tasks. To interpret model representations, we learned how to dissect neural networks and understand what representations of the data are learned by the intermediate or hidden layers in the network. We also learned how to visualize high-dimensional representations learned by the model using techniques like principal component analysis (PCA) and t-distributed stochastic neighbor embedding (t-SNE).

We finally focused on the topic of fairness and learned various fairness notions and how to make use of interpretability techniques to measure fairness. We also learned how to mitigate fairness using various preprocessing techniques, such as fairness through unawareness and an iterative label bias correction technique.

In this book, we made a strong distinction between interpretability and explainability. Interpretability is mainly about answering the *how* question—*how* does the model work and *how* did it arrive at a prediction? Explainability goes beyond interpretability in that it helps us answer the *why* question—*why* did the model make one prediction as opposed to another? Interpretability is mostly discernible by experts who are building, deploying, or using the AI system, and these techniques are building blocks that will help you get to explainability. We will focus on the path to explainable AI in this chapter.

9.1   *Explainable AI*

Let's look at a concrete example of an explainable AI system and what is expected of it. We will use the same example from chapter 8 of predicting the income of adults in the United States. Given a set of input features such as education, occupation, age, gender, and race, let's assume that we have trained a model that predicts whether an adult earns more than $50,000 per year. After applying the interpretability techniques learned in this book, let's assume that we can now deploy this model as a service. This service could be used by the public to determine how much they can earn given their features as input. An explainable AI system should provide functionality for the users of this system to question the predictions made by the model and to challenge the decisions made because of those predictions. This is illustrated in figure 9.2, where the functionality of providing an explanation to the user is built into the explanation agent. The users can ask the agent various questions regarding the predictions made by the model, and the onus is on the agent to provide meaningful answers. One possible question that the user could ask, as illustrated in figure 9.2, is why the model predicted that their salary would be less than $50K.

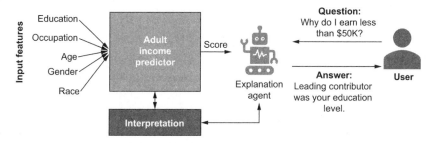

Figure 9.2   An illustration of an agent explaining the prediction made by a model to the user of the system

The question asked by the user in figure 9.2, for illustration purposes, is focused on understanding how various feature values influence the model prediction. This is just one type of question that could be asked of the system. Table 9.1 shows a few broad classes of questions that we can ask of the system and techniques that we have learned in this book that could be applied for such questions. As can be seen in the table, we are well equipped to answer questions on how the model works, what features are important, how the model arrived at a prediction for a specific case, and whether the model is fair and unbiased. As highlighted earlier, we are not well equipped to answer the *why* question and will briefly touch upon that in this chapter.

Table 9.1   Question types and explanation methods

Category of methods	Question types	Explanation methods
Explain the model	– *How* does the model work? – *What* features or inputs are the most important for the model?	– Model-dependent descriptions. (This book provides good descriptions on how various broad classes of models, both white-box and black-box, work.) – Global feature importance (chapters 2 and 3). – Model representations (chapters 6 and 7).
Explain a prediction	– *How* did the model arrive at this prediction for my case?	– Local feature importance (chapter 4). – Visual attribution methods (chapter 5).
Fairness	– *How* does the model treat people from a certain protected group? – *Is* the model biased against a group that I belong to?	– Fairness notions and measurements (chapter 8).

Table 9.1   Question types and explanation methods *(continued)*

Category of methods	Question types	Explanation methods
Contrastive or counterfactual	– *Why* did the model predict this outcome for me? – *Why not* another outcome?	– Counterfactual explanations (to be discussed in this chapter).

Although the interpretability techniques that we have learned in this book will help us come up with answers to most of the questions highlighted in table 9.1, there is more that goes into providing the answer or explanation to the user. We need to know what information is relevant to the question being asked, how much information to provide in the explanation, and how the user receives or understands explanations (i.e., their background). A whole field, called explainable AI (XAI), is dedicated to solving this problem. The scope of XAI, as shown in figure 9.3, is not just artificial intelligence, of which machine learning is a specific subfield, but also looks to other fields such as human-computer interaction (HCI) and social science.

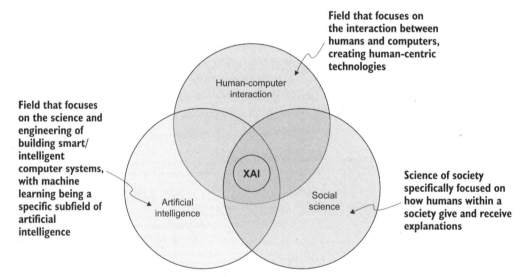

Figure 9.3   Scope of explainable AI (XAI)

Tim Miller published an important research paper (available at https://arxiv.org/pdf/1706.07269.pdf) on insights from social sciences that are relevant to XAI. The following are key findings in this paper:

- *Explanations are contrastive*—People usually do not just ask *why* the model predicted a specific outcome but rather *why not* another outcome. This is highlighted as the contrastive or counterfactual explanation method in table 9.1, and we will briefly discuss this in the next section.

- *Explanations are usually selected in a biased way*—If a lot of explanations or causes for a prediction are provided to the user, then the user typically selects only one or two and the selection is usually biased. It is, therefore, important to know how much information to provide and what information is most relevant for the explanation.

- *Explanations are social*—The transfer of information from the AI system to the user must be interactive and in the form of a conversation. It is, therefore, important to have an explanation agent, as illustrated in figure 9.2, that can comprehend questions and provide meaningful answers. The user must be at the center of this interaction, and it is important to look to the field of HCI to build such a system.

In the following section, we will specifically look at a technique that can be used to provide contrastive or counterfactual explanations, that is, answer the why and why not questions.

9.2 Counterfactual explanations

Counterfactual explanations (also known as contrastive explanations) can be used to explain why a model predicted a given value as opposed to another. Let's look at a concrete example. We will use the adult income prediction model, which is a binary classification problem, and focus on just two input features—age and education—for ease of visualization.

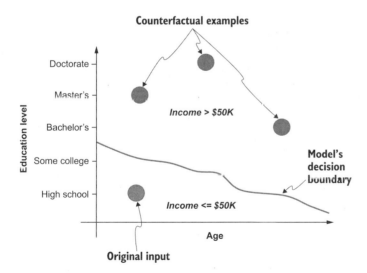

Figure 9.4 An illustration of counterfactual examples

These two features are shown in figure 9.4 as a two-dimensional plane. The decision boundary for the adult income model is also shown as a curve on the plane that separates the bottom part from the top part. For adults in the bottom part of the plane, the model predicts an income that is less than or equal to $50K, and for adults in the top part of the plane, the model predicts an income of greater than $50K. Let's assume that we have an adult who provides inputs to the system to predict how much income they will earn. This is labeled "Original Input" in figure 9.4. This adult has a high school education, and let's assume that the age is 30 (this is irrelevant for this example). Because this input falls below the decision boundary, the model will predict that the adult will earn an income that is less than $50K. The user then poses the question: why is my income less than $50K and not greater than $50K?

A counterfactual or contrastive explanation will provide examples, where in a counterfactual world, if that user satisfied certain criteria, then it will result in their desired outcome—earn an income greater than $50K. The counterfactual examples are marked in figure 9.4. They show that if the user's education level was higher—bachelor's, master's, or doctorate—then they would have a higher chance of earning more than $50K.

How do we generate these counterfactual examples? The whole process, described in figure 9.5, consists of an explainer that takes the following as input:

- *Original input*—The input provided by the user
- *Desired outcome*—The outcome desired by the user
- *Counterfactual example count*—The number of counterfactual examples to show in the explanation
- *Model*—The model used for prediction to obtain the predictions for the counterfactual examples

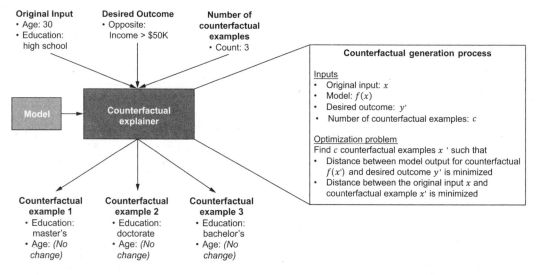

Figure 9.5   Counterfactual generation process

The explainer then runs an algorithm to generate the counterfactual examples. It is essentially an optimization problem of finding counterfactual examples such that the following criteria are met:

- The model output for the counterfactual example is as close to the desired outcome as possible.
- The counterfactual example is also close to the original input in the feature space, that is, the values of a minimum set of high-value features are changed to obtain the desired outcome.

In this chapter, we will focus on one popular technique called diverse counterfactual explanations (DiCE) to generate the counterfactual explanations. In DiCE, the optimization problem is formulated as we did earlier. Features are perturbed in such a way that they are diverse and feasible to change, and the desired outcome of the user is attained. The mathematical details are beyond the scope of this book, but let's use the DiCE library to generate counterfactual explanations for the adult income prediction problem. The library can be installed as follows:

```
$> pip install dice-ml
```

The following code snippet shows how to load the data and prepare it in a way that the DiCE explainer can process:

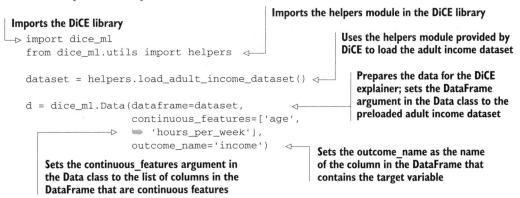

The next step is to train the model to predict the adult income. Because we have already done this in chapter 8 using the random forest model, we will not show the code for that here. Once you have trained the model, we are now ready to initialize the DiCE explainer, which we can do using the following code snippet:

Initializes the DiCE Model class by setting the model argument to the trained adult income model

Also sets the back-end argument in the Model class to "sklearn" because the model was a RandomForestClassifier provided by the Scikit-Learn library

```
m = dice_ml.Model(model=adult_income_model,
                  backend="sklearn")
```

Also sets the method to "random" in the DiCE explainer

```
exp = dice_ml.Dice(d, m,
                   method="random")
```

Initializes the DiCE explainer by passing the DiCE data and model

Once we have initialized the DiCE explainer, we can generate the counterfactual examples using the next code snippet. The function essentially takes in as input the original input, the number of counterfactual examples, and the desired outcome. For the input picked here, the model predicts a low income (i.e., <$50K) and the desired outcome for the user is a high income (i.e., >$50K):

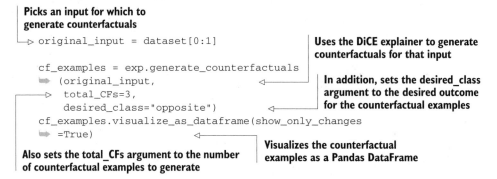

Picks an input for which to generate counterfactuals

```
original_input = dataset[0:1]

cf_examples = exp.generate_counterfactuals
  (original_input,
   total_CFs=3,
   desired_class="opposite")
cf_examples.visualize_as_dataframe(show_only_changes
  =True)
```

Uses the DiCE explainer to generate counterfactuals for that input

In addition, sets the desired_class argument to the desired outcome for the counterfactual examples

Also sets the total_CFs argument to the number of counterfactual examples to generate

Visualizes the counterfactual examples as a Pandas DataFrame

The output of this code snippet will print the counterfactual examples as a Pandas DataFrame. This output has been reformatted as a table and is shown in figure 9.6. We can see in figure 9.6 that the key contributor for why the model predicted a low income was the education level. If the education level was higher—doctorate, master's, or professional school—then there is a higher chance for the user to earn the desired outcome. The features that are not changed are shown as "–" in the figure.

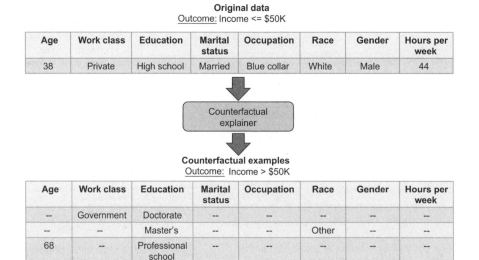

Original data
Outcome: Income <= $50K

Age	Work class	Education	Marital status	Occupation	Race	Gender	Hours per week
38	Private	High school	Married	Blue collar	White	Male	44

Counterfactual explainer

Counterfactual examples
Outcome: Income > $50K

Age	Work class	Education	Marital status	Occupation	Race	Gender	Hours per week
--	Government	Doctorate	--	--	--	--	--
--	--	Master's	--	--	Other	--	--
68	--	Professional school	--	--	--	--	--

Figure 9.6   Output of the DiCE counterfactual explainer

We can also use the DiCE counterfactual explainer for regression models. For classification, we specified the desired outcome by setting the `desired_class` parameter in the `generate_counterfactuals` function when generating the counter-factual examples. For regression, we must instead set a different parameter in the same function, called `desired_range`, to a range of possible values that is desired for the model prediction.

Counterfactual examples are a great way of providing explanations that are contrastive. A counterfactual explanation of the form, "The model prediction was P because features X, Y, and Z had values A, B, and C, but if feature X had values D or E, then the model would have predicted a different outcome, Q," is more causally informative and helps us understand why the model predicted a certain outcome as opposed to another. As mentioned earlier, more goes into providing a good explanation to the user of an AI system. XAI is an intersection of multiple fields such as AI, social sciences, and HCI and is a very active area of research. It is beyond the scope of this book, but the techniques that you have learned should provide you with a solid foundation, especially in the AI domain, to venture into the world of XAI.

This brings us to the end of the book. With a wide range of interpretability techniques in your toolkit, you are well equipped to understand how complex machine learning models work and how they arrive at a prediction. You can use this to debug and improve the performance of models. You can also use it to increase transparency and build fair and unbiased models. This book should also pave the way for you to build explainable AI systems. You should have a solid foundation to learn more about this very active area of research. Happy building and learning!

Summary

- Interpretability is all about understanding how the underlying models in an AI system come up with predictions, understanding how the predictions change with modifications to the input or algorithmic parameters, and understanding when the models have made a mistake.
- Explainability goes beyond interpretability in that it helps to answer the *why* question—*why* did the model make a specific prediction as opposed to another? Interpretability is mostly discernible by experts who are building, deploying, or using the AI system, and these techniques are building blocks that will help you get to explainability.
- The scope of explainable AI is not just artificial intelligence, of which machine learning is a specific subfield, but also looks to other fields such as human-computer interaction (HCI) and the social sciences.
- From the social sciences, the following three key findings are relevant for explainability:
  - Explanations are usually contrastive—people usually do not just ask *why* the model predicted a specific outcome but, rather, *why not* another outcome. Counterfactual explanations can be used to answer these types of questions.

– Explanations are usually selected in a biased way. It is important to know how much information to provide and what information is most relevant for the explanation.
– Explanations are social. The transfer of information from the AI system to the user must be in the form of a conversation or interactive. It is important to look to the field of HCI to build such a system.

appendix A
Getting set up

A.1   Python

In this book, all the code is written in Python. You can download and install the latest version from the Python language website (https://www.python.org/downloads/) for your operating system. The version of Python used in this book is Python 3.7, but any later version should work just as well. Various open source Python packages are also used in this book for building machine learning models and interpreting and visualizing them. Let's now download all the code used in this book and install all the relevant Python packages.

A.2   Git code repository

All the code in this book can be downloaded from the book's website (https://www.manning.com/books/interpretable-ai) and also from GitHub in the form of a Git repository. The repository on GitHub (https://github.com/thampiman/interpretable-ai-book) is organized into folders, one for each chapter. If you are new to version control using Git and GitHub, you can review material (http://mng.bz/KBXg) provided by GitHub to learn more about it. You can download or clone the repository from the command line as follows:

```
$> git clone https://github.com/thampiman/interpretable-ai-book.git
```

A.3   Conda environment

Conda is an open source system used for package, dependency, and environment management for Python and other languages. You can install Conda on your operating system by following the instructions on the Conda website (http://mng.bz/9Keq). Once installed, Conda allows you to easily find and install Python packages and export your environment from one machine and recreate it on another. The Python packages used in this book are exported as a Conda environment so that you can easily recreate them on your target machine. The environment file is exported in the YAML file format and can be found in the `packages` folder in the repository. You can then create the Conda environment by running the following command from the repository directory downloaded on your machine:

```
$> conda env create -f packages/environment.yml
```

This command will install all the necessary Python packages required for this book and create a Conda environment called `interpretable-ai`. If you have already created the environment and would like to update it, you can run the following command:

```
$> conda env update -f packages/environment.yml
```

Once you have created or updated the environment, you should activate the Conda environment by running the following command:

```
$> conda activate interpretable-ai
```

A.4   *Jupyter notebooks*

The code in this book is structured into Jupyter notebooks. Jupyter is an open source web application used to easily create and run live Python code, equations, visualizations, and markup text. Jupyter notebooks are widely used in the data science and machine learning communities. After downloading the source code and installing all the relevant Python packages, you are now ready to run the code in the book on Jupyter. From the repository directory downloaded on your machine, you can run the following command to start the Jupyter web application:

```
$> jupyter notebook
```

The Jupyter web application can be accessed from your browser at http://<HOST-NAME>:8888. Replace <HOSTNAME> with the host name or IP address of the machine that you are running from.

A.5   *Docker*

The Conda package/environment managed system does have some limitations. It sometimes does not work as expected across multiple operating systems, different versions of the same operating system, or different hardware. If you do encounter issues while creating the Conda environment detailed in the previous section, you can instead use Docker. Docker is a system used for packaging software dependencies, ensuring that the environment is identical for everyone. Docker can be installed on your operating system by following the instructions on the Docker website (https://www.docker.com/get-started). Once installed, you can then build the Docker image from the command line by running the following command from the repository directory downloaded on your machine:

```
$> docker build . -t interpretable-ai
```

Note that the `interpretable-ai` tag is used for the Docker image. If this command runs successfully, Docker should print the identifier of the image that was built. You can also view the details of the built image by running the following command:

```
$> docker images
```

Run the next command to run the Docker container using the built image and start the Jupyter web application:

```
$> docker run -p 8888:8888 interpretable-ai:latest
```

This command should start the Jupyter notebook application, and you should be good to run all the code in this book by accessing http://<HOSTNAME>:8888 from your browser. Replace <HOSTNAME> with the host name or IP address of the machine that you are running from.

appendix B
PyTorch

B.1 What is PyTorch?

PyTorch is a free, open source library used for scientific computing and deep learning applications such as computer vision and natural language processing. It is Python based and was developed by Facebook's AI Research (FAIR) lab. PyTorch is widely used by the research community and industry practitioners. Horace He conducted a recent study (available at http://mng.bz/W7Kl) that shows that the majority of the techniques published in major machine learning conferences in 2019 were implemented in PyTorch. Other libraries and frameworks like TensorFlow, Keras, CNTK, and MXNet can be used to build and train neural networks, but we will use PyTorch in this book. The library is pythonic and utilizes Python idioms well. It is, therefore, easier for researchers, data scientists, and engineers who are already familiar with Python to use it. PyTorch also provides great APIs to implement cutting-edge neural network architectures.

B.2 Installing PyTorch

You can install the latest stable version of PyTorch using Conda or `pip` as follows:

```
# Installing PyTorch using Conda
$> conda install pytorch torchvision -c pytorch

# Installing PyTorch using pip
$> pip install pytorch torchvision
```

Note that along with PyTorch, the torchvision package is also installed. This package (https://pytorch.org/vision/stable/index.html) consists of popular datasets, implementations of cutting-edge neural network architectures, and common transformations done on images for computer vision tasks. You can confirm the installation has succeeded by importing the libraries in your Python environment as follows:

```
import torch
import torchvision
```

B.3 *Tensors*

A tensor is a multidimensional array that is very similar to NumPy arrays. Tensors contain elements of a single data type and can be used on a graphics processing unit (GPU) for fast computing. You can initialize a PyTorch tensor from a Python list as follows. Note that the code in this section is formatted in such a way so as to reflect a Jupyter notebook or iPython environment. The line where you input a command is prefixed with In:, and the output of a command is prefixed with Out::

```
In: tensor_from_list = torch.tensor([[1., 0.], [0., 1.]])
In: print(tensor_from_list)
Out: tensor([[1., 0.],
             [0., 1.]])
```

For machine learning problems, NumPy is widely used. The library supports large, multidimensional arrays and provides a wide range of mathematical functions that can be used to operate on them. You can initialize a tensor from a NumPy array as follows. Note that the output of the print statement shows the tensor along with the dtype, or data type, of the elements. We will cover this in section B.3.1:

```
In: import numpy as np
In: tensor_from_numpy = torch.tensor(np.array([[1., 0.], [0., 1.]]))
In: print(tensor_from_numpy)
Out: tensor([[1., 0.],
             [0., 1.]], dtype=torch.float64)
```

The size of the tensor or the dimension of the multidimensional array can be obtained as follows. The tensor initialized previously consists of two rows and two columns:

```
In: tensor_from list.size()
Out: torch.Size([2, 2])
```

We can initialize an empty tensor of any size as follows. The next tensor consists of three rows and two columns. The values stored in the tensor are random, depending on the values that are stored in the bits in memory:

```
In: tensor_empty = torch.empty(3, 2)
In: print(tensor_empty)
Out: tensor([[ 0.0000e+00, -1.5846e+29],
             [-7.5247e+03,  2.0005e+00],
             [ 9.8091e-45,  0.0000e+00]])
```

If we want to initialize a tensor consisting of all zeros, we can do that as follows:

```
In: tensor_zeros = torch.zeros(3, 2)
In: print(tensor_zeros)
Out: tensor([[0., 0.],
             [0., 0.],
             [0., 0.]])
```

A tensor consisting of all ones can be initialized as follows:

```
In: tensor_ones = torch.ones(3, 2)
In: print(tensor_ones)
Out: tensor([[1., 1.],
             [1., 1.],
             [1., 1.]])
```

We can initialize a tensor with random numbers as follows. The random numbers are uniformly distributed between 0 and 1:

```
In: tensor_rand = torch.rand(3, 2)
In: print(tensor_rand)
Out: tensor([[0.3642, 0.8916],
             [0.4826, 0.4896],
             [0.9223, 0.9286]])
```

If you run the previous command, you may not get the same result because the seed of the random-number generator may be different. To get consistent and reproducible results, you can set the seed of the random-number generator using the `manual_seed` function provided by PyTorch as follows:

```
In: torch.manual_seed(24)
In: tensor_rand = torch.rand(3, 2)
In: print(tensor_rand)
Out: tensor([[0.7644, 0.3751],
             [0.0751, 0.5308],
             [0.9660, 0.2770]])
```

B.3.1 *Data types*

Data types (`dtype`), like NumPy `dtypes` (http://mng.bz/Ex6X), describe the type and size of the data. Common data types for tensors follow:

- `torch.float32` or `torch.float`: 32-bit floating point
- `torch.float64` or `torch.double`: 64-bit floating point
- `torch.int32` or `torch.int`: 32-bit signed integer
- `torch.int64` or `torch.long`: 64-bit signed integer
- `torch.bool`: Boolean

The full list of all the data types can be found in the PyTorch documentation at https://pytorch.org/docs/stable/tensors.html. You can determine the data type of a tensor as follows. We will be using the `tensor_from_list` tensor initialized earlier:

```
In: tensor_from_list.dtype
Out: torch.float32
```

You can initialize a tensor with a given data type as follows:

```
In: tensor_from_list_float64 = torch.tensor([[1., 0.], [0., 1.]],
                                      dtype=torch.float64)
In: print(tensor_from_list_float64)
Out: tensor([[1., 0.],
            [0., 1.]], dtype=torch.float64)
```

Sets the dtype parameter to torch.float64

A tensor initialized as a 64-bit floating point

B.3.2   *CPU and GPU tensors*

Tensors in PyTorch are by default loaded on the CPU. You can see this by checking the device that the tensor is on as follows. We will be using the random tensor (`tensor _rand`) initialized previously:

```
In: tensor_rand.device
Out: device(type='cpu')
```

For faster processing, you can load the tensor on a GPU. All the popular deep learning frameworks, including PyTorch, use CUDA, which stands for compute unified device architecture, to perform general-purpose computing on GPUs. CUDA is a platform built by NVIDIA that provides APIs to directly access the GPU. A list of GPUs that are CUDA-enabled can be found at https://developer.nvidia.com/cuda-gpus#compute. You can check whether CUDA is available on your machine as follows:

```
In: torch.cuda.is_available()
Out: True
```

If it is available, you can now initialize a tensor on the GPU as follows:

First checks whether CUDA is available

If yes, obtains the CUDA-enabled device

Initializes the tensor and sets the device to be the CUDA-enabled device

```
if torch.cuda.is_available():
    device = torch.device("cuda")
    tensor_rand_gpu = torch.rand(3, 2, device=device)
```

The following code snippet shows how to transfer a CPU tensor to the GPU:

```
if torch.cuda.is_available():
    device = torch.device("cuda")
    tensor_rand = tensor_rand.to(device)
```

B.3.3   *Operations*

We can perform multiple operations on a tensor. Let's look at a simple operation of adding two tensors. We will first initialize two random tensors, x and y, as follows:

```
In: x = tensor.rand(3, 2)
In: x
Out: tensor([[0.2989, 0.3510],
             [0.0529, 0.1988],
             [0.8022, 0.1249]])

In: y = tensor.rand(3, 2)
In: y
Out: tensor([[0.6708, 0.9704],
             [0.4365, 0.7187],
             [0.7336, 0.1431]])
```

We can obtain the sum of the two tensors using the add function, as shown next, or by just running x + y:

```
In: torch.add(x, y)
Out: tensor([[0.9697, 1.3214],
             [0.4894, 0.9176],
             [1.5357, 0.2680]])
```

Various other mathematical operations and functions are also provided by PyTorch. For an up-to-date list of all the operation, please refer to https://pytorch.org/docs/stable/torch.html. PyTorch also provides a NumPy bridge to convert a tensor into a NumPy array as follows:

```
In: x_numpy = x.numpy()
In: x_numpy
Out: array([[0.29888242, 0.35096592],
            [0.05293709, 0.19883835],
            [0.8021769 , 0.12490124]], dtype=float32)
```

B.4   *Dataset and DataLoader*

PyTorch provides a Dataset class that allows you to load and create custom datasets to be used for model training. Let's look at a contrived example. We will first create a random dataset using Scikit-Learn as follows:

Imports the make_classification function to create a random n-class classification dataset

```
In: from sklearn.datasets import make_classification
```

Sets the number of samples to 100

```
In: X, y = make_classification(n_samples=100,
                               n_features=5,
                               n_classes=2,
                               random_state=42)
```

Sets the number of input features to 5

Sets the number of classes to 2 to generate a binary classification dataset

Sets the seed for the random-number generator

The dataset consists of 100 samples or rows. Each sample consists of five input features and one target variable consisting of two classes. The values for each feature are sampled from a normal distribution. We can inspect the first row of input features as follows:

```
In: X[0]
Out: array([-0.43066755,  0.67287309, -0.72427983, -0.53963044, -0.65160035])
```

We will now create a custom dataset class that inherits from the `Dataset` class provided by PyTorch. This is shown in the next code snippet:

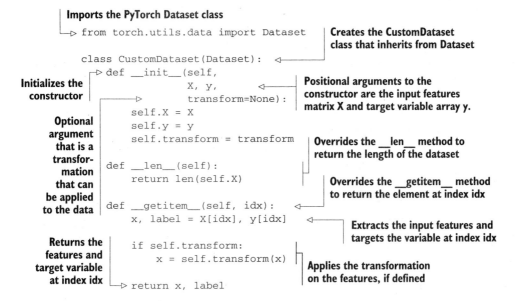

The constructor for the `CustomDataset` class takes in two positional arguments to initialize the input feature matrix X and the target variable y. There is also an optional argument called `transform` that we can use to apply a transformation function on the dataset. Note that we need to override the __len__ and __getitem__ methods provided by the `Dataset` class to return the length of the dataset and to extract the data at a specified index. We can initialize the custom dataset and inspect the length of the dataset as follows:

```
In: custom_dataset = CustomDataset(X, y)
In: len(custom_dataset)
Out: 100
```

Let's now also inspect the first row of input features as follows:

```
In: custom_dataset[0][0]
Out: array([-0.43066755,  0.67287309, -0.72427983, -0.53963044, -0.65160035])
```

We will now create a custom dataset and apply a transformation function to it. We will pass in the `torch.tensor` function to transform the array of input features as tensors. This is shown next. We can see that the first row of input features is now a tensor consisting of 64-bit floating point values:

```
In: transformed_dataset = CustomDataset(X, y,
                                        transform=torch.tensor)
In: transformed_data[0][0]
Out: tensor([-0.4307,  0.6729, -0.7243, -0.5396, -0.6516],
     dtype=torch.float64)
```

Some common image transformation functions like crops, flips, rotations, and resizing are also implemented in PyTorch as part of the `torchvision` package. The full list of transformations can be found at https://pytorch.org/vision/stable/transforms.html. We will use them in chapter 5.

Another useful data utility class to know about is `DataLoader`. This class takes as input an object that inherits from the `Dataset` class and a few optional parameters that allow you to iterate through your data. The `DataLoader` class provides features like data batching and shuffling and data loading in parallel using multiprocessing workers. The following code snippet shows you how to initialize a `DataLoader` object and iterate through the custom dataset created earlier:

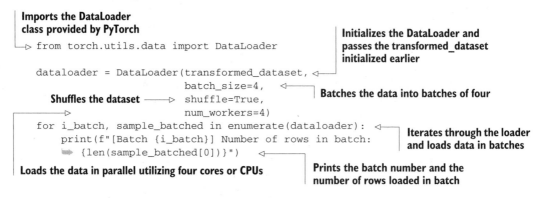

By executing this code, you will notice 25 batches and four rows in each batch because the input dataset has a length of 100 and the `batch_size` argument in the `DataLoader` class is set to 4. We will use the `Dataset` and `DataLoader` classes later in section B.5.3 and in chapter 5.

B.5   *Modeling*

In this section, we focus on modeling and how to build and train neural networks using PyTorch. We start off with automatic differentiation, which is a way to efficiently compute gradients and is used to optimize the weights in a neural network. We then cover model definition and model training.

B.5.1 *Automatic differentiation*

In chapter 4, we will learn about neural networks. Neural networks consist of many layers of units that are interconnected with edges. Each unit in a layer of the network performs a mathematical operation on all the inputs to that unit and passes the output to the subsequent layer. The edges that interconnect units are associated with weights, and the objective of the learning algorithm is to determine the weights for all the edges such that the prediction of the neural network is as close to the target in the labeled dataset.

An efficient way of determining the weights is using the backpropagation algorithm. We will learn more about this in chapter 4. In this section, we learn about automatic differentiation and how it is implemented in PyTorch. Automatic differentiation is a way to numerically evaluate the derivative of a function. Backpropagation is a special case of automatic differentiation. Let's look at a simple example and see how we can apply automatic differentiation in PyTorch. Consider an input tensor represented as *x*. The first operation that we do on this input tensor is to scale it by a factor of 2. Let's represent the output of this operation as *w*, where *w* = 2*x*. Given *w*, we now perform a second mathematical operation on it and represent the output tensor as *y*. This operation is shown here:

$$y = w^3 + 3w^2 + 2w + 1$$

The final operation that we perform is to simply sum all the values in tensor *y*. We represent the final output tensor as *z*. If we now wanted to compute the gradient of this output *z* with respect to the input *x*, we need to apply the chain rule as follows:

$$\frac{dz}{dx} = \frac{\partial z}{\partial y} \cdot \frac{\partial y}{\partial w} \cdot \frac{\partial w}{\partial x}$$

The partial derivates in this equation are given here:

$$\frac{\partial z}{\partial y} = 1$$

$$\frac{\partial y}{\partial w} = 3w^2 + 6w + 2$$

$$\frac{\partial w}{\partial x} = 2$$

The computation of these gradients can be complicated for more complex mathematical functions. PyTorch makes this easier using the `autograd` package. The `autograd` package implements automatic differentiation and allows you to numerically evaluate the derivative of a function. By applying the chain rule as shown earlier, `autograd` allows you to compute the gradient of functions of arbitrary order automatically. Let's see this in action by implementing the previous mathematical operations using tensors. We first initialize the input tensor x of size 2×3, consisting of all ones. Note that an argument called requires_grad is set to True when initializing the tensor. This argument lets autograd know to record operations on them for automatic differentiation:

```
In: x = torch.ones(2, 3,
                    requires_grad=True)
In: x
Out: tensor([[1., 1., 1.],
             [1., 1., 1.]], requires_grad=True)
```

We now implement the first mathematical operation that scales tensor x by a factor of 2 to obtain tensor w. Note that the output of tensor w shows grad_fn, which is used to record the operation that was performed on x to obtain w. This function is used to numerically evaluate the gradient using automatic differentiation:

```
In: w = 2 * x
In: w
Out: tensor([[2., 2., 2.],
             [2., 2., 2.]], grad_fn=<MulBackward0>)
```

We now implement the second mathematical operation that is used to transform tensor w into y:

```
In: y = w * w * w + 3 * w * w + 2 * w + 1
In: y
Out: tensor([[25., 25., 25.],
             [25., 25., 25.]], grad_fn=<AddBackward0>)
```

The final operation simply takes the sum of all values of tensor y to obtain z, as shown here:

```
In: z = torch.sum(y)
In: z
Out: tensor(150., grad_fn=<SumBackward0>)
```

We can easily compute the gradient of tensor z with respect to the input x by calling the backward function as follows. This will apply the chain rule and compute the gradient of the output with respect to the input:

```
In: z.backward()
```

We can see the numerical evaluation of the gradient as follows:

```
In: x.grad
Out: tensor([[52., 52., 52.],
             [52., 52., 52.]])
```

To verify whether the answer is right, let's mathematically derive the derivative of z with respect to x as provided by the earlier equations. This is summarized next:

$$\frac{dz}{dx} = \frac{\partial z}{\partial y} \cdot \frac{\partial y}{\partial w} \cdot \frac{\partial w}{\partial x}$$

$$\frac{dz}{dx} = 2.(3w^2 + 6w + 2)$$

As an exercise, I encourage you to evaluate this equation using the tensor. The solution of this exercise can be found in the GitHub repository associated with this book at https://github.com/thampiman/interpretable-ai-book.

B.5.2 *Model definition*

Let's now see how to define a neural network using PyTorch. We will focus on a fully connected neural network. The contrived dataset that we generated in section A.4 consisted of five input features and one binary output. Let's now define a fully connected neural network consisting of one input layer, two hidden layers, and one output layer. The input layer must consist of five units because the dataset contains five input features. The output layer must consist of one unit because we are dealing with one binary output. We have flexibility in choosing the number of the units in the two hidden layers. Let's use five and three units for the first and second hidden layers, respectively. We take a linear combination of the inputs at each unit in the neural network and use the rectified linear unit (ReLU) activation function at the hidden layers and the sigmoid activation function on the output layer. See chapter 4 for more details on neural networks and activation functions.

In PyTorch, we can use the `torch.nn.Sequential` container to define units and layers in the neural network in order. Each layer of units in PyTorch must inherit from the `torch.nn.Module` base class. PyTorch already provides a lot of the commonly used layers in neural networks that include linear, convolutional, and recurrent layers. Common activation functions like ReLU, sigmoid, and hyperbolic tangent (tanh) are also implemented. The full list of layers and activation functions can be found at https://pytorch.org/docs/master/nn.html. We are now ready to define the model using these building blocks as follows:

```
model = torch.nn.Sequential(
    torch.nn.Linear(5, 5),
    torch.nn.ReLU(),
    torch.nn.Linear(5, 3),
    torch.nn.ReLU(),
    torch.nn.Linear(3, 1),
    torch.nn.Sigmoid()
)
```

The Sequential container here defines the layers in order. The first Linear module corresponds to the first hidden layer that takes in the five features in the dataset and produces five outputs, which are fed into the next layer. The Linear module performs a linear transformation on the inputs. The next module in the container defines the ReLU activation function for the first hidden layer. The following Linear module then takes in five input features from the first hidden layer, performs a linear transformation, and produces three outputs that are fed into the next layer. Again, the ReLU activation function is used in the second hidden layer. The final Linear module then takes in three input features from the second hidden layer and produces one output, the output layer. Because we are dealing with binary classification, we use the Sigmoid activation function at the output layer. If we print the model by executing the command, print(model), we will get the following output:

```
Sequential(
  (0): Linear(in_features=5, out_features=5, bias=True)
  (1): ReLU()
  (2): Linear(in_features=5, out_features=3, bias=True)
  (3): ReLU()
  (4): Linear(in_features=3, out_features=1, bias=True)
  (5): Sigmoid()
)
```

We can now see how to define the neural network as a class where the number of layers and units can be easily customized, as shown in the code snippet that follows:

The BinaryClassifier class that extends the Sequential container

The constructor takes in an array called layer_dims that defines the architecture of the network.

```
class BinaryClassifier(torch.nn.Sequential):
    def __init__(self, layer_dims):
        super(BinaryClassifier, self).__init__()

        for idx, dim in enumerate(layer_dims):
            if (idx < len(layer_dims) - 1):
                module = torch.nn.Linear(dim, layer_dims[idx + 1])
                self.add_module(f"linear{idx}", module)

            if idx < len(layer_dims) - 2:
                activation = torch.nn.ReLU()
                self.add_module(f"relu{idx}", activation)
            elif idx == len(layer_dims) - 2:
                activation = torch.nn.Sigmoid()
                self.add_module(f"sigmoid{idx}", activation)
```

Initializes the Sequential container

Iterates through the layer_dims array

Adds the Linear module for all layers and names it "linear," followed by the index of the layer

For all hidden layers, adds the ReLU module and names it "relu," followed by the index of the hidden layer

For the output layer, adds the Sigmoid module and names it "sigmoid," followed by the index of the output layer

The BinaryClassifier class inherits from torch.nn.Sequential. The constructor takes in one positional argument, which is an array of integers called layer_dims that defines the number of layers and units in each layer. The length of the array defines the number of layers, and the element at index `i` defines the number of units at layer `i+1`. Within the constructor, we iterate through the `layer_dims` array and add a layer to the container using the `add_module` function. The implementation uses a linear module for all the layers and names them `linear`, followed by the index of the layer. We use the ReLU activation function for all hidden layers and the sigmoid activation function for the output layer. With this custom class in place, we can now initialize the binary classifier and define the structure easily using an array as follows:

Sets the number of input features to 5

Sets the number of outputs to 1

Initializes the layer_dims array that defines the structure of the network consisting of five units in the input layer, five units in the first hidden layer, three units in the second hidden layer, and one unit in the output layer

```
num_features = 5
num_outputs = 1
layer_dims = [num_features, 5, 3, num_outputs]
bc_model = BinaryClassifier(layer_dims)
```

Initializes the model using the BinaryClassifier class

We can see the structure of the network by executing `print(bc_model)`, which gives us the following output. We will be using a similar implementation in chapter 4:

```
BinaryClassifier(
  (linear0): Linear(in_features=5, out_features=5, bias=True)
  (relu0): ReLU()
  (linear1): Linear(in_features=5, out_features=3, bias=True)
  (relu1): ReLU()
  (linear2): Linear(in_features=3, out_features=1, bias=True)
  (sigmoid2): Sigmoid()
)
```

B.5.3   Training

With the model in place, we are now ready to train it on the dataset we created earlier. At a high level, the training loop consists of the following steps:

1. Loop over epochs: For each epoch, loop over batches of data.
   a. For each mini batch of data
      - Run the data through the model to obtain the outputs
      - Calculate the loss
      - Run the backpropagation algorithm to optimize the weights

An epoch is a hyperparameter that defines the number of times we propagate the entire training data in the forward and backward directions through the neural network. During each epoch, we load a batch of data, and for each batch, we will run it through the network to get the outputs, calculate the loss, and optimize the weights based on that loss using the backpropagation algorithm.

PyTorch provides lots of loss functions or criteria for optimization. Some of the commonly used ones follow:

- `torch.nn.L1Loss`—This computes the mean absolute error (MAE) of the output prediction and the actual value. This is typically used for regression tasks.

- `torch.nn.MSELoss`—This computes the mean squared error (MSE) of the output prediction and the actual value. Like L1 loss, this is also typically used for regression tasks.
- `torch.nn.BCELoss`—This computes the binary cross entropy, or log loss, of the output prediction and the actual label. This function is typically used for binary classification tasks.
- `torch.nn.CrossEntropyLoss`—This function combines the softmax and negative log likelihood loss functions and is typically used for classification tasks. We will learn more about BCE loss and cross-entropy loss in chapter 5.

You can find the full list of all the loss functions at http://mng.bz/Dx5A. Because we are dealing with only two target classes in the dataset we have created, we will use the BCE loss function.

PyTorch also provides various optimization algorithms that we can use during backpropagation to update the weights. We will use the Adam optimizer in this section. A full list of all the optimizers implemented in PyTorch can be found at https://pytorch.org/docs/stable/optim.html. The following code snippet initializes the loss function or criterion for the optimizer and the Adam optimizer on all the parameters or weights in the model initialized in the previous section:

```
criterion = torch.nn.BCELoss()
optimizer = torch.optim.Adam(bc_model.parameters())
```

We can implement the training loop as follows. Note that we are training for 10 epochs. During each epoch, we use the `DataLoader` object initialized in section A.4 to load the data and labels in batches. For each mini batch of data, we first need to reset the gradients to zero before computing the gradients for that mini batch. We then run through the model in the forward direction to obtain the output. Then we use these outputs to compute the BCE loss. By calling the `backward` function, the gradient of the loss function is computed with respect to the inputs using automatic differentiation. We then call the `step` function in the optimizer to update the weights or model parameters based on the gradients computed:

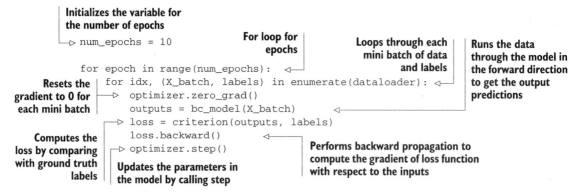

Once we have trained the model, we can get a prediction for a data point as follows. Note that we are switching the format of the following code snippet to mimic a Jupyter notebook or iPython environment:

```
In: pred_var = bc_model(transformed_dataset[0][0])
In: pred_var
Out: tensor([0.5884], grad_fn=<SigmoidBackward>)
```

The output of the model is a tensor consisting of a probability measure. This probability measure corresponds to the output of the sigmoid activation function in the final layer in the neural network. You can obtain the prediction as a scalar as follows:

```
In: pred_var.detach().numpy()[0]
Out: 0.5884
```

This ends our whirlwind tour of PyTorch, and we hope you are equipped with enough knowledge to be able to implement and train neural networks, and to understand the code in this book. There are a lot of books and online resources dedicated to PyTorch available at https://bookauthority.org/books/new-pytorch-books and http://mng .bz/laBd. The PyTorch documentation at https://pytorch.org/docs/stable/index .html is also a great resource to get a much deeper understanding of the library.

index